CALIFORNIA STYLE

Joseph Koret, early 1960s. [Koret private collection]

CALIFORNIA STYLE

THE JOE KORET STORY

BY REED BUNZEL

In collaboration with
the San Francisco Museum and Historical Society

CHRONICLE BOOKS

SAN FRANCISCO

In this life, I have wanted nothing more than for my husband's love for people and peace to endure. With this in mind, I wanted to publish a book that would tell the story of the real Joe Koret, and illustrate how his tremendous rise from poverty to fortune made the Foundation that bears his name possible. This is that book.

— *Susan Koret*

═══ CONTENTS ═══

FOREWORD 9

PREFACE 13

1 NEW YORK, NEW YORK 21

2 THE STREETS OF SAN FRANCISCO 37

3 CALIFORNIA DREAMING 51

4 THE POSTWAR BOOM 73

5 THE BIRTH OF THE CONSUMER 93

6 THE FIFTIES: A NEW GENERATION 119

7 THE SIXTIES: A DECADE OF TURMOIL 135

8 KORATRON: HOLD THE PRESS 161

9 KORACORP: IN THE PUBLIC EYE 179

10 THE SEVENTIES: THE END OF AN ERA 193

11 THE OLD MAN AND THE SEA 215

12 NOT YOUR AVERAGE JOE 241

13 WEDDING BELL BLUES 269

14 URBANE COWBOY 291

15 A FOUNDATION OF TRUST 307

SOURCES 325

ACKNOWLEDGMENTS 331

INDEX 334

Foreword

IN 1948, THE SAME YEAR THE STATE OF ISRAEL came into existence, Joseph Koret was just beginning to experience success with his women's sportswear company, Koret of California. He knew all too well the hard work and commitment it took to build a business from the ground up, and over the years he was able to achieve success beyond his wildest dreams. As his fortunes grew, he became a strong supporter and friend of the State of Israel, and in his later years he actively looked for ways to invest in the country's future.

Joe's personal history is one of a young Russian immigrant who grew up poor and hungry, shivering from the ravages of cold and starvation. Determined and tenacious as the legendary phoenix, he rose up from the ashes and transformed himself into a globally recognized business leader and humanitarian. Through diligence and considerable perseverance, he defined women's fashion and style for nearly a half century, and at the same time, he touched everybody around him with the gentle hand of generosity and compassion.

It could be said that Joe was a "start-up man" long before "start-up" became part of our business lexicon.

As much as Joe enjoyed the challenge of business, he was driven even more by goodness and charity. Across the decades, his hard work earned him millions of dollars, and he came to realize that his heart and soul could not be measured by his wealth. Rather, he knew the world would view him by his desire to help those in need, and to make the world a better place.

One notable example of this philanthropic benevolence was the creation of the Koret School of Veterinary Medicine. While visiting Israel in the early 1980s, Joe and his wife Susan realized that the State of Israel lacked a decent facility for studying, teaching, and learning the intricacies of animal science. During his visit, Joe saw the need to establish a top-line veterinary college, and he immediately set about making it a reality. Later, at a meeting that that took place in the Korets' home in California, Joe pointed to his black Labrador, and said "my dog will be one of the first to be treated at my school there." He analyzed what was required to begin such a project, and then—through the Koret Foundation—he pledged the financial resources necessary to get it done. Joe was involved in every aspect of the construction process, from developing the overall blueprints of the hospital itself, to making sure that the school would be financially secured forever.

The Koret School is, by far, the leading school of veterinary medicine in the Middle East, and often is contacted by doctors and officials in neighboring Jordan and other countries for advice and assistance. Additionally, it has been approved by the European Association of Establishments for Veterinary Education (EAEVE), and it has more internationally board-certified veterinarians than any veterinary school on the continent.

The Jewish people will forever recognize Joe as a man of pure heart and true dedication, an individual who embodied their spirit and self-determination. The King of Jordan, the Bedouins of the desert, the farmers of the entire State of Israel, and hundreds of thousands of beneficiaries of the Koret School of Veterinary Medicine and affiliated

Veterinary Teaching Hospitals all over the world know the Koret name because of his great mind and deeds. However, until now no one has ever had the opportunity to learn about Joe's personal life journey, and how he earned the dollars that would make the Koret School of Veterinary Medicine possible.

California Style: The Joe Koret Story is an educational eye-opener, a portrait of a selfless man who propelled the meaning of generosity to a new level. Its pages serve as an instruction manual for any innovator or entrepreneur, as well as a spiritual guidebook for those who wish to live a life as large as his. Through these pages you will have the opportunity to get to know the origins and motivations of this modern-day phoenix, and I am certain you will come to appreciate Joe the way we at the Koret School of Veterinary Medicine appreciate him.

In the collective eyes of the State of Israel, Joseph Koret is seen as an innovator, pioneer, businessman, and philanthropist without parallel. Thank you, Joe, for indeed making the world a better place.

Professor Menahem Ben-Sasson
Chancellor, The Hebrew University of Jerusalem
Former President of Hebrew University (2009–2017)

Joseph Koret waving at reporters after returning to California after a business trip to New York. [Bancroft Library collection]

Preface

AMERICA IN EARLY 1980 WAS CAPTIVATED BY A world that was shape-shifting before its very eyes. A rogue nation in the Middle East that few voters could point out on a map was holding fifty-two Americans hostage. Cold War rhetoric between the United States and the Soviet Union was ratcheting up day by day. The Winter Olympics had opened with much fanfare in Lake Placid, and the "Miracle on Ice" medal-round hockey game was about to be played. Interest rates were over 15 percent, a gallon of gas cost 86 cents, and the average home was priced at $68,000.[1] California was in the middle of a winter drought, and a series of modest earthquakes had just rocked the San Francisco Bay Area.

None of that seemed to matter to the elderly man in the passenger seat of a black Volkswagen bug that was darting through traffic on Lake Street. Each time its driver swerved to avoid another car or bicycle, the senior citizen grabbed the "oh-my-God" bar in front of him and hung on for dear life.

"Honey, you have to get a bigger car!" he admonished the attractive woman driver who kept shifting the German transmission. At five-nine,

Joe Koret was not a tall man, but his large frame filled every inch of the car's tiny seat. "How do you fit in this thing?"

"*This thing*, as you put it, is humble, and the people we will be meeting with today will be humble, too," she rebuked him. "If you don't like it, you should have driven that ugly Cadillac of yours."

Koret gave her an admiring side-eye glance, reminded once again why he had hired JoAnne Vente as his executive assistant. Besides her stunning looks, she was smart, quick, and not afraid to serve back whatever he might dish out.

"I've driven past this place every day for almost thirty years," he said, almost dreamily. "I never thought I actually might be giving them some of my money one day."

Them was the Little Sisters of the Poor, an international order of Roman Catholic nuns founded over 170 years ago by Saint Jeanne Jugan. Also known as Sister Mary of the Cross, Saint Jeanne was a Frenchwoman who had dedicated her life to taking care of the very neediest elderly poor. The San Francisco chapter of this organization had followed her lead by establishing St. Anne's Home for the Elderly, an assisted-living facility that provided around-the-clock care for people who, in addition to material poverty, suffered from a lack of human and spiritual support. In 1977, the facility had been declared unsafe in the event of a fire or earthquake, and two years later the sisters had begun an extensive seismic retrofit. Because of the expense involved, they were in dire need of a philanthropic angel who could help them finish the building, which would include a new residential wing.

"These women are very dedicated to helping the poor, and they really need the money so they can expand their outreach," JoAnne replied to Koret.

He nodded blithely as he gazed out the window—until the VW bug bounced through a pothole and yanked him back to the reality of city driving. "Honey—!"

"I know, Mr. Koret. I didn't see that one. We're almost there."

There was the intersection of Lake Street and Fourth Avenue, where St. Anne's was nestled under the shade of towering cypress trees that lined the edge of San Francisco's Presidio Golf Course.

"And just who are we seeing again?"

"Our appointment is with the Mother Superior and several of the sisters," JoAnne explained patiently. They had already reviewed the meeting before setting off in the car, but Joe Koret was the sort of man who liked to commit every fact and nuance to memory.

"I'm looking forward to meeting them," he told her, and he meant it.

In fact, as much as Koret was anticipating their pending visit with delight, he also was more than a touch apprehensive. Over the past forty years, he had amassed a considerable fortune from Koret of California, the women's sportswear company he had founded with his late wife, Stephanie, in 1938. *Resolute, tenacious, determined, driven, ambitious, rich*—all were adjectives that came to mind when people described the man who undeniably had merged "style" with "California." The challenge he had recently begun to face was that, after a lifetime of toiling for every possible dollar, he now was positioned to give his substantial wealth away. He enjoyed the notion of providing financial assistance to those less fortunate, but when the time came to sign the checks approved by the young Koret Foundation, his hand still trembled visibly.

That morning, Joseph Koret and JoAnne Vente, the foundation's director of grants, met up with Ken Moline, who not only served as the entity's chief financial officer but also was JoAnne's husband. Within minutes of arriving at St. Anne's, they were taken on a walking tour by the Mother Superior, who explained that the facility provided residential nursing care to San Francisco residents who could not afford to pay for these services themselves. While the Little Sisters of the Poor were aligned with the Catholic Church, the residents who lived at St. Anne's came from a variety of faiths and ethnic backgrounds.

Joe Koret liked that.

After the tour, the small group made their way to a room where they sat down around a table. Everyone knew why they were there: the Mother Superior had contacted the Koret Foundation a few days before in search of capital funding for the new residential-care wing. In turn, Joe Koret was actively seeking community-based organizations that were in need of monetary help. Poverty, homelessness, and hunger were his primary concerns, and the needs of St. Anne's Home for the Elderly seemed to address all three goals. The Mother Superior patiently explained what she and her order were hoping to do and who they were trying to help. "So many folks in this community need full-time care but can't afford it," she explained in a hopeful, plaintive voice. "That's what this building project is all about, but in order to finish it we need money."

Joe knew this was why he was there, and he began to soften under the Mother Superior's humility and good-natured earnestness. While he was Jewish, his former Koret of California employees represented a vast melting pot of religious and ethnic groups and origins. He also knew that a number of those people were now elderly and facing the sort of health-care issues that had just been explained to him.

"What sort of money are you looking for?" he asked.

"We need five hundred thousand dollars to complete the building," she replied. Phrasing it that way made it sound less than the half million they were seeking.

"Well, I think we can help with part of that," he said. "Up to half of it, in fact."

JoAnne Vente and Ken Moline tried their best not to stare at him. It was Koret Foundation policy not to tell any potential beneficiary how much, if any, funding they might receive before the board made a decision. The foundation was still in its infancy, and they were all new to this. Joe Koret clearly was being swept up by the charm of these genuine and open devotees of God.

"That would be very generous, sir," the Mother Superior replied serenely.

"But—" Joe raised a hand and gave this some thought. "If I agree to do this, where will you get the other half of what you need?"

The Mother Superior offered him a warm smile and looked him in the eye with complete sincerity. "The Lord will provide if he deems us worthy," she told him. "We're going to pray a lot."

He nodded at what she said, but said no more.

Joe Koret was an avid card player and liked to think of himself as the master of the bluff. Even though JoAnne and Ken admired him for his patient forbearance, they knew that he was also loath to give away the money he and his wife had worked so hard for, so in this case neither of them was sure what he was up to. Was he fully committed to helping the Little Sisters, or was he setting them up for a hard fall?

He returned the Mother Superior's smile and stood up from the table, signaling to the others that it was time for them to go. "We'll be back in touch with you soon," he told the nuns as they all filed out of the room.

A few minutes later, JoAnne and Joe climbed back into the VW bug that was as black as a nun's habit. He had been silent on the walk out to the car, and she had no idea where his mind might be taking him. She turned the key, and the small German engine sputtered to life; only then did she glance over at her boss.

That's when she noticed the tiny stream of tears trickling out of the corner of his eye.

Without saying a word she backed out of the parking space and pulled out onto Lake Street. Koret was silent for a long while before he turned to his trusted assistant and said, "Honey, we're going to do this."

"Sir?" she said, half-question, half-statement.

"I don't care what the board might say—we're going to help those wonderful ladies."

"They certainly need it, and it's definitely a good cause."

He turned to her and said, "All this money I have? My house, my boat, all my real estate? It means nothing, not really. Yes, I worked hard. And I got lucky. I was even a bit ruthless when I thought I had to be. But everything I have today—each and every joy and even the setbacks I've experienced in life—have made me a very happy man."

JoAnne had never seen him quite this reflective, at least not in years. "You should be very pleased, sir. Think of all the good you can do in this world."

"Those lovely sisters have made me see that," he said. "There were times I didn't have a proper pair of shoes for my feet, or a cold potato to put in my stomach. Now I have more money than any man can ever hope for, and it's time to give it back. I'm a very fortunate man, but none of this would have been possible if not those early struggles—and the hard-fought dreams of my father . . ."

Koret family photo, taken in New York sometime in 1903. Pictured (l-to-r): Mrs. Sarah Koret, sons Alexander and Joseph, and Mr. Abram Koret. [Koret private collection]

1

New York, New York

ABRAM KORETSKY PRESSED AGAINST THE RAILING of the crowded steamer as it slowly chugged toward the ice-choked pier. The year was 1901, and a bitter chill cut through the collar of the tattered overcoat tucked up around his neck, keeping out the harsh bite of winter. Flurries drifted down like white ashes from the caul of gray clouds that cloaked the sun. All around him people were jostling each other, murmuring with friends and family, many of them pointing at what lay before them.

Shadowy buildings lined the point of land that rose from the water in the distance, where boats of all sizes and countries of registry were lined up at the docks. Small ships, skiffs, and ferries plied the cold, leaden harbor, while wisps of smoke curled up from the streets of the frozen city. A scent of hope and opportunity drifted on the winter wind—or maybe it was just a collective sigh of relief of those who had spent two weeks at sea in the bowels of a cramped and putrid steam vessel.

Abram fixed his eyes on the skyline of this bustling city and wondered what his new life would bring. He gave no credence to the stories that the streets of New York were paved with gold, but even here—on the slick deck of this creaky old ship—he sensed an air of optimism and possibility that had not existed in the burdened streets of Odessa. He'd bid farewell to the city of his birth just two weeks before, knowing he would never set eyes on its teeming waterfront or towering churches or famous Potemkin Steps again. Since then, he'd been packed into a crowded compartment in the dank hold among the seasick and the infirm and buckets of sewage that slid about all day and all night. He'd paid the steamship company the equivalent of thirty dollars for a narrow bunk that he shared with his father's old suitcase, into which he'd stuffed virtually all of his worldly possessions. Whatever didn't fit he'd left behind: his childhood home, his livelihood, his mother and father. And especially his beautiful wife, Sarah, and their two young sons.

How he missed them now as the ship turned toward a space along the crowded dock. He wished Sarah could be standing beside him on this first cold afternoon in New York. He pictured her in his mind, cradling their infant son Joseph in her arms as two-year-old Alexander pressed against the railing with eyes widened in amazement at the big green goddess standing watch over the harbor: the *Statuya Svobody*—Statue of Liberty—given by France to the United States and dedicated to its people just fifteen years earlier. From day one, her iconic torch, raised high above the harbor, had become a welcoming inspiration to immigrants arriving in the United States from all over the world. Abram had wanted his entire family to join him here in America from the very start, but he'd only scrounged up enough money to purchase a single ticket.

He would have to be patient.

At long last, the steamship nudged up against the quay, and the deckhands heaved large knotted ropes over the pilings. The engines ground to a halt, and a modest cheer rose up from the hundreds of Russians who pressed forward. They had arrived in America. Now all that stood between them and freedom was the immigration processing center at Ellis Island.

As with most ships bringing immigrants to America, this vessel offered three types of accommodations: first class, second class, and steerage. Those individuals and families who could afford the steep rates of a first- or second-class ticket were deemed suitable for entry into New York with an almost cursory on-board medical examination. Inspectors kept an experienced eye open for all sorts of contagious diseases, including smallpox, typhoid fever, cholera, yellow fever, scarlet fever, plague, diphtheria, and measles. After these fortunate passengers were deemed disease-free, they were certified to disembark once the boat was docked. That exam had been completed earlier that morning at the official quarantine area in the Lower Bay of New York Harbor. Once the inspectors had departed, the steamship was free to move through the Narrows into the Upper Harbor at the tip of Manhattan. After some official paperwork was finalized, the privileged classes would be allowed to disembark directly into the city and travel on to wherever their fates might carry them.

Those who had crossed the ocean in the stultifying confines of steerage, however, were a different story altogether. These passengers were viewed as the lowest of the low: the indigent, the disenfranchised, the persecuted. They also represented a huge profit for the steamship companies, which designed their holds to accommodate up to two thousand immigrants per trip representing a potential net profit of $60,000 for a single one-way voyage.[1] Almost anyone could board the ship with a cheap ticket in hand, but if for some reason an immigration official turned any passengers away after their arrival in the States, they were forced to return to Europe at the steamship company's expense. Not pleased with having to ferry these rejects back across the ocean, the captain often would dump them at the first return port they entered.

The routine this cold afternoon was no different than usual. As soon as the first- and second-class passengers were gone, the remaining immigrants were collected into groups of thirty and herded onto barges while their meager possessions were loaded into the cavernous holds below. Abram watched a deckhand hurl his father's old suitcase into a pile with all the others, then pressed forward into the throng of fellow passengers on the barge.

Like many new immigrants, the first solid ground Abram Koretsky touched in America was the stone quay at Ellis Island. After two weeks at sea, he was unsteady on his feet, but he anxiously followed the orders of the interpreter who was there to greet them. Unlike many of the "processing officials" at the immigration center, these interpreters often were supportive and empathetic, providing new arrivals with valuable insights on how to survive the grueling entry process that lay ahead. Immigration officials had almost complete control over whether a person was granted entry or sent home, so following the rules—and showing some deference to American authority—was critical to admission.

Abram's group was led through the main entryway and ordered to climb a steep set of stairs that led to the Registry Room. Thus began the evaluation process, and over the next few hours every steerage passenger was examined for the same diseases as the "cabin" passengers who had already disembarked. They also were assessed for lameness, heavy breathing that could indicate a heart condition, or "bewildered gazes" that might be symptomatic of a mental condition.[2] At twenty-four years of age, Abram was a healthy, strong young man who had survived the ocean voyage with little difficulty. He had no known ailments and easily passed all the medical phases of the examination. This was the stage that most new immigrants feared the most, because they would not be allowed entry if they were determined to be physically or mentally ill.

Abram patiently endured the slow parade through the medical exam station, then moved on to the "primary line" inspector. Because of the sheer number of immigrants, this government official usually had only a minute or two to decide whether to allow a person to pass. Each immigrant was required to verify thirty-one items of information listed on his or her manifest but, because of the time crunch, most of them were given entry after only a perfunctory question or two. Rare was the individual who got tripped up at this stage, and a quick flick of the inspector's wrist waved Abram onward.

The next and final stop along the line was the currency exchange station, where Abram turned in his few remaining rubles for American dollars and coins—mostly coins. Every new immigrant was required to have at least $25 to his or her name, but few new arrivals possessed much more than that. Abram Koretsky—now anglicized to Abram Koret by an immigration official—was one of them. He stuffed the few pieces of new money into his pocket and moved through a doorway that took him back out into the icy March afternoon. Before he was quite able to grasp the reality of it, he had made it through registration and into a new country.

The sign painted over the door read "Welcome to America."

ABRAM KORET QUICKLY CONFIRMED—JUST AS logic had told him—that the streets of America were not paved with gold. That was simply a metaphor for the rumored riches that awaited those who worked hard and were not afraid to get their hands dirty. The streets of New York were a hive of human activity and free enterprise, and no one really cared whether you were Jewish or Catholic or Greek or Russian or German. Historically, the most recent wave of American was always feared and despised by those who had arrived before them—Chinese, Italian, Irish, or otherwise. But the prejudices and preconceptions that had haunted Abram's fellow Jews throughout western Russia were nowhere near as pronounced here in the United States of America.

That's not to say that hate and bigotry weren't alive and well in America; they were. At the turn of the nineteenth century, the United

States was still burdened by Jim Crow restrictions and Bible Belt prejudice. Interracial marriage was still against the law in many corners of America; separate but equal arguably was anything but; and the nation was still almost two full decades away from granting women the right to vote. Anti-Semitism was highly prevalent in a country where ignorance and fear contributed equally to social intolerance, but it was not institutionalized as it had been in Russia and many parts of Europe. Religious freedom was a cornerstone of the U.S. life, fully guaranteed by a document known as the Constitution. That tiny variance made all the difference in the world to Abram Koret and other Jewish refugees.

At the time Abram set sail for America in March 1901, Jews had become the targets of deadly pogroms that killed thousands of people from one end of Russia to the other. Progressive reforms that had been instituted by Tsar Alexander II in the second half of the nineteenth century came to a grinding halt upon his assassination in 1881, an event that was wrongly (and thought to be intentionally) blamed on Jewish dissidents. Within weeks, a number of violent anti-Semitic uprisings erupted throughout the country, as more and more people blindly blamed the country's ills on the Jewish population. Hate and anger quickly spread, and many Jews were physically attacked and their homes burned. The government ignored these vicious outbursts as the violence grew more frequent and intense, establishing a brutal sense of normalcy.

Additionally, almost all men of military age were required to serve six years in the Army, followed by an additional nine-year stint in the reserves. Feeling no loyalty to an empire that continued to persecute and oppress them, many Russian Jews looked for ways to avoid conscription and flee the despotic government forever. Many sought out relatives who had settled elsewhere in Europe, while others used their last rubles to buy passage across the Atlantic Ocean to the United States. The journey was characterized by illness and discomfort, but those seeking freedom to work and live outside the sphere of Russian discrimination and violence found the risk worthwhile.

All this was true for Abram Koret. He certainly professed no allegiance to a government that sought to oppress him and his fellow Jews, and he had no taste for serving in its military. He was married and had two sons, and forced conscription was counter to everything he believed in. Still, Russian officials could be brutal in their enforcement measures, so he had made a bold and deliberate decision to find his way out of the country. His own parents—and those of his wife— were saddened by, but supportive of, what they viewed as a courageous choice and eagerly contributed whatever rubles they could spare for the cause.

This largess provided young Abram with just enough money to not only pay for his passage to New York but also to motivate a Russian official to look the other way when he boarded the boat in Odessa. As Joe Koret recalled in a television interview taped in the late 1970s, "One of the reasons my father left Russia was at that time you served in the Army whether you liked it or not. It was compulsory. He already had an established family, and he didn't want to serve in the Army. There was a lot of bribery in Russia in those days, and he took the last of his money to bribe his way out of the country."

REALITY INVARIABLY TURNS OUT TO BE FAR different from the dream. As Abram Koret quickly discovered, by the turn of the century tens of thousands of Jewish immigrants had descended on Manhattan's Lower East Side. Many of them lived in squalid conditions in densely packed tenements, numbed by bone-chilling cold in the winter and languishing in fly-infested humidity in the summer. Living quarters were overcrowded and filthy, and the streets were rife with disease and crime. While almost any able-bodied young man could find work, the pay was low and food was scarce.

With an average seven hundred residents per acre, the neighborhood was regarded as one of the most densely populated areas on the planet.

In order to make ends meet, many immigrants—men, women, and children—toiled in factories under appalling working conditions. It was a hand-to-mouth existence of twelve-hour work days, usually six days a week, and most new arrivals barely earned enough money to keep food on the table. Entry-level America was defined by long hours loading and unloading ships on the docks, washing clothes in steaming laundries, or hefting shovels to clean up after the thousands of horses that polluted the city's streets. Still, these newcomers were able to practice their faith without fear of violent reprisals, and this made the living conditions more than worthwhile. Opportunity continued to fuel the dreams of thousands.

Abram Koret was a tailor by trade, and he quickly found work at one of the many garment factories that dotted lower Manhattan. Conditions were just as abysmal inside the walls as they were out on the streets, and the pay was shameful. Women worked side-by-side with men in the factories and mills, and while earning less money than their male counterparts, they achieved a new independence they had not felt in the old country. According to the New York census of 1900, women comprised 70 percent of the city's garment workforce. Half of them were not yet twenty years of age, and half were Jewish.[3]

Inside these apparel factories, women typically were assigned tasks of assembling and finishing garments, while their higher-paid male coworkers were responsible for cutting fabric and pressing the finished clothes. According to historian Howard Sachar, many workers supplied their own materials, "including needles, thread, and sewing machines. Workers could be fined for being late for work or for damaging a garment they were working on." Additionally, at some factories, such as the Triangle Shirtwaist Company, steel doors were locked in order to prevent workers from taking breaks.[4] (In a terrible twist of irony, the building was the site of a devastating fire in 1911 that killed

146 workers, a tragedy that to this day remains one of the city's largest industrial disasters.)

While it's not known exactly where Abram Koret first found work on arrival in New York, these would almost certainly have been the conditions of his employment: he would have trudged to work before sunup and labored for unbearably long hours before tucking his paltry salary into his pocket and slogging home again long after sundown. Like so many workers around him, he was surely determined to make a good life for himself and the rest of his family as soon as he was able to bring them over. He must have scrimped and saved, eating just enough to stay healthy and fit, and probably sleeping in a corner of a rented room with other Russian immigrants. During that first year in America, his mind was doubtlessly preoccupied by one goal: to be with his wife, Sarah, and their two young boys again.

That opportunity came the following year. Abram had been able to save most of the ninety dollars he needed to purchase three one-way tickets, and what he didn't have he borrowed from newfound friends. A strong sense of selfless camaraderie and shared purpose was the norm throughout the neighborhood, and no cause was greater than being united with loved ones who had been left behind. One day in 1902, Abram handed a steamship ticket officer enough money to buy passage for his wife and sons to board another ship bound for America. With the vouchers pre-paid in full, word was sent to Odessa, and within weeks Sarah, Alexander, and Joseph were waving goodbye to a throng of relatives cheering from the dock.

Two weeks later, Sarah and her two sons watched from the rail as their steamship chugged through the outer harbor of New York. They experienced the same medical quarantine and examination Abram had endured eighteen months before, and were finally processed through Ellis Island along with thousands of other new arrivals. There were probably some tense moments as the inspectors poked and pried at the two young boys, but eventually all three Korets were found to be in good health and waved through under the same sign that read "Welcome to America."

Life was no easier for a family of four than when Abram had been toiling endlessly as a lone man. He now had four mouths to feed, and sleeping on a straw mattress in the corner of a tiny room no longer would suffice. Sarah Koret was able-bodied and willing to work, but she had two small children to care for. Abram's take-home pay had not changed with the arrival of his family, and food was more scarce than ever. Men and women in the factories constantly grumbled about the poor conditions, but only among themselves. Any signs of discontent or resentment, and they were readily reminded that they were easily replaced.

Headstrong and principled, Abram was known to support the growing workers' movement that was beginning to take hold in factories across America. Labor organizations had existed in Europe since the industrial revolution began in the late eighteenth century, and many Jews in Manhattan had been members of the Jewish Labor Bund, which was active in Russia between 1897 and 1920. Conditions in New York sweatshops made those businesses obvious targets for organizing workers, and the International Ladies Garment Workers Union (ILGWU) eagerly accepted the challenge.

Each day on the job caused Abram Koret to witness more and more horrors, and over time he became active in labor recruitment and organizing. As his son Joseph many years later would recount, Abram would come home from the picket lines beaten and bloodied. Factory owners were loath to pay higher wages to new immigrants who barely spoke English and had little choice but to submit to their heavy-handed rule. Few workers could risk being kicked out into the street, and at times entire families—children included—labored under abhorrent conditions just to make ends meet.

In 1909, the Triangle Shirtwaist factory was hit with a walkout as Jewish workers voted for a general strike after reciting a traditional

Yiddish oath: "If I turn traitor to the cause I now pledge, may this hand wither from the arm I now raise." Approximately twenty thousand of the thirty-two thousand workers in the New York shirtwaist trade walked out over the next two days.[5]

"My father's sojourn in New York was particularly hard," Joe recalled in the 1970s video interview:

> In those days it was the beginning of the fight—and when I say fight, I really mean fight—to install unions in the shops. He worked as a tailor. He never made a good living for his family when he worked as a tailor. Finally, the grueling experience of getting into continual battles and actual fights, and his activities as an organizer, began wearing a little on him. My mother kept pressuring him all the time to get out of that.

Eventually, he did. Almost a decade after arriving in New York, Abram Koret grew weary of the low pay and mounting violence associated with being a New York garment worker. He quit his job as a tailor and, borrowing a small sum of money from a relative, opened a modest grocery store. This was not a completely unexpected move; approximately one-third of immigrants to New York in the early 1900s worked in retail sales at some point.

You would think that, in such a crowded neighborhood, a grocery store would thrive. But since most people in the area lived on subsistence wages, they had no more money than did the Korets, so times continued to be hard. Meanwhile, the Koret family continued to expand. A third son, Harold, was welcomed in 1907, followed just over a year later by a fourth son, Solomon. With six mouths to feed, pennies were stretched thin and food became even more scarce. Fresh meat and vegetables were almost nonexistent, especially in winter, and bread was several days old by the time it got to the Korets' table. Although Abram was a grocer, he and Sarah often went without so they could provide food for their four growing sons.

There is some evidence that the Korets moved to Brooklyn at one point during their time in New York, but life remained hard and the struggles continued. Like other immigrants, they lived in deplorable conditions in dilapidated buildings with dozens of other struggling families. There was no running water in tenement apartments, and the only toilet facilities were located outside—usually marked by a long and desperate line to get in. As Joe recalled in the taped interview:

> The early days in New York were hard days. Up until the time I was seventeen, our winters were cold and slushy. They were particularly cold to me because my shoes weren't so good. They had holes in them. What you read about in some of the storybooks was true. You took newspaper and lined the inside of your shoes so you weren't exposed to the cold so much on the frozen sidewalks.

The grocery business turned out to be one failure after the other. No matter how hard Abram Koret tried, he simply could not get ahead. "There was a succession of grocery stores," Joe said. "[My father] would buy one and it was unsatisfactory, so he'd sell it and buy another, and sell it. Four of us working didn't even make the salary of one. It was a terrible cut-rate business, and the profit margin was almost nil. It was as bad as a tailor's hours. From sunup to sunset, and then beyond sunset. The average closing time was ten o'clock at night. It was a lousy business."

Many years later, Joe shared the memory of how he occasionally would venture to the shore of the East River or up to the lake in Central Park to see if he could supplement whatever his mother might be able to scrounge up for dinner. One day when he was around twelve, he was collared by a police officer, who inquired why he was carrying a fishing pole and some string. "I had a fish, a big bluegill, which I shoved down the front of my shirt," he recalled. "I never went to jail. My motivation for keeping the fish was simply hunger."[6] Although he didn't know this at the time, fishing would become a lifelong obsession. No other pursuit would be as relaxing and gratifying, and yield such comforting and nutritious results.

Because they both had to work to help support the family, Joe and his older brother, Al, never completed a formal education. This didn't keep either of them from dreaming, as both were innately intelligent, ambitious, and determined to make a better life for themselves and the rest of the family. As months turned into years, however, it became clear that New York City was not the place where any of them would find their fortune.

Eventually, fate intervened. In 1917, midway through the first Great War, an uncle from California traveled east to New York and paid the Korets a visit. This uncle, whose name is lost to history, found Abram and his family living in squalid conditions, not much better than when they had first arrived in America fifteen years before. Abram had bought and sold several retail operations, never making a profit and never getting a toehold in life. Now in their teens, Joe and Al continued to work side-by-side with their father, but their prospects for prosperity were growing dim. On top of that, their abiding love and loyalty to family prevented them from striking out on their own.

The uncle from the West Coast changed all that.

"Come out to California," he told Abram during a family dinner toward the close of his visit. "Things are better there, and you can get ahead."

The two older Koret sons were eager to chase this opportunity, but their father wasn't nearly as enthusiastic.

"Listen to him, Papa," Joe urged his father. "For all the work we've done we have nothing to show for it."

"Joseph's right," Alexander agreed. "I'm tired of living like this. We can do better."

But their father was tired after decades of hard work, and he still felt responsible for feeding and clothing his wife and two younger sons. Life had not turned out as his dreams had promised, but at least New York was a known quantity.

"This is where we live," Mr. Koret reminded them.

"This is not living, Abram," the uncle persisted. "This is poverty. If you stay here you will never pull yourself out of it."

"Besser ain ku in shtal aider tsen in feld," the stubborn man replied. Better one cow in the stable than ten in the field.

"What do you know from cows?" the uncle said.

"New York is our home—"

"So was Odessa, but you saw fit to leave," Joe reminded him. "And I want to leave New York. There's nothing for me—for any of us—in this city."

Abram Koret was faced with a serious dilemma. New York was where he and his family lived, but it also was a place of severe hardship. He had worked diligently the past sixteen years but had nothing tangible to show for it. Plus, his two eldest sons were mature enough to strike out for themselves and seek their own fortune—just as he had done when he was only a few years older than they were. He could hardly blame them for wanting to try something new, something that promised them more than the paltry existence that currently defined their lives. Abram Koret was reluctant to start over and reinvent himself, but the not-so-gentle reminder of his own desire for a better life struck home with him. Joe and Al made it clear they were ready to follow their dreams, and they had every right to do so.

To the end a family man, Abram saw the writing on the wall. He took a deep breath, then agreed to pack up his family and their meager belongings and head west.

Young Joe Koret's hosiery stall was one of the original shops in the Crystal Palace Market when it opened its doors on Market Street in 1922.

[San Francisco Historical Museum/San Francisco Public Library]

2

The Streets of San Francisco

IN LATE 1917, THE KORET FAMILY BOARDED A train at Penn Station in New York with their minds set on making a new life in California.

They traveled by second-class day coach, which meant they had to sleep on hard wooden seats rather than in the more expensive first-class berths. The family changed trains twice along the way, in Chicago and Ogden, Utah, and disembarked five days later at the Southern Pacific station located at Sixteenth Street in Oakland. They brought very few belongings with them, but there was little need for the threadbare winter coats and ragged gloves that had served as grim reminders of their poverty in New York City. It was California's rainy season, which meant the rolling hills were as green as mounds of emeralds. Even inside the rattling train car, the sun seemed brighter and the air cleaner. Except for the long climb through the Rocky Mountains and then the Sierra Nevada, there was no sign of snow. No ice, no slush. No need to stuff paper into shoes or stand in line in a blizzard in order to use a toilet.

As the mother, father, and four boys stepped down from the car, they were struck by the lack of cold. This was winter, yet the temperature was unbelievably mild. In the days before the massive infilling of the bay, the train station was just a stone's throw from the Oakland waterfront, and the scent of the Pacific Ocean hung in the air. There was a sense of optimism and hope everywhere; even the porters and conductors were smiling as they greeted the new arrivals. Things were beginning to look up for the Korets, even more so once they took the ferry across the bay to San Francisco, where they marveled at all the new construction and thriving businesses springing up everywhere they looked.

The building boom was one of necessity, not indulgence. Just over a decade earlier, the catastrophic earthquake of 1906 had demolished hundreds of structures and ignited a destructive inferno that ravaged the entire city. By the time the dust and smoke finally settled, as many as three thousand people were dead and over 80 percent of the city had been demolished. Insurance losses from the quake, thought to have been a 7.9 as measured by today's Richter Scale, were estimated at $400 million, or approximately $12 billion today.[1]

As deadly and destructive as the quake was, the building boom that followed transformed San Francisco into the world-class city it is today. Within weeks of the near-total devastation, streetcars were running up and down Market Street. The banks reopened, and thousands of tons of rubble from crumbled buildings was carted to the bay each week, part of a continuing expansion of the city's waterfront. As the *San Francisco Chronicle* reported the following year, "The new city looked different—more modern, cleaner. The old Victorian downtown was gone; the slums South of Market had been burned out. It was as if the board had been wiped clean. The push was to build steel-framed, Class A buildings."[2]

In 1909, three years after the earthquake, San Francisco held a three-day bash called the Portola Festival, to show off its nearly twenty thousand new buildings. As an extension of this celebration, in 1915—just nine years after its near-destruction—the city hosted the Panama-Pacific International Exposition, a world's fair erected on top of earthquake rubble in the new Marina District. "The fair was a daydream of a lost past, at once an elegy and a picture of what was to come," historian Kevin Starr wrote in the *Chronicle*.[3]

Within weeks of the Koret family's arrival, Abram opened a small second-hand clothing store and the family settled into a considerably more comfortable life on Russ Street in San Francisco. Since most of the city had been destroyed just over a decade before, their accommodations were relatively new and could only have been better than what they'd experienced on the Lower East Side of Manhattan.

Several months later they moved again, and the 1920 federal census of San Francisco reports all six were living in a residence on Moss Street, one block over from their previous home. The area was an emerging neighborhood South of Market Street, home to many of the city's newly arriving working-class families. Because of the area's growing economy, suitable employment for Abram and his two eldest sons was easier to come by than in New York. At age nineteen, Alexander found work in the railway office just blocks from home, while Joseph—who had turned seventeen just months before—was employed as a salesman in the ladies' division of the popular Hale Brothers Department Store.

The earliest public record of the Korets in San Francisco is a tiny squib in the *Chronicle*, dated March 24, 1918: "The Jolly Bachelors Club, recently formed in San Francisco, held its monthly get-together in the form of a banquet last night. The evening was taken up by speeches and discussing affairs of benefit to the club." One of the dozen or so members who attended the Jewish men's club event was Al Koret. Later this same year, both Al and his father registered for the U.S. draft, but neither was called to serve because World War I was already beginning to wind down.

In 1920, the post-war economy was flourishing, and emerging financial and religious opportunities continued to draw a sizable Jewish population to San Francisco. Many of the city's original Jewish settlers had landed in the South of Market neighborhood near downtown San

Francisco, where the Korets lived when they arrived. Following the earthquake, however, many of the more established families opted to relocate about twenty blocks farther west. As a result, several sizable Jewish neighborhoods had taken root, particularly in the Fillmore District near the intersection of Fillmore and McAllister Streets, just a couple blocks from where the now-famous Victorian "Painted Ladies" stand today.

The new streetcar system extended beyond the Fillmore District, but the Korets usually stayed close to home. Market Street was teeming with life, and while not viewed as quite as up-and-coming as the Fillmore neighborhood, this was where they lived, worked, and shopped. With three industrious men now bringing home a paycheck, there was a little more financial freedom. Mrs. Koret could buy fresh produce grown just a few hours away in the Central and Salinas Valleys, which were earning the reputation of "the salad bowl of the nation." The boys had new trousers and shirts rather than the ragged hand-me-downs they were forced to wear in New York. The two younger sons, Harold and Solomon, were enrolled in school, and everything their uncle had told them about California during his visit to New York was turning out to be true.

Then tragedy struck. In June 1921, fifteen-year-old Harold fell gravely ill with an undiagnosed illness. Since school had just ended for the summer, he stayed in bed the first day to recuperate, but the next day he seemed to be getting worse. A doctor came to visit, but there was little he could do except recommend that the child get a lot of rest. Mrs. Koret hovered over Harold, and on the morning of June 18 she briefly stepped out of the house in search of medicine that might help him get better. While she was gone, Alexander looked in on his little brother, and found him to be completely unresponsive. Harold had just died.

Little is known of the exact reason for the boy's death, which the coroner listed as "natural cause." It's very likely that Harold's immune system had been weakened while the family was still living in New

York, or he could have contracted pneumonia or some other type of insidious bug. As Stephen Miller, a professional genealogist based in Oakland, notes, "It was not very unusual for a child that age to die back then. Since antibiotics were still decades away, Harold probably had a lingering infection which may have been exacerbated by an opportunistic infection such as pneumonia, which pushed him over the edge."[3]

Another scenario—one that seems highly likely—is that he had contracted tuberculosis, which arrived in San Francisco during the Gold Rush days. Known as the "scourge of the city," this highly infectious disease was spread via microscopic droplets in the air and attacked the lungs of those who inhaled it. A project initiated by the University of California San Francisco identified those neighborhoods where early cases of the disease had been reported, and the Koret's apartment was located directly in the center of the several-block area that was hardest hit.[4]

Harold's death cast a dark cloud over the Koret household. The journey west was supposed to unlock myriad new opportunities, but instead it brought grief to the struggling family. The heartache Mrs. Koret felt over the loss of her youngest child almost immobilized her, and Mr. Koret found himself paralyzed with guilt as well. His business suffered, and everyday life was riddled with anguish and sadness. It was as if the Korets had lost their own Tiny Tim, and none of them would ever be the same.

EARLY THE FOLLOWING YEAR, ABRAM KORET gave up his second-hand store and returned to his earlier trade as a tailor, this time in a modest shop located on Fourth Street, just south of Market. He continued in that line of work for a number of years, at least through the 1930 federal census, which lists it as his place of business. Today, the shop on Fourth Street has been replaced by contemporary mixed-use retail and office space just a half block-from the city's popular Metreon complex.

Despite his early years of poverty and hunger, Joe Koret grew up with an eye that always viewed the glass as half-full rather than half-empty. Census reports indicate that his education in New York was spotty at best, since he usually worked long hours in his father's store and often peddled stale food and yesterday's newspapers to passersby. As Joe reached adulthood, he realized that the lack of a formal education would prevent him from succeeding in such traditional occupations as doctor or accountant. This didn't bother him, for he was an entrepreneur at heart who imagined himself creating an independent enterprise where his street smarts and innate talents could be tested. He had seen his father slave sixty and seventy hours a week in New York sweatshops with no chance of ever getting ahead and wisely decided that life was not for him. While Abram Koret's efforts to own his own a series of retail stores led to a parade of failures, his son developed a strong sense of self-reliance and a keen instinct for business. Instilled with an innovative spirit and boundless enthusiasm, Joe envisioned a world in which he toiled for himself rather than as a salaried worker tied to another man's greed.

Fortunately, Joe was a quick study and absorbed everything he saw and heard. He learned from his father's mistakes and saw them as lessons to improve upon. He would prove to be unafraid to put his last dime on the line for a business prospect, and would readily admit when he had miscalculated or made a poor decision. By the time he turned twenty-one, he was itching to leave his sales job at the department store and seek whatever fortune he could find, so he began evaluating the marketplace. The risk of quitting his department store job was small; he still lived at home with the rest of the family, so he wouldn't find himself out on the street if he failed. And the upside was significant, since San Francisco was booming and the sky was the limit for those who worked hard.

Around this time, two enterprising brothers, Oliver and Arthur Rousseau, purchased four acres of prime San Francisco real estate at the corner of Market and Eighth Street. Earlier in the city's history, the site had housed the Mechanics Institute Pavilion, after which it became home to the first ballpark constructed for the new California Baseball League. Eventually the league outgrew the park and it was replaced by a theater, which was destroyed in the earthquake. For the next sixteen years, the vacant lot hosted a variety of traveling festivals and carnivals, including the world-famous Ringling Brothers and Barnum & Bailey Circus.

The Rousseau brothers had a different plan in mind for the plot of land. Their father, Charles Rousseau, was a highly regarded San Francisco architect who had schooled his sons in the design elements and building techniques of the day. To Oliver and Arthur, a piece of land was a blank slate for opportunity, and that corner lot was a chance to deliver on a dream. Realizing that Market Street was exploding as a central commerce district, the brothers erected a seventy-one-thousand-square-foot marketplace designed to sell goods from every corner of the United States and around the world.[5] According to writer/historian Gail MacGowan, the new Crystal Palace Market—named after the famous structure built in London seventy years before—featured virtually every kind of food and dry good imaginable: "Sixty-five shops included four dairy stands, four poultry stands, six butcher shops, three fish markets, and seven fruit and vegetable stands. It featured a pet shop, a five and dime, two tobacco shops, and a phonograph record store."[6]

The Crystal Palace Market also offered silk stockings, socks, garters, and other hosiery goods in a small stall owned and operated by a young entrepreneur named Joseph Koret. Taking advantage of his department-store salesmanship, as well as the close proximity to where he lived, Joe signed on as one of the original merchants when the Crystal Palace Market opened its doors in December 1922. Comfortable footwear had been a persistent issue for Joe since his early days in New York, and it seemed natural that he would go into business selling goods designed to keep feet warm and looking fashionable.

The hosiery stall was a modest success, but over time Joe came to realize he was not going to find his fortune simply by selling stockings. Ever watchful and always learning, he studied his customers and the clothes they wore as they walked by or stopped in to shop. Friendly and talkative, he would strike up a conversation to see what people liked and didn't like. Fashion in the early 1920s was taking on a notable postwar flair as women abandoned the restrictive designs that were regarded as relics from Victorian England, and shifted to apparel that was more comfortable. Despite the enactment of Prohibition—the Eighteenth Amendment to the Constitution had gone into effect on January 17, 1920—social customs were becoming more progressive. More and more women were entering the workforce, and the Nineteenth Amendment to the Constitution had just granted them the right to vote.

One day, Joe Koret struck up a conversation with a young woman who had a distinct eye for fashion. She was from a traditional Jewish family and lived with her parents in the Fillmore District. Like the Korets, her family had emigrated to the United States because of mounting religious persecution and the possibilities promised by a new life in America. Born in Bucharest, Romania, she had recently graduated from high school and was taking design classes at a local fashion institute. Like most women of the time, she welcomed the more relaxed cultural mores introduced at the end of the war, including a growing acceptance of women in the workplace. And like Joe, she was guided by unbridled optimism and hard work, and was possessed of a strong entrepreneurial drive.

She introduced herself as Stephanie Diana Brown (her last name had been changed from Braunstein during the immigration process) and by all accounts Joe was smitten immediately.

Despite the relatively permissive times, theirs was a traditional courtship that followed the customs of their respective homelands. Family dinners were important to both the Korets and the Browns, and Joe and Stephanie passed their respective parental tests with ease. A romantic duo from their first chance encounter, they did the things most couples in San Francisco did. They took the trolley out to Playland at the Beach and rode the new Bob Sled Dipper roller coaster and the wet and wild Shoot-the-Chutes. They took grainy pictures of themselves in the photo booth there (unfortunately, no images remain), and window-shopped up and down Fillmore Street. And on occasion, they rode the ferry to Marin County, where Joe also sometimes enjoyed a walk in the woods on his own to a quiet stream where he could drop a hook into the water.

Stephanie relished the tranquility of nature, but she neither understood nor possessed the patience it took to wait for what seemed like hours for a fish to jump on the line. Still, she adored Joe and it didn't take long for her to decide to follow wherever he led—and vice versa. More and more, their discussions involved women's fashion and the burgeoning garment business. Stephanie possessed a creative flair that could turn a simple pencil sketch into a stylish dress or skirt that was a pleasure to look at and comfortable to wear. Meanwhile, Joe was amassing a body of merchandising knowledge that gave him insight into new marketing and sales techniques. Through his discussions with suppliers and customers, he was starting to grasp the underpinnings of the San Francisco clothing industry, particularly women's apparel. Plus, his sales experience at the department store and hosiery shop put him face-to-face with women who were looking for the latest fashions.

As their romance blossomed, Joe and Stephy—as he liked to call her—came to the inevitable conclusion that any partnership between them would encompass both the home and the office. They were ambitious, determined, young people living in a city that knew no bounds. They also were blessed to have parents who supported the dreams of their children—the same dreams that had drawn them to the United States in the first place. Over the years, Joe became a champion of motivational maxims, such as "Plan your work and work your plan" and "Nothing ventured, nothing gained." These aphorisms had been instilled in him at an early age, and they guided his business sense throughout his career.

One of these sayings was a line widely attributed to Helen Keller: "Alone we can do so little; together we can do so much." That seemed to be the truism that directed Joe and Stephanie in the early months of their courtship. They considered themselves a team both in love and in business, for better or for worse, until death did them part. Their plan was to blend their respective passions for business and fashion and create an enterprise that would provide them a comfortable life. Little did they realize what they were getting themselves into, and the full scope of what that venture would become.

In June 1924, Joe Koret and Stephanie Brown applied for a marriage license. They were married a few days later in a festive ceremony at her family's synagogue and moved in with her parents on Golden Gate Avenue. The apartment, just a few blocks from the center of the bustling Fillmore District, was a jovial if somewhat crowded abode. Stephanie's two sisters, Anne and Mimi, still lived there as well, and her brother, Leo, occasionally dropped in for the evening.

During those early years, husband and wife worked hard, as they did for the rest of their lives. Joe gave up his hosiery shop at the Crystal Palace Market and found a job at Snyder Brothers, a popular knitwear manufacturer and distributor, selling women's sweaters to shops and department stores up and down the West Coast. Stephanie tried her hand at designing skirts and dresses for women in search of practical clothing they could afford, rather than simply gawk at in fashion magazines. The skyrocketing number of women in the workplace was creating a need for attire that was attractive, sensible, and comfortable—and available at a reasonable price.

Joe spent most of those early days traveling north to Seattle and south to San Diego as he peddled his sweaters. Initially, he worked exclusively for Snyder Brothers, where he enjoyed modest success, but he began to see that his sales opportunities were limited by his product line. The sweaters were popular and of good quality, but limited in their variety. Since Joe worked as a direct contractor paid completely on commission, he was not contractually bound to sell only Snyder Brothers' products. Thus, he began marketing several different lines of sweaters, which gave him the diversity of goods he needed in order to satisfy his direct customers—the store managers who knew what their customers were likely to buy. Comfort and fit were always at the top of the list, followed by style and price. Realizing that fashion was dictated by season, Joe took a commonsense approach to his sales, focusing on placing warmer sweaters in stores at the end of summer and selling lighter sweaters as soon as the December holidays were over. This gave manufacturers time to produce, pack, and ship the sweaters to stores long before demand hit its seasonal peak.

Ever watchful and mentally nimble, Joe tuned in to what customers had to say. He learned that some sweaters fit better than others. Some were comfortable, while others were made of wool that scratched, or they wore out at the elbows. Some were totally inappropriate for the office or on the factory assembly line. Sweaters that looked good on the rack often lost their shape after being worn just once. Dry cleaning was expensive, and the yarn from which many sweaters were made tended to pill or unravel. Joe listened carefully to his customers' concerns, and they eventually began to ask if he had anything besides sweaters in that big product case he lugged from store to store. Women shoppers were always looking for innovative ways to enhance their overall appearance, and an attractive sweater was just one part of the overall ensemble. They often seemed to find a few extra dollars to spend if they could pair one garment with something else that created a sharp new look. If Joe just had a skirt or even a new blouse that might match the sweaters—well, the opportunities could be endless.

Joe heard what these customers were telling him. No matter what the color, design, or fit, a sweater was designed to be worn over a shirt or blouse and paired with a skirt. It seemed so obvious: women rarely ventured into a store with the notion of buying just a sweater; most of the time they were looking for a complete outfit, top to bottom. Ideally, they wanted a two- or three-piece combination that gave them confidence in their appearance, whether going to work, the grocery store, or out to dinner with their husbands.

In other words, they wanted color coordinates. Mix and match. No-iron pleats. *Permanent press.* Qualities that would bring massive change to the women's apparel industry.

Joe and Stephanie board a plane for a sales and design trip
to New York in the early 1940s.
[Bancroft Library collection]

3

California Dreaming

ASK ANYONE WHAT SINGLE DEMOGRAPHIC MOST defined women's fashion in the 1920s, and nine times out of ten the response will be "flappers."

The flapper movement was a postwar cultural statement that allowed free-minded women to thumb their noses at the smothering garments and restrictive customs that had jumped the pond from Victorian-era England. Newly liberated and encouraged by enlightened modern-day thinking, flappers celebrated the perceived emergence of permissive social and sexual attitudes. Eschewing the toe-to-throat fashions of the past, they typically dressed in short, loose-fitted skirts. They wore their hair in short bobs and scorned what, at the time, was considered conventional behavior. More specifically—and largely intentionally—flappers were chastised by the social establishment as exhibiting loose morals, smoking cigarettes, wearing excessive makeup, and otherwise flouting long-held customs and values.

This fad, however, was just the visible tip of a cultural iceberg that was lurking beneath the surface of American progress. The end of the "The Great War" had brought hundreds of thousands of veterans home from Europe, where they had been exposed not only to the violence of combat but also to myriad cultural influences that inevitably shaped their lives and expectations back home. Meanwhile, their wives, mothers, and girlfriends had participated in the war effort by going to work in factories and assembly lines. These influences were bound to shake long-held traditions to the core, and within a few short years they did.

At the same time, new technologies were making the country seem smaller. The first commercial radio broadcast occurred in November 1920, introducing millions of American homes to a host of news and entertainment programming. Meanwhile, a burgeoning movie industry—fueled by D. W. Griffith's highly controversial three-hour film *The Birth of a Nation*—was changing the way Americans were entertained. Hundreds of "picture palaces" sprang up from coast to coast, many of them massive theaters that could hold several thousand moviegoers at a time. The first "talkies" were introduced around 1926, and shortly thereafter Hollywood became synonymous with show-biz glamour and fashion. Swashbuckling actors and romantic leading men caused women's hearts to melt, while bewitching actresses were idolized by millions of loyal fans who fantasized about their dazzling lives.

These movie stars quickly became leading ladies of fashion as well as on screen. In a decade already riddled with change, they challenged old-fashioned styles by flaunting their figures, shortening their hemlines, and painting their faces. Dozens of movie magazines regaled their readers with the latest gossip and fashions of such actresses as Greta Garbo, Joan Crawford, Clara Bow, and Gilda Gray. Hollywood's undisputed fashion influence, along with the shifting attitudes of women, led to a seismic social shift in America.

But dreams and reality typically travel separate paths that often don't intersect. Joe and Stephanie Koret knew this, and while they studied Hollywood to see what was influencing the fantasies of American women, they primarily looked to the sidewalks of San Francisco to gauge what the women of the day really were—and *were not*—wearing. Wriggling into a form-fitting silk gown draped with diamonds and emeralds for a celebrity party hosted by Douglas Fairbanks and Mary Pickford was a star-studded fantasy, but dressing for a long day in a smoke-filled office was the reality that drove America's true fashion industry.

For most women, this meant skirts, blouses, and sweaters. In other words, the basics.

That's what Joe Koret was all about. Ambitious by nature, he learned his sales craft one day at a time. While he initially represented sweaters manufactured by Snyder Brothers, he also served as a Pacific Coast salesman for Sebro Knit Sportswear, which at one time had been known as the Knit Sportswear Company. As long as Joe was making a profit, these companies didn't mind him spreading his sales talents across several product lines, and his West Coast business began to grow. Still, the rigors of being on the road took a toll on his marriage. Joe's young bride was tiring of life alone, and kept urging her husband to try to find work closer to home. After all, the San Francisco economy was thriving and there were more than enough women to be dressed in the Bay Area. There was no need to clothe every female form from Seattle to San Diego.

By the late twenties, the Korets had moved into their own small apartment on Fulton Street, in the heart of the Fillmore District. Stephanie's life was one of lonely nights highlighted by brief telegrams from the road. Not one to brood, however, she distracted herself by designing a line of attractive skirts and blouses during those long weeks her husband was gone. While she always looked forward to Joe's short visits home in between sales trips, she also found confidence in her creative abilities and a flair for fashion.

The long weeks spent on the road eventually began to pay off. Joe would come home with a notebook full of ideas he'd picked up on the road, and Stephanie was eager to hear them. At the top of this long list was the need for blouses that would match the sweaters he sold. Women were developing a strong sense of personal style, but their limited household budgets often left little room for an expensive wardrobe of pieces designed to go together. If it were possible to buy separate items of clothing—maybe several blouses to go with a single sweater, and possibly a skirt—they could seriously stretch their minimal clothing dollars.

Armed with this knowledge, Stephanie began designing a line of blouses that would be suitable for the sweaters in Joe's growing line. Again, the companies Joe worked with didn't mind if Joe sold blouses along with their garments, since he was able to convince retailers to increase their overall orders as women began to appreciate the ease of mix-and-match shopping. In fact, the folks at Snyder Brothers were so impressed with Stephanie's eye for design that they employed her as an assistant to their primary sweater designer. As her own line of blouses began to take off, the Korets introduced a coordinated line of skirts designed to be worn with the blouses and the sweaters, thereby expanding the shopper's wardrobe and wallet. Without even really realizing it, the Korets had turned their small apartment on Fulton Street into the headquarters of their first clothing enterprise.

In the late 1920s, Joe's entrepreneurial confidence began to kick in. He and three business acquaintances ponied up some hard-earned savings and formed the Sportswear Manufacturing Company. The goal of this new company was to produce and market a basic line of Stephanie's knitted suits, dresses, and blouses. She also was single-handedly responsible for designing the fledgling company's trendy sharkskin knit suit, which quickly gained regional popularity.

During its first months of operation, the Sportswear Manufacturing Company turned a modest profit, and Joe began to view it as his entrepreneurial ticket to the future. In his mind he now had the foundation on which to build a successful women's apparel firm: sweaters, skirts, blouses, and dresses. That, combined with his wife's eye for style and his own wealth of merchandising knowledge, meant that nothing could stand in his way. Except for some sort of unforeseen economic setback.

That setback came on October 29, 1929, when the bottom fell out of Wall Street. Almost overnight, the Dow Jones Industrial Average lost almost half its value and, by the time the worst of the crash was over three years later, the market had plunged almost 90 percent. Joe and Stephanie, and their business partners, struggled to keep the company afloat, but financial disaster was sweeping the country. Hard-working Americans lost their jobs by the millions; low crop prices forced farmers out of business; and over-extended investors watched their bank accounts evaporate. Consumer confidence fell off a cliff; banks closed; and family savings vanished. Household budgets were stretched to the limits, and when faced with the very real threat of not being able to put food on the table, men and women alike had to forget about that new pair of trousers or a fashionable sweater.

The Sportswear Manufacturing Company collapsed under the weight of the Depression, and Joe was forced to return to the road. He picked up where he had left off prior to the crash, selling garments for Westwood Knitting Mills of Los Angeles, Nuvelle of New York, and again for Snyder Brothers. Just as before, Stephanie designed and sewed a small line of complementary skirts such as one featuring a box pleat and another other with a flared hem. Later, as these pairings grew more successful, she added jackets to the skirts to make two-piece suits. Even in those early years, she was guided by the standard of "meticulous fit and finish," which was important because these garments were slightly more expensive than other competing merchandise.

Despite ongoing economic challenges and Joe's departure from the company, the Sportswear Manufacturing Company would continue to produce a limited range of apparel until early 1940, when the firm's partners liquidated its assets in an auction. An ad in the *San Francisco Chronicle* announced that the sale would be held at the company's Minna Street headquarters, offering used knitting machinery, sewing machines, cutting machines, a pressing machine, and even a cooling system.[1]

By the mid-thirties, Joe was finished with the road. Tens of thousands of miles spent on trains and, later, behind the wheel of his well-traveled Ford, had worn him out. He'd spent so much time away from home that he was like a father who never had time to see his children grow up. New buildings were shooting up in the booming financial district downtown, and automobiles had replaced the horses and buggies that had clogged the streets when he had arrived as a teenager fewer than twenty years before.

But that was just the façade. Beneath the surface, San Francisco was reeling financially, just like every other city in America. The Great Depression continued to squeeze the city that had seen decades of prosperity and expansion. Thousands of workers who had earned a decent living during the Roaring Twenties suddenly were jobless, with no means to support themselves or their families. Unemployment in San Francisco mushroomed, leaving many men, women, and children with little to eat and no place to seek shelter. At the same time, tens of thousands of people back east also had lost work and all hope, and many of them headed west to the Golden State. Some who had a few dollars to spare bought passage on one of the trains that snaked its way west, while those with nothing in their pockets either caught rides from passing motorists or hopped freight cars.

Still mindful of the extreme poverty and deplorable conditions he and his family had endured during those cold days of hunger in New York, Joe remembered the hollow, empty feeling in his stomach when all he and his family had to eat was a loaf of stale pumpernickel bread. "No man who wants to work should go hungry," he told his wife more than once. In fact, it was a notion that would remain in the forefront of his thoughts during those troubling times as breadlines and shanty towns sprang up across the country. No matter where he traveled, the signs of despair were all around him, and he pledged to himself that one day he would do all he could to make sure no one went hungry again. It was a tall order, but Joe was a principled man, instilled with the basic human values his father had taught him, and he stood on his convictions.

The Korets did not escape the hard times. As families faced financial ruin and jobs dried up, so did sweater sales. Clothing budgets vanished, and whatever money might have been available for a new skirt or sweater now was spent on food and shelter. Men and women alike found themselves without a paycheck, and many were forced to make do with what they had. They patched holes in trousers and repaired hems in threadbare skirts. Socks were darned until they could hold no more thread, and sweaters were repaired so often they puckered and pinched at the elbows. The boom times that had raged just a few years before had come to a screeching halt, and apparel sales were hard for a man who plied his trade up and down the seaboard selling goods no one could afford.

Despite the hard times, San Francisco remained critical to the U.S. economy. The opening of the Panama Canal in 1914 and the completion of the transcontinental railway a half century before had established the city as a major Pacific port. Dozens of ships sailed through the Golden Gate, and hundreds of boxcars full of goods arrived either in San Francisco or Oakland every week. Each of these ships and trains needed to be loaded and unloaded and—despite the Depression—the docklands and railroad yards were busy night and day.

By 1933, both widespread corruption and a plentiful supply of eager workers had caused the average weekly wage earned by longshoremen to plummet. If a worker protested the subsistence pay or long hours, he was shown the door and replaced by another strong back. At the same time, the National Recovery Act, signed by President Roosevelt, recognized the right of American workers to organize and engage in collective bargaining. The following February, the International Longshoremen Association convened in San Francisco and demanded that West Coast shipping companies raise the minimum pay of all dockworkers by a dollar and agree to other conditions.

The companies turned a deaf ear to their workers, and several months later thousands of longshoremen and sailors in every West Coast port walked off the job. "Strikebreakers" were brought in, which led to violent and bloody conflicts in San Francisco, as well as Oakland, Portland, and Seattle. The work shutdown lasted eighty-three days and helped to coalesce a nationwide labor movement, eventually organized through the Congress of Industrial Organizations.

Joe Koret, who could remember the days in New York when his father had served as a union organizer, sympathized with those strikers who were fighting for better wages and humane conditions in the shipyards. On a number of occasions, Abram Koret had come home from the garment factory bloodied and dispirited after standing up for those workers who made the goods that allowed their employers to live in posh Upper East Side brownstones. The blood on his father's shirt was just one of many images that would remain with Joe his entire life, fueling a compassionate work ethic for which he would be recognized by union leaders many years later.

By 1936, many of the effects of the Depression were beginning to wane. San Francisco recovered slightly ahead of the rest of the country, largely due to its position as the country's West Coast financial and shipping hub. With the creation of the Works Progress Administration in 1935, President Roosevelt—through executive order—directed that millions of dollars be spent on building roads, bridges, and other projects throughout the nation. San Francisco became one of the first cities in the country to receive funding from the WPA. New streets were paved, drainage systems were built, and public buildings were erected as part of this massive program. Thousands of people returned to work, and a city whose growth had been stalled by almost a decade of financial crisis began to move again.

A monument to this economic renaissance was the construction of the San Francisco–Oakland Bay Bridge in 1936. While it was not built with WPA funds, its completion provided a long-needed link between the East Bay and the city. The following year, the Golden Gate Bridge connected San Francisco with the Marin headlands to the north, ushering in yet another era of growth in the area. The Golden Gate Bridge also was not funded through the W.P.A., but the Lyon Street approach to the southern end of the bridge was one of the program's many citywide projects.

With the completion of these two bridges, the Bay Area grew—and at the same time got much smaller. Residents who previously had to spend up to an hour on passenger ferries now could commute to their downtown offices in almost half that time. The city continued to expand westward to the ocean, where the Bob Sled Dipper still rolled on its rickety wooden frame. New houses and apartment buildings began to emerge on streets that twenty years before had simply been grid lines on maps of dirt hillocks and sand dunes.

WHEN JOE FINALLY DECIDED TO BID THE ROAD farewell, he did so gradually. Because of his status as an accomplished salesman, he was able to restructure his accounts so he could cut back on his travel. He longed to start his own company once again and work exclusively for himself. The more he studied the clothing market and emerging fashion trends, the more he realized the phenomenal opportunities that existed. Plus, he had gained invaluable experience through the daily operations of the Sportswear Manufacturing Company. He knew the women's clothing business literally from collar to hemline. He had a notebook full of loyal customers who managed mom-and-pop shops and large department stores in every city and town on the West Coast. He possessed a firm grasp of effective sales techniques, and he'd developed unique merchandising strategies that he was convinced would give him an advantage over whatever competition he might encounter.

More than anything, however, he had Stephanie. Cut from the same entrepreneurial cloth, she possessed an innovative flair for design. With his input from the road, she'd already created a collection of simple but smart blouses and skirts that the "everyday woman" of the late thirties was looking for. An avid reader of Hollywood glamour magazines and fashion trade publications, she knew what styles were drawing the eyes (and pocketbooks) of women both regionally and nationally. More than anything, she saw the need for clothing that women could wear with comfort and confidence in almost any social setting.

In 1937, the young couple believed they were ready to strike out on their own, and Joe formed a company called Younger Set Sportswear. Not unlike the Sportswear Manufacturing Company, the new firm manufactured blouses and skirts, which he paired with sweaters from several of the best lines he'd sold on the road. The brand performed well enough to convince Joe and Stephanie that they were on the right path, but the term "Younger Set" by definition limited the company's target demographic. In fact, both Korets believed their primary customer was the average woman in her thirties or forties. She most likely was married with children, and was either a traditional housewife or employed as a secretary or assembly-line worker. She was dedicated to her family, had a wide circle of friends, and had an active social life. She also was smart when it came to finances, and—like most folks who had weathered the Depression—knew how to stretch a dollar to its limits.

Within a year, Joe realized the Younger Set brand didn't fill the fashion niche he and his wife had identified. While minimally profitable, it fell short of the cutting-edge sportswear company they initially envisioned. After much discussion ,they decided to fold the operation into a second firm that, for a very short time, was known as Koret Knits. Following a trademark complaint filed by Richard Koret, founder of the Koret Handbag Company of New York (and no known relation to Joe), the company name was changed to Koret of California. Logo and brand restrictions imposed in the settlement initially were considered a hindrance to the company's growth plans, but in the years to come "Koret of California" would become synonymous with contemporary women's apparel.

The first years were difficult. Then, as now, most small businesses failed within the first twelve months of their existence. Joe and Stephanie knew this new firm would be faced with challenges, and these anticipated struggles burdened them from the start. They had already invested most of their meager savings in Younger Set, and additional start-up capital was scarce. In addition to hiring contract cutters and seamstresses, they needed to buy fabric, zippers, buttons, and thread in bulk—often months before seeing any returns from sales.

Koret of California opened its doors in 1938 in a small loft at 111 Sutter Street, across from the then-innovative Hallidie Building. The Korets paid $30 a month for their space, which was just large enough to accommodate the two of them and a small area to display the latest fashion line. Most of the clothing was manufactured by contract workers employed at other firms in the Bay Area. Unlike many San Francisco company owners, however, Joe was proud to boast that all of his manufacturing was done by members of the local ILGWU, the same union for which his labor-organizer father had been beaten decades before in the New York sweatshops.

DURING ITS FIRST MONTHS ON SUTTER STREET, Koret of California struggled. Sales were modest, and the company just managed to break even. General overhead, manufacturing supplies, and the weekly payroll seemed to crush any progress the small firm was making. Joe was personally responsible for everything on the business end, while Stephanie took charge of all design functions. At one point during that first year, Joe examined the balance sheet and realized he was not going to be able to pay his contractors. This was a daunting prospect for a small firm with the odds of survival already stacked against it. If he couldn't pay his workers, the cutting and sewing machines would fall silent, and the company would go bust.

Joe couldn't let that happen. His name was the company's name, and he would not allow it to be associated with failure. He made an appointment with the branch manager of a large San Francisco–based bank to discuss the possibility of extending a small loan to tide him over until his accounts-receivable issues eased up.

"In 1939 I was doing business with contractors only because I didn't have enough money to put up a factory of our own," Joe recalled in the aforementioned video interview.

> I was trying to meet a payroll and I didn't have enough money. I went to one of the banks and told them I needed five hundred dollars for payroll. He asked me about nine trillion questions, and I filled out about 20 million papers. And they refused to give me $500. I felt terrible. I raised the $500 anyway, but it was a tremendous disappointment. Here's a young man and a young woman—my wife was dedicated, she worked like a dog—and this bank thought we weren't worth five hundred dollars.

While disappointed by—and disenchanted with—the financial world, Joe understood where the bank was coming from. Just ten years before, hundreds of financial institutions had been at the core of the Black Thursday crash. The subsequent run on the banks had wiped them out by the hundreds. That experience, and tighter scrutiny by federal regulators, made banks skittish about loaning money without collateral to back up the risk. Unfortunately, Joe had nothing to put up in return for the loan he was seeking.

"That's the way banking was in those days," Joe recounts in the video. "They'd be glad to lend you $500 if you had $5,000 worth of security for it. Fortunately, banking has changed since then."

Joe experienced profoundly different results with an upstart company from New York, whose business outlook was more forward-thinking. "The opposite of that was a meeting I had with Cohn-Hall-Marx," he observed. "At that time, they were extremely strong, they were a young outfit, and they were feeling their oats. And they had money."

The Cohn-Hall-Marx Company was founded in 1912 as a New York City textile "converter" that bought unfinished fabrics (known as "gray goods") from textile mills and sent them to finishing plants to dye or print the fabrics according to exact specifications. According to Funding Universe, a company that matches entrepreneurs with loans, "A converter requires no manufacturing facilities, so it can make a big return on small capital if it comes up with a popular design or color combination."[2]

One year before the 1929 stock market crash, investment bankers at Kidder, Peabody & Company in Boston proposed a merger between Cohn-Hall-Marx's converting business and their own wholly owned manufacturing plants. The deal was approved, and with a $20 million investment, United Merchants & Manufacturers was incorporated to acquire interests in various New York textile-selling houses or converters.[3] Cohn-Hall-Marx remained UM&M's core business, and by 1935 the company had net sales of nearly $35 million. Many of the firm's customers were poorly financed apparel manufacturers that couldn't obtain credit or supplies through regular financial channels.

Koret of California fit that description to a "T."

In 1939, the credit manager at Cohn-Hall-Marx was a genial and ambitious man named Sam Simon. He spent a substantial amount of time visiting knitting mills and apparel manufacturers on the West Coast, servicing existing accounts and drumming up new business. "I heard Sam Simon was helping build [the textile] industry in Los Angeles because of his liberality and his credits," Joe recalled. "A lot of those people didn't have any money and he was helping them."

One day, Joe got wind that Mr. Simon was in San Francisco, and he managed to track him down. "I told him my story," he said. "I told him what the bank had done, how terrible I felt. Here I was—myself and my wife were working so hard and trying to get ahead—and I don't seem to be able to get a start. 'I need credit,' I told him. 'I need textiles. I'm selling way more goods than I can deliver.' "

Sam listened intently to what Joe was telling him and said, "Let me buy you and your wife a lunch. I want to meet her."

Joe jumped at the opportunity and set up a lunch date for the next day. He reiterated what he had said in their previous meeting, and Mr. Simon pressed both Joe and Stephanie on their vision. At the end of the meeting Sam took Joe aside and said, "Look—I have faith in you and I have faith in your wife. I'd like to offer you a line of credit."

Joe was overwhelmed by the offer, but cautious at the same time. "That's marvelous," Joe replied, wondering what kind of catch there might be. There was *always* a catch. "What kind of credit line are we talking about?"

"We will open you up with a limit of $50,000," Mr. Simon told him. "Starting immediately."

As Joe Koret recounted nearly forty years later, the line of credit Sam Simon granted that day was the difference between success and failure. "One guy wouldn't give me $500, this guy gives me $50,000," he says in the video interview. "He really enabled us to get into business. Up to that time we were scratching for payroll. He made a very wise move."

The only catch in the deal was that the line of credit was good solely for materials purchased from Cohn-Hall-Marx or one of the companies owned by UN&M. But the growing conglomerate was in serious acquisition mode, so this was not an issue since most of the fabrics Koret would use in manufacturing its skirts and blouses came from those mills anyway. The credit line meant that Joe no longer had to pay for materials up front; he now could order up to $50,000 worth of fabric and pay for it after his own accounts had paid for the finished garments they received. The company's ledgers from the early 1940s indicate that Cohn-Hall-Marx was one of Koret of California's biggest suppliers, with Koret purchasing several thousand dollars' worth of critical materials from the firm every month.

WITH THEIR FINANCIAL CHALLENGES SOMEWHAT alleviated, Stephanie and Joe Koret were able to focus their respective attentions on designing and merchandising a full line of clothing that would appeal to the contemporary woman of the time.

Koret of California skirts and sweaters quickly earned a reputation of practical functionality; that is, they were comfortable, stylish, and were designed to be mixed and matched easily. Their price point, while slightly higher than that of some of their direct competitors, was budget-friendly, especially to women who were still sensitized to the lingering financial hardships of the 1930s. Essentially, any woman with a touch of fashion sense could create a functional wardrobe around just a couple of colors and fabrics.

Still, Koret of California—along with most clothing manufacturers— was challenged by one seemingly insurmountable hurdle: the amount of time it took a woman to iron a skirt after it was cleaned. These were the days before the words "machine wash, tumble dry" were found on magazine ads and clothing labels. In fact, most homes in the 'thirties were equipped with a laundry appliance known as the "wringer/mangler," or wringer washer. These devices washed clothing in a tub that agitated out the accumulated dirt and grime, after which the user fed the wet clothing through the wringer to squeeze out most of the water. Fingers often became a painful casualty of this tedious and thankless task.

In the absence of electric dryers, the wash then was hung up to dry, usually on clotheslines in the backyard. On top of that, almost every garment then had to be hand-pressed to remove wrinkles and to straighten pleats and creases. Housewives spent hours performing this mundane work, often listening to the radio as they ran the hot iron back and forth over dresses, skirts, and trousers. Broadcasters amassed a captive and loyal audience of women who tuned in to the "serial" story lines, and advertisers hawked soap and other cleaning products during the commercial breaks. Cleanliness existed side-by-side with godliness, and the daily "soap opera" was born.

Stephanie Koret was no different. Despite being a working woman, she was faced with the chores of washing and ironing every garment by hand. She understood what women were up against, and she fully empathized. Because of her focus on practical fashion she continually fussed over the challenge of keeping the pleats in a pleated skirt. This was long before the days of permanent press, and if a pleat was left to its own devices, it quickly ceased being a pleat.

While many couples would sit at the dinner table reviewing their respective days and talking about plans for the upcoming weekend, Joe and Stephanie were different. They worked, ate, and slept together. They spent their days discussing the challenges of the office, puzzling over whether a zipper should be placed on the side of a skirt or in the back. The color of buttons or a particular blend of fabric could occupy an entire dinner conversation. The length of a hemline or the width of a waistband was far more critical to them than any office gossip or newspaper headline.

Nowhere was this dedication to work more pronounced than the concept of pleats. Stephanie was obsessed with them. Pleated skirts were popular casual wear at the time, and she believed the American housewife would beat a path to Koret of California clothes racks if there was just a way to keep the creases straight—and permanent. The key was to design a better mousetrap, and then build it.

Enter the Trikskirt. According to Koret legend, one day Stephanie Koret (or, depending on who was telling the story, her husband) was sitting in the chair at the dentist's office. The doctor had stepped out of the exam room for a moment, and she began studying the window in the wall opposite her. Like many office windows at the time, it was fitted with venetian blinds, two-inch wood or metal slats held together by cloth webbing. They could be adjusted with pull cords that angled the slats or, with just a gentle tug of the cord, draw them upward and collapse them completely.

As the story goes, Stephanie raced back to the office and sketched out an idea that incorporated the same simple mechanics into a pleated garment. Instead of individual slats of wood or metal, however, her creation used folded sections of fabric stitched into individual pleats at the waistband. A drawstring then was inserted through eyelets in each pleat, so when the skirt was removed from the body the cord could be pulled and conveniently flatten the folds into layered pleats. The garment then could be placed in a dresser drawer or rolled up and tucked into in the bottom of a woman's handbag. The next time it was to be used the pleats would be allowed to unroll, the cord was loosened, and—voilà!—it looked as if it had just been pressed yesterday.

That was the story, but the reality is a little more complicated. Around the same time, a garment manufacturer named Arthur Heyman was living in Oakland, across the bay from the Korets. Heyman came from a family that, over the years, had created and patented a number of inventions ranging from collapsible stairs to innovative eyewear. It is not known whether Heyman and the Korets were business acquaintances, but Heyman and his wife, Bebe, owned a clothing manufacturing company known as Bab'nart. In the early 1940s, Arthur—who had considerable experience as a fabric cutter and clothing designer—created a "women's skirt pleated across the waistband portion," which he began manufacturing and selling under the name Trik Skirt.

Heyman applied for a design patent on October 13, 1941 (U.S. No. D135,819), noting in his application that "the characteristic feature of my design resides in the combination on the skirt disclosed of the stitched pleats extending through the waistband portion on the major portion of the skirt in association with oppositely disposed gores

Patent drawing of Arthur Heyman's Trikskirt, issued 1943. [U.S. Patent Office]

connecting the pleated portions, all as shown."[4] The patent was issued in 1943, along with a trademark for the Trik Skirt name.

Unbeknownst to the Heymans, around this same time Joe Koret filed for a patent of his own for a pleated skirt that took Arthur's Trik Skirt to another level. Joe's patent application was based on a garment sketched and actually manufactured in the Koret of California design studio. Described simply as a "Pleated Skirt," the six separate illustrations contained in the application depict not only how the garment was constructed so as to fold flat, but also to demonstrate how the ingenious drawstring system could pull the skirt closed in two seconds. As Joe's patent application described it, the system really was similar to the one used in venetian blinds:

> The pleats are accordion-like sections and extend from the lower edge of the skirt to the extreme upper edge of the skirt and arranged in such a way that the skirt folds flat into two

adjacent stacks of pleats connected across the top and bottom of the stacks by flat or out-folded sections, all held in this folded relation by a draw-string or tape. [This] passes in and out of the pleats around the waistband and is clearly exposed to view while the skirt is being worn.[5]

By this time, the United States was involved in World War II. A veteran of the first Great War, Arthur Heyman had dutifully reenlisted in the military, leaving his wife home in Oakland with a house to run and a greatly reduced household income. Pressed for cash, she met with Joe and Stephanie Koret, who, through the Bay Area fashion grapevine, had almost certainly heard of the Trik Skirt. Joe quickly recognized the value of the Trik Skirt trademark, and also grasped the potential similarities between his and Heyman's patents. For an undisclosed sum, Mrs. Heyman assigned the patent to Joe, and in June 1943 the Patent Office officially transferred it to the Korets.

Joe's patent for the "Pleated Skirt," filed in March 1943, was granted one year later (U.S. No. 2,344,462). With these two patents in hand, Joe and Stephanie geared up to create what they intuitively knew would revolutionize the women's clothing business. Stephanie set about designing the new Trikskirt with overall style and taste in mind, but she knew from experience that no woman would buy it if it wasn't comfortable to wear. She was obsessed with quality and fit. Long before any garment was considered ready for mass production, she took it through an exacting sketch process, repeatedly tweaking the design until she considered it perfect. Next, she created a number of mock-ups that she and other women in the office would try on and wear as everyday garments. Only when she was satisfied that the dress or skirt would fit all her personal style criteria did she sign off on its final production.

The design process for the Trikskirt took almost two full years. The Korets simply had to get it right the first time; there would be no second chance to introduce what they viewed as a ground-breaking

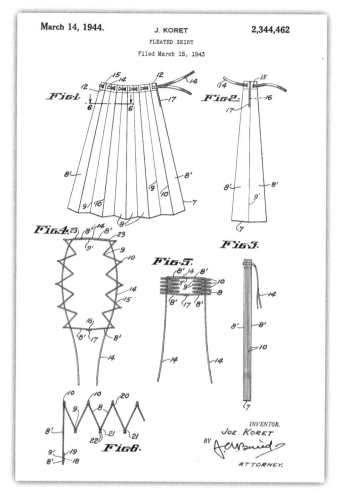

Patent drawing of Joe Koret's "pleated skirt," filed 1943. [U.S. Patent Office]

product. Joe worked tirelessly to develop a radical marketing and merchandising plan calculated to successfully pair the Trikskirt with the company's existing line of blouses and sweaters. Meanwhile, Stephanie devoted six—sometimes seven—days a week to the project until she was convinced it was perfect. During this process, the hard-driving couple still had to design, manufacture, and sell clothing lines already in the market, upholding the company's high standards and customer satisfaction.

The launch of the Trikskirt also was delayed by wartime manufacturing. After the attack on Pearl Harbor, virtually every factory in the

States was pressed into some kind of military production. Eager to help defeat the enemy forces in the Pacific and Europe—especially the madman in Germany who was persecuting and killing his fellow Jews—Joe zealously retooled his company to produce thousands of much-needed parachutes. A.P. Giannini, the founder of the Bank of America, personally extended a line of credit so Koret of California could make this critical switch. "The war transformed the Koret company from a locally oriented enterprise into a venture that was geared up for national markets and distributors," historian Kevin Starr would write years later in the *San Francisco Examiner*.[6]

As the war wound down and victory appeared assured, Joe and Stephanie refocused their attention on the Trikskirt. Through their arrangement with Cohn-Hall-Marx, they were able to purchase large quantities of fabric, eyelets, thread, and color-coordinated drawstrings to create a wide variety of garments. Also, as the government's need for parachutes subsided, Koret was able to shift his cutters and seamstresses back to civilian production. Through the summer of 1945, the company began manufacturing the Trikskirt timed to introduce it strategically in target markets, adequately fill advance retail orders, and generate consumer buzz.

Koret of California introduced the Trikskirt in late 1945 in select retail shops and department stores, and within a year it was a best seller from coast to coast. Actual sales figures no longer exist, but the company claimed that over three million were sold during the garment's decade-long run. With strong sales of blouses and sweaters to match, the Trikskirt earned Koret of California the status of a nationally recognized apparel company.

Employees in the Koret of California shipping department pack the company's popular "Trikskirt" for nationwide distribution in the mid 1940s.

4

The Postwar Boom

AMERICA'S ENTRY INTO WORLD WAR II CREATED
a seismic shift at home as well as on the battlefront.

Immediately after the Japanese attack at Pearl Harbor, President
Franklin Roosevelt proclaimed, "No matter how long it may take us to
overcome this premeditated invasion, the American people in their
righteous might will win through to absolute victory." Within days,
the entire nation had mobilized, with virtually every citizen taking
whatever patriotic measure he or she could in order to ensure that the
United States and its allies emerged victorious. All Americans, young
and old, men and women, were expected to sacrifice and contribute
to what the President termed the "Arsenal of Democracy."

In those early days of U.S. involvement, the deployment of millions
of American men took a toll on factories and assembly lines, drawing
hundreds of thousands of women into the workplace. This was particularly true of the aviation industry, which saw the greatest wartime
increase in the number of female workers. Prior to the attack on Pearl
Harbor in December 1941, less than 1 percent of the aircraft industry's employees was female, but by 1943 their numbers totaled over

310,000—almost two-thirds of the workforce. The government specifically targeted women with ads that suggested, "If you can use an electric mixer, you can learn to operate a drill."[1] The munitions industry also served as a major employer of women, spawning the U.S. government's "Rosie the Riveter" recruitment campaign. Loosely inspired by the lives of two women—Rosalind Walter and Rose Will Monroe—the bandana-wearing icon became synonymous with the nearly 19 million women who held jobs during the war.

The millions of women either returning to the workforce or entering it for the first time proved to be a boon for Koret of California. The company's garments were specifically tailored for the woman who led a double life: worker by day, housewife and mother by night. Koret purposely did not manufacture clothing to be worn on the assembly line, but once the five o'clock whistle blew and workers punched out, women preferred not to wear their overalls and work shirts home. Whether they had a husband or children waiting for them, they wanted to look presentable when they walked through the front door. Koret of California helped them do that.

As noted earlier, Stephanie's creations were designed with this duality in mind. Koret of California offered women the style they wanted after stuffing artillery shells all day long. Even before the inception of the Trikskirt, the company stressed that many of its garments could be placed in the bottom of a handbag and still be fresh at the end of the day.

Workplace demographics changed with the war, and so did Koret of California's fortunes. In July 1943, Joe signed a new lease that moved the company from its $30-per-month loft on Sutter Street to much larger space at 611 Mission Street, just a few blocks south of Market. The new rent was a whopping $200 per month, but the move allowed the company to consolidate a number of facilities that were scattered around the area. The expanded operation soon housed two new manufacturing facilities that Joe said would handle increased garment orders with maximum efficiency.

As Koret of California grew, so did its retail base. Initially viewed as a West Coast clothing company, Koret's designs and merchandising programs began to spread from one coast to the other. Over the next few months, the company launched a sales office in Dallas, and early in 1944 it opened a display area in New York City. While considered a temporary move overseen by salesman Arthur Oster, the showroom at the Hotel New Yorker was critical to Joe's plan to market the fall line of shirts, blouses, cardigans, pullovers, and weskits which were fashionable waistcoats for women.

Closer to home, Joe's family ties to—and support of—organized labor were starting to be recognized. Just before Christmas in 1943, Henry Zaharin, manager of the joint board of the International Ladies' Garment Workers' Union of San Francisco, lauded the city's future as a California garment center. "Manufacturers now have a greatly augmented market here in the Pacific slope, and the quality and styling of their merchandise has rightly won many of them national recognition," he proclaimed in a speech commemorating a new five-year agreement between workers and business owners. Singling out Joe's ongoing dedication to his employees, Zaharin noted that Koret of California "takes a direct interest in developing the efficiency of workers and ironing out technical details." Furthermore, Koret's record "shows a relatively small labor turnover, and [the company is] producing excellent merchandise at low unit cost. Koret might aptly be called the Henry Kaiser of the San Francisco apparel industry."[2]

THE REALITIES OF WORLD WAR II CHANGED San Francisco in ways that could hardly have been foretold. With the destruction of so many ships during the Japanese attack on Pearl Harbor, the entire Bay Area became a core component of the country's seagoing arsenal. Pristine marshland was replaced with massive boat-yards that constructed new battleships, which, within just a few years, would hasten America's victory in the Pacific. During the height of this construction boom, almost a quarter million Bay Area residents worked in these shipyards.

Fort Mason, on San Francisco's northern waterfront, became the main port of embarkation for the Pacific war. According to U.S. military records, over 1.6 million soldiers, sailors, and non-military personnel boarded ships here and headed west into the Pacific theater. Tens of thousands of these young men never made it home, but many of those who did traveled back through the Golden Gate at war's end. Faced with the option of returning to the family farm in Iowa or the dusky coal mines of Kentucky, many decided to remain in California and make a new life for themselves in a booming post-war America.

On the fashion front, the end of the war meant rations were eased and more fabric was available. Patterns and colors also changed, as designers created brighter and livelier styles. Cotton remained a favorite material for housedresses, but rayon—a synthetic fiber commercially developed in the mid-twenties—found a wider audience in post-war fashion. Essentially a semi-synthetic fiber, rayon is a manufactured cellulose product made from wood pulp that, through a combination of chemical and spinning processes, is turned into silk-like filaments.

Fashion designers quickly found that rayon was almost as com-fortable as natural fibers, although it tended to be slippery, like silk or nylon. Depending on how it was manufactured, it could take on the characteristics of cotton, linen, silk, and even wool. Material made from rayon could be dyed easily, and it tended to feel cool and comfort-able when worn. It also was highly absorbent, a critical factor in warm, humid climates where perspiration might be a fashion faux pas.[3]

The introduction of the Trikskirt and a post-war surge in consumer optimism helped to bolster Koret of California's bottom line. The small company still faced some manufacturing and distribution hurdles, often because it was difficult to keep up with demand. Through Joe's astute ability to read the marketplace and Stephanie's aptitude at the drawing board, the company came to be a leader in West Coast fashion styles and trends. At a public fashion show presented at the San Francisco Opera House in May 1946, the company introduced a fall line of sportswear that, "although barer than ever, was softened by ruffles, shirring, draping, or bows. Ensembles with separate skirts, scarves, and jackets were strongly endorsed as seen in the Koret of California's horizontal stripe and plain wool jersey playsuit. The extended shoulder midriff bra and snug boomer panties had a matching drawstring skirt."[4]

As more styles were added to an ever-increasing line of clothing, Koret of California created what it billed as a "style and research salon" at its Mission Street headquarters. This facility, which comprised just one sector of Stephanie's fashion department, occupied part of the fifth floor where her design offices were located. The new space housed a luxuriously furnished display showroom, with adjacent dressing rooms for models. Stephanie also installed his and hers restrooms for employees and visitors, as well as a fully equipped kitchen. The rest of the newly defined area was relegated to the styling and operational section, which held proprietary cutting tables and a variety of machines used in creating original styles and market samples. An additional display room was connected to the styling department's general office array, which was located next door to Stephanie's private office and apartment suite. When in the public eye, Stephanie was outgoing and buoyant, but privately she was somewhat of a recluse who enjoyed long stretches of solitude. To satisfy this occasional need for seclusion, she designed her own private boudoir, to which she would retire for a little "time out" or a much-needed nap.

The purpose of the new style-and-research department was twofold: to streamline the ongoing seasonal design process, and to provide educational resources that could assist in understanding past trends and create new apparel lines. According to a news release issued at the time, one of the features of the department was a library of rare editions of fashion books and manuals, some dating back as far as the twelfth century.[5] Stephanie was almost fanatical about women's and men's clothing, and spent countless hours studying the various cultural and social factors that influenced fashion trends through the centuries.

Around the same time, Joe opened a new factory at 375 Freemont Street, just a few blocks from the company's headquarters on Mission. The new plant consisted of 80,000 square feet—almost two full acres—and housed several ninety-foot cutting tables and the latest mass-production sewing machines designed for assembly-line manufacturing.

AFTER THE WAR, WHICH HAD PROVIDED RICH material for hundreds of patriotic action films and tearjerker romances, the glitz of Hollywood began to fuel new fashion trends as never before. Magazines and newsreels were bursting with Hollywood hyperbole and daily gossip about such actresses as Lana Turner, Lauren Bacall, Rita Hayworth, and Ingrid Bergman. Once again, the movies were fueling the imaginations of American women both young and old, and Hollywood costume designers were fashioning new fads every few weeks.

While Koret of California's clothing was designed for middle-class women who lived relatively modest lives, Stephanie knew these loyal customers also entertained rich fantasies. Most women were adept at separating their personal lives from their imaginations, and they knew that the gowns worn by Olivia de Havilland or Bette Davis on screen were not suitable for the office or grocery store. Still, the silver screen allowed them to live vicariously through the flashy automobiles these superstars drove, the rakish actors they kissed, and the dazzling jewelry and sequined dresses that defined the "tinseltown" image.

That gave Stephanie an idea. Working in tandem with Koret of California's expanded publicity department, she developed a national radio program titled *Hollywood Preview*. Though broadcast from NBC's Radio City facilities in Hollywood, the program actually originated at the network's San Francisco station, which had recently switched its call letters from KPO-AM to KNBR-AM. The program offered listeners a behind-the-scenes look at new films being shot and exclusive interviews with the major stars of the time. During the program the hostess—not-so-subtly named "Diana Stephanie"—would chat with set technicians, designers, makeup men, and such stars as Dick Powell, Ann Shirley, Ann Harding, and Binnie Barnes. Each week, the show introduced a new song by the ever-popular Eddie Cherkose and Jacques Press, and on-air correspondent Coins Leonard reported on the latest show-biz gossip.[6]

Hollywood Preview launched in late 1945 and, at its peak, aired every Sunday on 150 stations across the country. During the commercial breaks, of course, listeners were treated to advertisements about the latest fashions from Koret of California. While the company's sensible styles could not compete with the silk gowns and ermine stoles that swirled through the ballrooms at lavish Hollywood parties, Stephanie believed the ad placement would create a mental association that, in turn, would lead to increased sales. There are no accounting statistics to illustrate whether this indeed turned out to be the case, but Stephanie and Joe both were convinced that Hollywood could provide a solid marketing platform for their fashion lines.

The following year, the enterprising couple sat down with executives at Monogram Pictures in Hollywood. Considered one of the smaller cut-rate studios on Hollywood's Poverty Row, the production company was housed in a large brick building at 4376 Sunset Drive, which subsequently housed KCET-TV and today is part of the Church of Scientology's Media Center. Monogram Pictures (now Allied Artists International) was a low-budget studio formed in the early 1930s through the merger of Rayart Productions and Sono Art-World Wide Pictures. Its stature rose somewhat in the mid-thirties when independent producer Paul Malvern's Lone Star Productions released its John Wayne westerns under the Monogram name.

Joe and Stephanie approached the Monogram studio execs with an idea that, at the time, was still in its infancy: product placement in a feature-length film. In the mid-1940s, the average budget for a Hollywood picture ran about $800,000, while a typical Monogram film could be produced and distributed for about one-tenth of that amount. With a few glittering stars and some dollar signs in their eyes, the Korets sat down with studio head Steve Broidy and made an interesting proposition.

"You want to do what?" Broidy asked.

"We want to costume a movie that features fashions created exclusively by Koret of California," Joe told him.

"That's your company?"

"It is," Stephanie assured him. "I design all our clothing. Like Edith Head." Head was one of the preeminent costume designers at the time, and during her illustrious career she won eight Academy Awards. (She was nominated for thirty-five.)

"Who's paying for this?" Broidy wanted to know.

"We'll have to discuss that," Joe replied.

It's not known how much the Korets invested in the film venture, but Broidy agreed to produce a test picture, titled *High School Hero*. The movie targeted a teen audience—not necessarily the company's primary customer—and was a feature-length film "of the lighter entertainment type, affording plenty of opportunity to show sportswear in action." Starring the popular duo of June Preisser and Freddie Stewart, the film highlighted new fashions personally designed by Stephanie and subsequently mass-produced for retail outlets across the country.[7]

Broidy reportedly was pleased with the box office receipts, and the Korets were more than satisfied with initial in-store sales. Both parties were eager to move forward, so Broidy gave the thumbs-up for a more ambitious film titled *Vacation Days*. This low-budget venture was a semi-musical film featuring a group of teenagers who were convinced to spend their summer vacations at a western ranch. The mystery-thriller again starred Pressier and Stewart, and the inclusion of catchy musical numbers and some mild comedic scenes expanded the film's anticipated audience.

A credit line that read "Wardrobe by Stephanie Koret" told movie-goers just who was responsible for designing the costumes, but any further connection to Koret of California was the responsibility of local retailers. Marketing materials forwarded to merchants prior to the film's release boasted that "Never before in the history of the motion picture has window shopping been possible at a movie theater—until now." One flyer claimed the movie was "loaded from beginning to end with sportswear designed for the high school, college, and business girl."

Al Citron in the Koret of California publicity department developed sales materials that provided marketing guidance to the company's retail customers: "Every link in a merchandising chain reaction has been carefully forged to show returns to the store, theater, and advertising in the town booked for a showing of a specially produced film highlighting Koret garments," he wrote. The plan further informed retailers that, "Your merchandise shares the limelight with the glamour of Hollywood and a famous designer, [and] your customer is pre-sold at the theater. She will be in a buying mood when she enters your shop. For those reasons, 'Vacation Days' is a natural for lively promotion and sparkling publicity."[8]

According to a subsequent company news release, Koret of California also was involved in costuming the cast of Columbia Studios' 1946 picture *Betty Co-Ed*, starring Rosemary LaPlanche and Jean Porter. A more ambitious picture with a larger budget than Monogram Pictures could produce, the film by all accounts was wildly unspectacular. As film critic Leonard Maltin noted years later for Turner Classic Movies, it was "an inexplicably dull grade-B musical about a professional singer who decides to go to college, where she's snubbed by sorority girls. Cute as ever, Porter can't save this turkey."[9] An additional film featuring Koret of California fashions also was planned by United Artists, but its fate is unknown.

DESPITE THESE HOLLYWOOD-THEMED MARKETING efforts, Koret of California never lost sight of what "brought it to the dance." From the beginning, the company's strength lay in Stephanie's steadfast belief that women wanted smart, stylish mix-and-match designs that could be worn wherever she might go. By the mid-1940s, Joe's sales acumen had turned the company into a multimillion-dollar enterprise, fueled largely by the success of the hugely popular Trikskirt. The "trick" now was to adapt the folding-skirt concept to other garments that were trending heavily at the time.

That meant culottes.

Culottes have been around since before the French Revolution. These "bifurcated skirts" originally were created to give the impression that a woman was wearing a skirt while also enabling her to straddle a horse or ride a bicycle. In early years, ruffles or folded panels of fabric concealed the fact that the skirt or dress actually was closer in design to wide trousers, which were strictly forbidden by the conservative customs of the day. Initially worn only by upper-class sportswomen who were concerned about style, culottes became increasingly popular despite the strict social dictates of Victorian England.

Still, fashion trends come and go. By the 1930s. culottes had fallen out of favor in Europe, and tennis star Lilí Alvarez was soundly booed for wearing them in a match at Wimbledon. Culottes actually were outlawed in Paris, where women were forbidden to wear them unless they were "holding a bicycle handlebar or the reins of a horse."[10]

The story was different in the States. The war years and a fresh sense of independence gave women a new freedom to express themselves through fashion. While trousers still were not fully acceptable at the office or PTA meetings, culottes quickly gained popularity. They began flying off department store racks, and Joe and Stephanie quickly realized that what Koret of California had done for the pleated skirt could easily be applied to culottes, as well. Once again, Stephanie went to the design table and sketched out a garment that could be folded flat with a drawstring, while Joe fired off patent and trademark applications for what was to become known as the Trikulotte.

No company, however, can grow on the success of just one product, and Koret of California was no "one-Trik pony." Even while the Trikskirt and its culotte cousin were taking the retail fashion world by storm, the company was developing several other products that would augment its fashion lines. One of these was the "Koretigan," essentially a cardigan sweater with a sewn-in elasticized waistband and cuffs to ensure permanent fit and to hold the garment in place during active sports. According to company marketing materials, the two initial styles were "executed in 100 percent wool jersey, had gold metal buttons and simulated shoulder pockets, and retailed for about $9. Both fabrics were preshrunk."

Uniform elastic stitching—as used in the Koretigan line—proved to be a manufacturing challenge, but the new Koret of California research team developed a custom-designed attachment for its multi-needle sewing machines to guarantee constant elastic shirring. "Stitching is done on six needle machines, with the amount of elastic regulated in proportion to size in the 12 to 18 range offered," a company publicity one-sheet explained. "Even extreme stretching of the waistband will not break stitches."

BY 1946, STEPHANIE WAS THE QUEEN BEE OF the Koret fashion world. "Mrs. K," as she was called by her staff, oversaw every aspect of the production of two fashion lines each year. Almost every garment started as a simple sketch, with an emphasis on practicality and functionalism—and what she called "free-form traditionalism." For instance, an innovative two-way blouse was designed to be worn frontward or backward; other inventive techniques transformed a blouse into a midriff bra or converted collars into collarless necklines. Always conscious of the customer's wallet or pocketbook, Stephanie designed every garment with both price point and perfect fit in mind. It was customary at the time for many garments to be purchased off the rack and then finished by a tailor, but Stephanie and Joe knew they could eliminate this often-costly step if they focused on "sound lines, clean tailoring, and careful detail."

To this end, Stephanie would implement adjustable features—waist drawstrings or elastic shirred panels—to make a garment fit the first time, every time. For instance, many Koret garments were designed with a back center seam that would allow for a perfect fit simply by easing or taking it in, while other seams and darts remained in proper alignment.

During these creative spells, Stephanie's mind was described as having the agility of a Mexican jumping bean and what today would be considered the epitome of multitasking. "Being a dramatic type, Mrs. Koret can talk into the four telephones on her desk at once—and does," wrote *San Francisco Chronicle* reporter Evelyn Hannay in 1946. "At the same time she can approve color swatches by the peek; consult on tricky points with cutters; greet friends, buyers, and relatives (all by the name of 'darling'); and keep up a running commentary on her life and love and work in a deep Tallulah Bankhead voice."[11]

Stephanie's office was a walnut-paneled beige-and-chartreuse retreat tucked away in a corner of the fifth floor of the Mission Street headquarters. It was her private realm, and she guarded that privacy carefully. Friendly and generous to a fault, always sharing ideas and working with her staff to create the absolute best designs Koret of California could manufacture, she was very much an introvert who often preferred to withdraw into the safety of her own nest. At one moment, she would be playing big sister to the company's staff, and ten minutes later she was be resting on the bed in her private studio.

Stephanie was said to design a new garment the way a musician is inspired to write a new song. She would start in a "frenzied fit" with just a hint of an idea, and she would madly sketch it out until she had the framework of a new style. Then she would painstakingly go back and add smaller features that either ended up as a finished skirt or dress, or a pile of stitched fabric on her office floor. Since she was her own target customer, she would create every new design to match her personal taste and fit her petite form. "I make everything first to fit me," she would say. "I try to be original without being extravagant, and stick to functional, sportswear clothes. I design three ways—on a sketch pad, on a dummy, and on myself. Every garment has to feel comfortable before I am satisfied with it."[12]

OVER THE NEXT EIGHTEEN MONTHS, THE COMPANY would expand its horizons and take a few design risks. Always listening to what company salesmen were telling him, Joe had a good feel for the next emerging trend. Stephanie was equally tuned in to the fashion marketplace, and by the end of 1947 the company rolled out a publicity program intended to draw attention to a wide selection of new designs. These included garments that would fit "tiny waistlines, rounded hips, and natural shoulders. . . . Dresses, playsuits, slacks, and coordinates are included in the functional group of classic and high-style playclothes which have a distinctly feminine look."[13] Tailored one-piece romper-type playsuits in seersucker or poplin were matched to full skirts with huge pockets, while cuffed shorts had matching midriffs or contrasting striped sweaters.

Koret of California also expanded into short coats, suits and matching blouses, and dressy blazers. Always focusing on mix-and-match pragmatism, the company stressed its simple styling and tailoring details, concentrating on basic wearable designs at volume prices. With fabrics now more available than in the war years, Stephanie branched out to incorporate "wool jersey, Kasha, flannel, sheer wool plaids and stripes, a frosted Challis in wool and rayon, corduroy, homespun type woolens, and rayon 'suitings.' "[14]

By the end of 1947, Koret of California was on track to become the largest women's sportswear manufacturer in the United States. At a company sales conference in held in December, Joe made the bold prediction that unit volume for 1948 would increase 25 percent over 1947 sales, which in turn showed a substantial gain over the $12 million in gross dollar volume earned in 1946. Ray Allanius, the company's director of sales, boasted that in just under nine years the company had grown to the point where it operated seventeen factories in the Bay Area. Through a network of twelve thousand retail stores, the firm now produced and sold "a basic sportswear line of moderately priced bread and butter items" on a steady year-round basis.[15]

While Koret of California was enjoying year-over-year sales growth, a number of its retail partners were having difficulty breaking even. As Joe knew from his face-to-face visits with banking executives in the late thirties, operating capital for small businesses with little to no collateral was hard to come by. It was difficult for them to order adequate stock to fully satisfy their own customers, and many limited their seasonal orders to just a few select items from the Koret line. Their thinking was that the fewer skirts and sweaters they ordered, the greater their chance of selling them all, and therefore ending up with fewer returns at the close of the sales cycle.

A quarter-century of merchandising experience told Joe differently. A store that limited its stock of skirts, dresses, and sweaters to what the retailer believed were most likely to sell never lived up to the consumers' expectations.

"The moment a woman enters that store she is looking for something new," he would tell his wife. "She doesn't want the same old skirt, in the same old colors."

"Or made from the same fabric," Stephanie would agree.

"The store owners are afraid—simple as that."

"It's human nature, dear. A lot of people fear what they don't know."

"Like FDR said, 'The only thing we have to fear is fear itself.' "

Thus Joe Koret's concept of "fear psychology" was born. He firmly believed that retailers' worries when ordering new inventory worked against them and caused fiscal pain in the long run. At one point in the late forties, he booked a fact-finding tour of small shops and large department stores across the country. After meeting with scores of retail customers, he confirmed his suspicion that many simply were guided by irrational anxiety and panic. "Their lack of courage reflects itself in improper planning of stock, which can do more damage in loss of sales than making mistakes," he told a reporter for *Women's Wear Daily*.[16]

To Joe's way of thinking, retailers needed to accept that common items and special sales cannot be expected to drive business. "Stores must have well-rounded stocks for repeat business and cannot depend entirely on 'one-shot' items," he told the publication. "They have allowed their stocks, in many instances, to become dangerously low and their assortments are starved. Retailers must show courage in business and must have the courage of their convictions. [They must] get over the fear psychology which has been haunting them . . . and buy merchandise with confidence."[17]

Ultimately, that was easier for Joe to say than for the retailers to do. If they lacked sufficient credit and operated on month-to-month cash flow, it was challenging for them to order more stock than their quarterly sales would allow. By contrast, Joe's firm grasp of business and motivation to succeed had transformed Koret of California from a modest clothing manufacturer into a multi-million-dollar corporation that was supplying women's sportswear to most of the country's major department stores. Macy's, the Emporium, Dillard's, City of Paris—all prominently featured Koret fashions, and cash registers rang like a carillon of bells.

Meanwhile, Joe Koret was beginning to make merchandising inroads outside the United States. Grand'Mere Knitting Company in Quebec signed a deal that granted it exclusive Canadian manufacturing rights for all Koret designs. Grand'Mere had manufactured most of the Canadian military berets during World War II, but peacetime sales had dropped off a cliff. As the market for headgear began to wane, company officials decided to expand into ladies' and men's sportswear. The tenure of the initial contract with Koret of California, which was on a strict royalty basis, was for one year, expiring September 1, 1950.

Joe completed a similar deal with Garment Industries Ltd. of Great Britain. In a move that he said was "in line with the firm's expanding policy of cooperative trade agreements with international apparel industries," he negotiated a licensing arrangement that also gave the British company a one-year license to manufacture and distribute specific Koret garments. An identical deal was made with Three Star Manufacturing Pty. of Australia, which licensed the Koret name with the intention of producing and distributing the greater portion of the company's sportswear line on a straight royalty basis.

FROM HIS FIRST YEARS IN SAN FRANCISCO, JOE Koret had grown to appreciate the Bay Area just north of the Golden Gate. In the 1920s and thirties, Marin County was still adorned with pristine forests and bubbling streams teeming with fish. It was a far cry from Joe's dismal memories of the cold, slushy streets of New York, and just a short journey from the Ferry Terminal at the head of Market Street. Not much of a boat person, Stephanie often stayed home when her husband would venture out on one of his Marin excursions, but when the Golden Gate Bridge was completed the small villages of Sausalito and Tiburon suddenly seemed a lot closer.

After the war, Joe convinced Stephanie that, despite the commute, the quietude of Marin County would give them the peace of mind they both craved. Away from the noisy bustle of downtown San Francisco,

Stephanie could lose herself in her new creations, while Joe would be closer to his second-greatest love: fishing. After considerable stealthy trips north he found a spacious home in the village of Larkspur, where he and Stephanie moved with a small menagerie of animals. They lived in this home, known affectionately as "The Ark," for about a year until Joe's real motive for moving north was attained.

In 1947, the Korets packed up and moved a few miles away to a twenty-seven-acre tract of land on the east side of Tiburon known as Paradise Cove. Set on a forested hillside and encompassing several hundred feet of pristine waterfront, the Koret Estate included a custom-built home with panoramic views of San Francisco Bay and the glimmering lights of Richmond. The hills were lush with coastal redwoods, cypress, and pine, and Joe planted the open areas with bottlebrush, salvia, and aloe. He installed a deep-water dock large enough to accommodate a sizeable fishing boat and constructed a massive swimming pool that, at a cost of $20,000, was considered an extravagance few could afford in the late forties. While quite a distance from the Mission Street headquarters, Paradise Cove was right in the heart of the solitude and tranquility of Marin. It also was just a short boat ride from one of Joe's favorite weekend hangouts, a fishing retreat on the Napa River known as Napa Val Resort.

On many an evening, Joe would come home from the office and sit on the deck of his new home. He enjoyed gazing out at the lights of the expanding skyline, marveling at how far he had come since that boat set sail from the port of Odessa almost half a century before. A man who had not yet turned fifty, he was amazed at where life had taken him, and he pondered what still lay ahead. He was the cofounder of a phenomenally successful women's clothing company, he had a beautiful and gregarious wife at his side, and he was rich beyond his wildest dreams. Even more important, he had been able to share his wealth with both of his parents, whose lives were also drastically different from when they had stepped off that train in Oakland thirty years before.

But on top of the many casualties the country suffered during World War II, the forties would bring death to Joe's family. After the Korets had headed west to San Francisco in 1917, Joe's older brother, Al, eventually opened his own clothing manufacturing business on Second Street in the heart of the city. The company was incorporated in 1941, with Al; his wife, Lenore Koret; and her brother Maurice Rosenberg listed as the primary officers. Al and Joe shared marketing and merchandising insights with each other, and over the next few years Al was able to grow his business quickly. Soon, the Koret Manufacturing Company was producing a line of quality menswear, most notably a collection of handsome suits that soon become popular up and down the West Coast.

One morning just three years after the company opened its doors, Al walked into his office on Second Street and suddenly collapsed on the floor. He had suffered a stroke a year earlier, and his coworkers suspected he was experiencing another one. He was rushed by ambulance to Harbor Emergency Hospital, where doctors immediately treated him for left hemiplegia, or paralysis of the left side of the body. He died three hours later at the age of forty-five.

Joe's brother Solomon had died just one year before Al, at the age of thirty-five. A hosiery salesman, Sol had contracted tuberculosis in 1930 and, as the years progressed, his lungs became increasingly compromised. By now a resident of Southern California, he was admitted to the Los Angeles Sanitorium (now the City of Hope National Medical Center) in the community of Duarte. He lived in the facility for the next two years, and on October 10, 1943, he underwent surgery in an attempt to repair a bronchopleural fistula. The procedure was fraught with risk, and Sol died nine days later. His death from this chronic disease, which at one point had killed 100,000 Americans a year, suggests that it also could have been what took the life of his brother Harold twenty-two years previously.[18]

DESPITE THE LOSSES, JOE WAS STILL OPTIMISTIC and upbeat about his life. On New Year's Eve 1949, he and Stephanie hosted a grand party at their Paradise Cove estate, inviting close friends and family to celebrate the past and toast the future. As the clocks struck midnight, with the glittering lights of Richmond stretched out like a diamond necklace across the bay, they raised glasses of champagne to welcome a new decade—and all that it might bring.

Joseph Koret seated at his desk sometime in the early 1950s. [Koret private collection]

5

The Birth of the Consumer

AS THE POPPING OF CORKS AND DIME-STORE noisemakers ushered in the second half of the twentieth century, the country welcomed a newfound sense of hope and confidence.

War was almost five years in the past, and the U.S. economy was hit with a strain of affluenza. More and more young men and women were tying the knot, having babies, and moving out of American cities to new suburbs that seemed to be sprouting like mushrooms. A new invention known as television was replacing the time-honored radio as the centerpiece of living rooms around the country. Families now gathered around primitive black-and-white screens to gape at the weekly offerings of *Ed Sullivan*, *Your Show of Shows*, and *Your Hit Parade*. Automobiles became larger and more powerful, and on average set back their owners $1,510. A gallon of gas cost 18 cents, the average price of a new home was $8,450, and the median family income was just over $3,300 a year.[1]

Meanwhile, much of the independence and freedom women had gained during the war and the years to follow became ingrained in American culture. Men were still seen to rule the roost financially and traditionally, but the involvement of women both in the work-place and household decision-making gave them more autonomy than ever before. They dressed in relaxing skirts and dresses, and some even began to wear slacks to work. Heavier cottons were out, and newer rayons and other synthetic fibers were de rigueur.

But a funny thing happened on the way to the fifties. Even though times were gentler and money more plentiful—at least within main-stream white-bread America—the country also was riddled with worry. The dawn of the nuclear age that had brought a swift but hor-rific end to the war also introduced a new sense of anxiety. Not long after the United States dropped bombs on Hiroshima and Nagasaki, the Soviet Union acquired nuclear technology, spawning an arms race and the prospect of global annihilation. Geopolitical tensions that began shortly after the war spurred a growing distrust of the Soviet Union and other eastern-bloc nations that had fallen under communist influence. On the streets of America, this distrust evolved to suspicion of friends and neighbors, and a growing fear of the destruction of "life as we know it" gave rise to a new sense of nationalism.

As the political pendulum began to swing toward more conservative ideals, Koret of California prospered on the notion that the American consciousness remained steady and true. Year after year, this had proved to be the case, and neither Joe nor Stephanie had any reason to expect any major shift in fashion taste just because of the Cold War and Hollywood blacklists. Historically, the American woman had sac-rificed her own needs as other household matters took priority, but as the overall economy brightened, many families had more money in the bank. That meant wives and mothers finally were able to attend to their own needs, in addition to those of their husbands and children.

Joe and Stephanie Koret spent an inordinate amount of time assessing not only the most current fashion trends, but also the socio-economic state of the contemporary American woman. She was their primary target, and her tastes and perceptions would dictate—more than any single fashion designer—what would sell next season. Stephanie eagerly pored through the pages of *Life*, *Look*, and *The Saturday Evening Post* and devoured the fashion magazines of the day. She constantly analyzed and critiqued the work of other designers, then sketched out her own concepts for what would lead next year's fashion marketplace.

An example of Stephanie's fashion vision is found in a news release that accompanied some of her designs being displayed at a fashion show at the Gotham Hotel in late 1949:

> Koret of California places the promotional spotlight on denim and butcher rayon, repeating last year's success fabrics in the early Spring line of coordinated separates. . . . A sun dress has a lapel halter; its jumbo pockets and self buttons are typical details recurring throughout the butcher rayon separates, including a coat dress, new this year. Also added to the faded blue denim group is a double-breasted coat dress. . . . Other fabrics featured in the current showing are chintz, pique, cotton cord and rayon suiting, each shown in an all-inclusive range of separates. Cotton broadcloth makes a brief appearance in a Tattersall checked shirt and halter supplementing the butcher rayon items.[2]

The lapel halter mentioned in the above description was the second generation of a patent Stephanie had applied for almost six years earlier, in September 1944. The first "halter neck" garment ever commercially produced arguably was the top half of two-piece European swim suits, but in 1946 a Frenchman named Jacques Heim crafted a daring change to this ensemble. A couturier designer from Cannes, Heim raised the bottom of the halter and created what today is widely considered the first true two-piece bathing suit.[3]

Halter-top swimsuits were a little slow to catch on, although initially they were more popular than the more daring—and baring—bikini.

Stephanie Koret viewed the halter as a valuable fashion element, but as a slim size 2, she recognized a number of challenges in incorporating it into a marketable clothing line. As a designer of blouses and dresses, she knew that height, body mass, and bosom size all dictated fit and comfort. In other words, no two women's bodies were exactly alike.

Stephanie's 1944 patent application describes an invention related to "women's personal wearing apparel and in particular to a breast

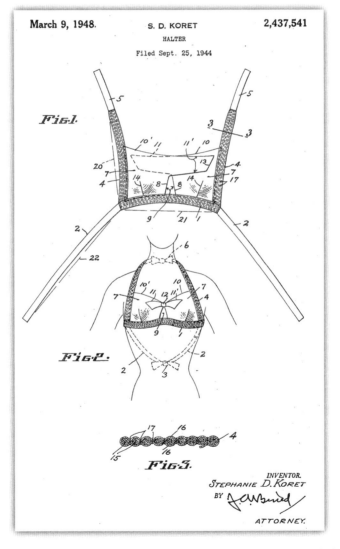

Patent drawing of Stephanie Koret's "adjustable halter," issued 1948.
[U.S. Patent Office]

covering and supporter of the type generally known as a halter." As she wrote, "The principal objects of the invention are to provide such a halter which will be simple, adjustable for any figure or breast position or development, yet preferably be free from buckles or mechanical take-up devices, will expose the back to maximum suntan, and withal be comfortable and stylish so that it may be worn at bathing beaches and swimming pools with a pair of trunks to constitute a bathing suit." Stephanie received her patent for the adjustable halter on March 8, 1948 (Patent No. 2,437,541).

In just over a decade, Koret of California had carved out a solid position in the woman's casual and sportswear field. The name became synonymous with style, comfort, fit, and freedom, and the Korets exuded an air of confidence just as the age of American consumerism took hold. Shifts in media usage and marketing strategies increasingly induced people to buy things, whether they needed them or not. Consuming goods had almost become a patriotic duty, and manufacturers used every means available to gain general consumer awareness. Product placement, which the Korets had pioneered in the late forties, became more common. This was particularly true on television, where such programs as *Texaco Star Theater*, *Philco Television Playhouse*, *Colgate Comedy Hour*, and *Kraft Television Theatre* served to cement their brands in the American consciousness.[3]

People had money to spend, and a virtually unlimited number of products on which to spend it. In 1949, a quarter million television sets were purchased every month, a number that exploded with the new programming that took hold in the early fifties. Madison Avenue advertising agencies were brazen in their direct appeal to "buy, buy, buy," developing simple slogans to effectively imprint a product's benefits in the consumer's mind. Such catchphrases as "You'll wonder where the yellow went" still evoke strong memories of toothpaste among early viewers who became addicted to the tiny screen.

Nineteen-fifty also saw the introduction of the credit card. While individual department stores and retailers already issued their own charge cards, Diners Club—established in February 1950—paved the way for other independent card companies to front money to consumers. American Express and Carte Blanche quickly followed with their own versions. All three required their members to pay the charged balance in full at the end of the month; cards that offered revolving credit were still a few years off. In any event, the "buy now, pay later" concept allowed consumers to satisfy the craving for a product today, with the hope that when the eventual bill arrived in the mail there would be sufficient funds in the bank to cover it.

Television also proved to be a boon for the fashion industry. For the first time outside the movie theater, men and women could see what other red-blooded Americans were wearing. Such programs as *I Love Lucy*, *Ozzie and Harriet*, and *Dragnet* exposed an entire population to skirts, dresses, trousers, and shirts that perpetuated a conservative, yet oddly independent, look.

In keeping with this theme, Koret of California introduced a spring 1950 fashion line that offered women's clothing designed to feel both familiar and liberated. The company produced an eight-piece sailcloth coordinated set sporting a nautical look known as "Ship Ahoy." Stephanie worked up a palette of fabric colors that offered navy, red, and pink–mocha brown for the progressive-minded buyer, and standard black and white for traditionalists. The "pair-offs" featured medium-wide pocket flaps and rounded boyish collars, plus a waist-length bolero also fitted with pocket flaps on the shoulders and below the bust. Rounding out the line were pedal pushers, brief shorts, a button-front skirt, and two trouser styles with fly fronts and horizontal double-button center front fastenings.

In anticipation of an expected post-Trikskirt sales surge, Joe Koret reorganized the San Francisco head office. He concentrated the company's entire San Francisco sales department on the first floor so it would catch the eye of any business customer who walked through the front door. Joe's office sat in the middle of this sales area and was adjacent to a series of sales showrooms where garments could be displayed. The upper floors housed the shipping department, where mass orders would be processed and goods dispatched directly out the back door.

To keep up with expanding demand and changing merchandising strategies, Joe also made a strategic realignment to the Koret of California sales team. He placed veteran sales manager Leo Brown (Stephanie's brother), in charge of the Los Angeles and Dallas districts, while San Francisco stalwart Abe Goldberg took on the additional duties of overseeing the southeast region. The company also joined the Brand Names Foundation, an organization that championed the use of advertising and the protection of trademarks and company brands. Noting how the group worked tirelessly to persuade smaller retailers to use national brand-name goods instead of those that were regionally produced, Joe observed, "We have joined in this effort because we believe the apparel field merits the same brand name recognition enjoyed by the hard goods. It has been proven conclusively that women are becoming increasingly aware of labeled merchandise. Now it is up to us not only to live up to this trust, but to go forward in every manner possible."[4]

While Koret of California was growing organically, Joe was always keeping his eyes open for critical acquisitions. In the fall of 1950, he was contacted by Sam Menzin, cofounder of a dress manufacturing company known as Marilyn Inc. Menzin had entered into a manufacturing partnership with another businessman named Harry Golson, but after several months of inactivity that arrangement soured and the two businessmen parted company. Using $200,000 in new funding acquired as a result of the split, Menzin incorporated the firm and inquired whether Joe might be interested in becoming business partners with him. The under-capitalized venture had struggled from the beginning, and Menzin viewed Joe as a potential savior. After examining the financials and studying the existing Marilyn Inc. dress lines, Joe agreed and made an investment that brought Marilyn under Koret's protective wing.

The following summer, Koret of California took over full owner-ship of Marilyn Inc. The company operated as a separate Koret affiliate under the control and management of Koret executives, although it maintained its own sales staff and occupied separate offices and a factory at 612 Howard Street. Sales distribution, type of merchan-dise, promotional effort, and overall policies were determined by Joe, while Stephanie planned new lines of women's sportswear, each of them adapting the same line of "dress groups" she had developed for a specific fabric category. These "dress groups" ranged from casuals to semi-dressy, with each series "balanced" around style and diversity.

BEFORE THE ATTACK ON PEARL HARBOR, FEW Americans knew much, if anything, about Hawaii. Lying almost twenty-four hundred miles off the coast of California, the island chain was a mystical place of leis and luaus, hula dancers and ukuleles. Palm trees swayed in the gentle breezes and massive waves washed up on black sand beaches. Storefront travel posters promised idyllic fantasies to those who stopped to look, but few people gave much thought about ever going there for real. Hawaii was just a distant speck in the middle of the ocean, and well out of most people's daily frame of refer-ence. Even in 1950, the small cluster of islands were best known as the tropical paradise that Bing Crosby crooned about in the 1949 hit song "Mele Kalikimaka."

Koret of California aimed to change all that. In the fall of 1951, a team of marketing executives accompanied Joe and Stephanie to Honolulu to use the island's distinctive scenery as the backdrop for the com-pany's 1952 spring clothing line. Advertising and promotion manager Al Citron, fashion expert Charlotte Field, two models, and a photographer spent nearly a week on the beaches of Oahu shooting the forthcoming fashion line against various tropical backdrops. To help offset the cost of the excursion and to offer women shoppers some tropical magic, the company worked with Pan American Airlines and the Hawaii Visitors Bureau to promote the overall theme "Season in the Sun." The new spring line was officially announced through in-store displays the following January—in the dead of winter—and the campaign ran through the end of June.

To dovetail with the company's ongoing Hawaii-themed marketing program, Joe Koret invited a select group of newspaper fashion editors and department store buyers to participate in an "experiential aviation junket" that stuck much closer to home. One of the many challenges for any clothing manufacturer was to design and produce fashionable sportswear that could fit inside a standard suitcase and then be worn as soon as it was unpacked. No pressing or steaming, no muss or fuss. Joe and Stephanie had become obsessed with no-iron pleats since before they introduced the Trikskirt, and they spent countless hours creating various designs manufactured from an assortment of fabrics that would be ready to wear as soon as travelers arrived at their final destination.

In March 1952, a party of fashion editors and retail buyers convened at San Francisco International Airport, where they boarded a specially chartered Pan Am airplane for a highly secret excursion. They were plied with pink champagne and teriyaki hors d'oeuvres, which *San Francisco Chronicle* fashion editor Mary Hampton, writing under the pseudonym Ninon, described as "an olive, a chunk of beef, and a mushroom." Properly plied with food and drink, they gazed out the window as the "smooth blue of the bay and rumpled billiard-table green of the Berkeley foothills sank beneath us, while we . . . swallowed rapidly to keep up with the popping ears."[5]

For the next two hours, Pan Am flight attendants proceeded to model a range of new sportswear designed to be unpacked from a suitcase wrinkle-free and worn immediately. To emphasize this point, the Koret marketing team had brought forty-four- and sixty-six-pound Samsonite bags on board, and, as the turboprop aircraft climbed over the Sierra foothills, the airborne audience was treated to an in-flight fashion show.

"Presently we turned our attention from the white-capped Sierra to a white Catalina bathing suit with a single strap and appliqued blossoms with rhinestone centers," the *Chronicle*'s Ninon wrote. A diminutive and sophisticated critic who lived in Marin, Ninon/Hampton was a fixture of the Bay Area fashion scene and enjoyed her role in shaping the region's sense of style. "Next came some one-piece play suits, one with a pearl gray and white removable skirt and red accessories," she continued. "A strapless print with yellow and brown figures and touches of persimmon followed, and then suddenly we were over Yosemite."

Eventually, the entourage was treated to an ensemble featuring a black pleated skirt and white blouse "that came out of a crowded bag quite un-mussed," as well as a white lace T-shirt modeled with pale yellow pedal pushers, with a purple scarf worn as a cummerbund. Ninon's general conclusions: nylon and Orlon acrylic traveled best and dried fast, regardless of climate. The airborne fashion show continued for well over an hour, and then the plane returned its models and guests to the airport from which it had departed.

IN THE EARLY 1950S, "READY-TO-WEAR" HAD become a mantra within the walls of Koret of California. New synthetic fabrics were making wrinkle-free clothes possible, but the challenge was keeping them crisp and fresh wash after wash. Joe and his sales team heard about this issue constantly from retail customers who, in turn, heard about it from women shoppers who simply didn't have time to iron every garment that came out of the dryer or off the clothesline.

Because of this fascination—borne out of the early design of the Trikskirt—Koret of California rapidly became one of the industry leaders in the mass production of ready-to-wear clothing. Joe Koret believed the apparel business was no different from automobile manufacturing or other heavy industries of the time. From the inception of the company in 1938, he and Stephanie took a methodic approach to the design and merchandising of their clothing. They identified what sold, discontinued what did not, and applied simple market research to every garment in the next year's clothing line. New fashion styles, fabric improvements, colors and patterns, and cultural trends were sorted into a massive database, and over time the company became exceptionally adept at anticipating customer's tastes and desires.

The implementation of a research department in the mid-1940s was part of the long view Joe had toward the future—and a deliberate plan to gain traction over his competitors and the fickleness of trends. By design, Joe had created a system that allowed him to blueprint an entire production line a full year in advance. He and his team would take a look at the previous year's sales data and determine what they could expect in year-over-year growth. They then divided the year into two distinct business "silos," representing the company's two major clothing categories: spring/summer and fall/winter. Each season then was further divided into specific lines, such as summer beachwear, back-to-school, and holiday. Each of these then was further separated into groups based on fabric, cruise- and-resort-wear, party, and sports.

Joe also instructed his entire sales team to survey their retail customers. Guided by Henry Weil, the company's merchandise director at the time, they were urged to learn as much as they could about shoppers' perspectives on garment styles, social trends, new fabrics, colors, timing, comfort, and fit. Joe was specifically interested in what these women liked and didn't like about the current Koret lines and, similarly, what they liked and disliked about the competition's merchandise and promotional strategies. The criteria he used when examining any garment or trend followed three simple questions: (1) Is it on the upswing and is it wearable?; (2) Is it a flash fad and therefore has limited, short-term appeal?; and (3) Is it on the way out?

As Weil told *Women's Wear Daily* in the spring of 1952, "[We] think in terms of what people want and what they don't want—the acceptance or rejection of fabrics and styles—and both these points are very important."[6]

Once all the survey data was analyzed, the department heads would recommend how to proceed with the next line of clothing. While Joe ultimately made the final business decisions, everyone's input was considered valuable—and was fully expected. If the company was going to commit millions of dollars and an entire sportswear line to a particular type of rayon or wool, Joe wanted to make sure his suppliers could commit to delivery. As new fabrics, patterns, and colors arrived from the mills, he insisted each of them be evaluated to determine whether they met the exacting standards established by both the company's own San Francisco laboratory and an outside testing facility. "Fabrics were tested for certain specifications, such as wearability, washability, shrinkage, color fastness, and heat-setting possibility," Weil said.

The final phase in creating a seasonal line was the actual styling. By this time, Stephanie and her team had already sketched out all the designs they envisioned for the coming season. Once the fabric was selected, the designers would cut and sew mock-ups of the actual garments, and then the female employees would wear them home. They would receive feedback from husbands, boyfriends, girlfriends, children, and anyone else who had a comment on how they looked. These in-house "models" would assess the clothing in terms of comfort and also how well they cleaned up in a standard washing machine. Only when a garment passed every test was it considered a candidate for the upcoming line.

As evidenced by a marketing plan released by the company in late 1952, "maximum wearability with minimum upkeep" was the overall objective of the company's design department. "Washability" and "ironability" had become key requirements across the entire merchandising chain, and Koret of California had just announced a new patent that allowed for wrinkle-free "drip-drying" of pleated skirts. The new process also permitted home-laundering of pleat-front and pleat-yoke blouses, which had been redesigned with "constructional detailing" intended to firm up the creases. The new lines were created and manufactured in such a way as to minimize unwanted wrinkles and creases, both through design elements and the innovative use of various fabric blends.

These innovations increasingly pushed the company's annual sales growth into double digits, eventually causing Joe to split the advertising department into two divisions. Al Citron, who for years had overseen all marketing duties, was named director of promotion and publicity, while Merv Brown, who most recently had been connected with Koret of California's Los Angeles sales department, took over the title of advertising director. As Joe told his customers at the time, "the volume of work and a stepped-up promotional program at local retail store levels" made the departmental separation a reasonable step forward.[7]

By now, Koret of California had firmly established a national reputation as a major manufacturer of sensible, mix-and-match sportswear. As the *San Francisco Chronicle*'s Ninon wrote, "Koret of California is a name that gains in prestige and popularity year after year, as sportswear fans well know. When Koret introduces its new designs for the forthcoming season, the event is fashion news. The Emporium will present Koret's new Fall styles in three fashion shows Monday in the sportswear department."

Founded in San Francisco in 1896, the Emporium was a chain of upscale department stores affectionately known as "the big E." It had been one of Koret's largest retail customers from the early days of the company, and Stephanie worked closely with its buyers to make sure its new seasonal lines would be the talk of the town. In the fall of 1952, the Emporium hosted three public fashion events that introduced a new line that, as Ninon wrote, could be "shuffled, assembled, and re-assembled to form more than 200 different ensembles."

While Koret of California was popular in its own backyard of San Francisco, New York remained the center of American of fashion. High-end gowns and dresses stole the attention of the fashion press, but "ready-to-wear" was becoming increasingly popular from coast to coast. By the mid-fifties, Manhattan's runways were walked not only by models draped in Christian Dior and Coco Chanel, but also those wearing the latest off-the-rack—"*pret-a-porter*"—styles created by such designers as Suzy Perette, Lilli Ann, Ceil Chapman, and Tina Leser.

Joe knew that in order to compete with these clothing lines he had to make a splash of his own. Believing the fashion industry was elitist and conceited, he suspected Koret of California was viewed by the New York establishment as merely a West Coast interloper. Joe's personal memories of ice-encrusted shoes and purloined fish reinforced a subjective distrust of Manhattan, and he enjoyed being viewed as an outsider. In a bold move that might have been considered a "thumbed nose" at the fashion stalwarts, he developed his own invitation-only fashion exhibitions and largely ignored the regularly staged Press Week events the elite design houses participated in. Created in 1943 by New York Dress Institute press director Eleanor Lambert, Press Week initially was designed to draw attention to American fashion designers and their creations. By the mid-fifties, the well-established soiree had become known as Press Week of New York, and today is simply referred to as Fashion Week.[8]

In coordination with Bob Weiss, who ran Koret of California's New York sales office, Joe and his team held a series of daily fashion shows in June 1954 in its New York showroom. Billed as "small and intimate," these presentations marked the first time the company had staged its own events in New York. To mark the occasion, two members of the cast of *The Fifth Season*—a popular Broadway play about the garment industry—were hired to model Koret clothing. While these events were the "off-Broadway" versions of the more mainstream New York runway extravaganzas, they helped to reinforce Koret of California's reputation as an independent manufacturer of stylish yet functional sportswear that emphasized comfort and fit.

Merv Brown, who spent more than forty years with Koret of California, recalls those early days at the company with great fondness. "We would all sit around the table so we could hear what Joe and Stephanie were saying about styles," he says.

> They would comment on the designs that were displayed on the walls, and they talked about the fabrics. They wanted to see their creations out there in the marketplace, and everything was geared to make that happen. Al Citron was great at publicity, while my job was to make the clothing look more fashionable. As long as I could carry it off without spending more money, Joe Koret was in favor of it. Back then there were no set practices on how to do that, so I had to ad lib the whole thing.

This "ad-libbing"—and the efforts Joe made in marketing Koret of California both in the United States and abroad—eventually caught the eye of an enterprising businessman named S. R. Back. Back was the chairman of I. L. Back & Company, a South African firm that at the time manufactured everything from bed linens to undergarments. Back's interest in Koret of California was predicated on fast-moving changes in the South African economy and cultural landscape. Racial discrimination—institutionalized with the passage of apartheid laws in 1948—had created a deeply segregated society, and Back anticipated social turmoil and fiscal uncertainty.

Economic differences between the white establishment and the vast black majority were stark and unambiguous, and government-imposed sanctions on foreign goods had created market instability. Koret products had been available in the Union of South Africa market for several years, but import controls and currency difficulties made dealing with any firm based outside the country increasingly problematic. Back had pleaded with government officials to protect the country's clothing industry in general, and eventually decided it would be wise to partner with Koret of California to establish a wholly owned company in which his company would hold a 50 percent interest. This new company—Koret of California, S.A. Ltd.—was designed to make it easier for both parties to compete in the South African apparel market, as well as to create designs more suited to the African climate than San Francisco weather.

Two decades later, Back would emerge as an advocate for racial inclusion in the divisive South African economy. In 1972, in his role as chairman of the Federated Chamber of Industry (similar to the U.S. Chamber of Commerce), he argued that any plan to stimulate South African productivity must include a plan to give black workers the opportunity to play a larger role. He also maintained it was imperative that the government train the country's non-white population in order to provide them opportunities for advancement.[9]

The completion of the deal with S. R. Back meant that Joe had wholly owned companies or license agreements with clothing manu-facturers on four continents. Now in his early fifties, he could look back on how his life had brought him to this point, beginning with that win-ter day in 1917 when the Koret family stepped down from a Southern Pacific railroad car and caught sight of San Francisco Bay for the first time. Thirty-five years later, Joe's hard work was paying off, and—with Stephanie working right beside him—he had much to celebrate.

But the times of joy also were shadowed by moments of sorrow. Not only had Joe outlived his three brothers, but on October 25, 1952, his father died at the age of seventy-six. The erstwhile tailor from Odessa had endured persecution and oppression in his native Russia and had raised a family in the squalor and near-starvation that was common to so many immigrants in the early part of the twentieth century. He had outlived three sons and had marveled at how his fourth had built a California clothing empire. The opportunities the Koret family had found in California had turned their lives around, and he and his loyal and devoted wife, Sarah, had celebrated their fiftieth wedding anniversary at Joe's waterfront retreat in Tiburon in 1948. Abram Koret was buried just a few miles south of San Francisco at the Eternal Home Cemetery in Colma.

RESOLUTE AND DETERMINED TO A FAULT, JOE always guided Koret of California with a keen mind and a firm hand. All company managers were invited to share their observations about new fashion lines or marketing programs, and Joe listened intently to what was being said. He asked question after question and demanded intelligent answers from his management team. He also kept his focus on one basic question: "What is the good business reason for doing this?" Every day, he placed considerable faith in the men and women who worked with him to grow the company, and he trusted each of them to always look out for the best interests of Koret of California.

One of these employees was an accountant named Herschel Silverstone. In the early 1940s, Joe needed a financial wizard who could oversee the company's accounting functions and implement fiscal control systems. Silverstone came highly recommended as a professional adviser skilled in both corporate and personal financial matters, and he kept meticulous books at a time when computerized spreadsheets were just a dream. Joe hired him as comptroller, and his skill at navigating complex tax codes endeared him to the board. Within a few months, Joe made him an officer of the company and offered him a sizable amount of Koret of California's privately held stock, making him one of the firm's principal shareholders.

As talented as Silverstone was in balancing books and calculating corporate earnings, one of his real strengths turned out to be identifying—and then exploiting—federal tax loopholes. In 1951, an eagle-eyed auditor at the Internal Revenue Service noticed that, in 1944, Silverstone had underreported Joe Koret's distribution income from Koret of California as $71,212 when the amount should have been $140,979. As a result, Joe had paid just $44,413 in federal taxes instead of the $107,116 the diligent auditor calculated was actually due. Since the undeclared (and untaxed) distributions went directly into Joe's private bank account, the discrepancy was identified as a personal issue, not a corporate liability for Koret of California.[10]

The error was quickly referred up the bureaucratic chain, and in March 1951 both Joe Koret and Herschel Silverstone were indicted by a Federal Grand Jury in San Francisco for income tax evasion. Joe's attorney at the time, A. J. Zirpoli—who later would become U.S. District Court judge for the Northern District of California—said his client had no statement to make on the indictment other than to insist he was innocent. Both men were ordered to appear before the United States IRS Commissioner to post bond—$5,000 for Koret and $2,500 for Silverstone—and released on their own recognizance. Neither was considered a flight risk.

Over the ensuing months, it became clear that Silverstone's complex scheme to underreport Koret of California distributions on Joe's personal returns had begun three years earlier, in 1941. At this point, Joe personally reviewed his tax returns and voluntarily notified the IRS that similar discrepancies probably existed for every year from 1941 through 1949. Because of this finding, A. J. Zirpoli contended the indictment against Joe should be dropped for reasons of "voluntary disclosure," and entered a "not guilty" plea for his client. Robert McMillan, chief assistant U.S. attorney, opposed the motion, and Judge Edward Murphy, who initially drew the case, ruled against both defendants. In a sternly worded ruling, he set a tax evasion trial date of August 17, 1953.[11]

Typical of the U.S. legal system, the case moved forward like the final two minutes of a football game. As McMillan and his team of investigators inspected Joe's tax returns, they confirmed the income discrepancies Joe had already revealed. One small error that had been red-flagged through a routine IRS audit now had become a legal albatross. Joe Koret and Herschel Silverstone both were facing maximum penalties of $20,000 and ten years' imprisonment; together they were liable for more than $160,000 in payments, penalties, and interest. That amount would soon grow to a seven-figure sum.

The writing on the wall was clear: this was serious business. Joe was wealthy enough to pay whatever fines and penalties were levied upon him, so he could handle the financial setback. What he couldn't handle was the prospect of actually going to jail. He was an upstanding American businessman with a company to run and thousands of employees who depended on him. Federal prison simply wasn't an option.

Just before the two cases were scheduled to go to court both men changed their pleas from not guilty to no contest. This move circumvented the need for a protracted trial, which their respective attorneys convinced them they were likely to lose. Federal Judge Oliver Carter, who had taken over the government's case, accepted the plea changes and set a date for sentencing. Legal delays and other issues pushed that date back until just two weeks before Christmas, making for a tense fall season at Koret of California headquarters.

On December 11, 1953, Judge Carter issued his long-awaited ruling. Herschel Silverstone, the architect of the tax evasion scheme, was fined $10,000 and sentenced to one year and one day in prison. A thirty-day stay of execution was allowed by the judge. For his part in the scheme, Joe Koret also received a $10,000 fine, but was spared any time in jail. Instead, he was assessed $1,384,957 by the government for taxes, penalties, and interest allegedly owed for the years 1942 through 1949. At the time of his sentencing, he had paid approximately $275,000 of that amount, and his attorneys argued that $752,000 of the deficiency Judge Carter had assessed was "very debatable."[12]

During sentencing, Judge Carter noted that even after the tax fraud was discovered by the IRS agent in 1951, Joe Koret had not stopped it. Then he looked at Silverstone and stated, "You have a capacity that approaches genius in financial matters. You set up this very compli-cated bookkeeping transaction that involved Koret and the company in the tax fraud scheme. [This is] one of the most artful schemes to defraud I have ever encountered on the Federal bench . . . a most remarkable and devious scheme."[13]

The entire ordeal left Joe personally ashamed and professionally embarrassed. He also faced financial hardship, if not potential ruin, since he was required to reimburse the government for unpaid back taxes, plus interest and penalties. The subsequent sale of his prized Paradise Cove estate (see Chapter 6) was, in part, initiated because of mounting tax bills. Mortified by seeing his name and reputation dragged through the mud, he vowed never to run afoul of the tax man again.

BY THE MID-FIFTIES, THE AGE OF AMERICAN consumerism was well underway. The G.I. Bill had given veterans the ability to pursue a college education and purchase their own homes with little credit or money down. Gasoline was cheap, a fact that drove the automobile industry and fueled the creation of a far-reaching inter-state freeway system. Advances in science and technology spurred productivity, and newly available credit and quick financing shifted the overall American outlook from one of thrift to self-indulgence. While a mild downturn in 1954 reined in some of this consumer exuberance, low unemployment—around 4.5 percent for most of the decade—kept people in a spending frame of mind.

Without question, this push toward consumerism was propelled by a surge in advertising dollars. The explosive introduction of tele-vision in the American household transformed not only the way families interacted with each other; it also shaped the character and attitude of virtually every generation of viewers to come. Parents and children alike gathered around the tiny screen to watch the latest adventures of *The Lone Ranger* or *The Honeymooners*, or to watch

Nat King Cole or Edith Piaf on *The Ed Sullivan Show*. Joe Friday, Danny Thomas, Clark Kent, and Howdy Doody became staples of everyday American life. Young boys dreamed of getting a Davy Crockett coonskin cap for Christmas, while girls wished for their very own Betsy McCall doll.

None of this could have happened, of course, without advertising. In order for people to buy something, they first needed to believe they couldn't live without it. To instill this perceived demand, marketers began to promote their goods and services in such a way that people of all ages were infected with "consumption anxiety." By blurring the previously distinct lines between "want" and "need," advertising agencies liberated billions of untapped dollars from consumers' wallets. Any baby boomer alive today knows the product that "melts in your mouth, not in your hand" or "takes a licking but keeps on ticking." While older Americans who had weathered the Depression proudly maintained a sense of frugality, younger folks saw no reason to save for a rainy day when the sun was shining today. Merited or not, a sense of financial freedom prevailed as Americans were lured by temptation in this new era of spending.

Joe and Stephanie Koret benefitted greatly from this surge in consumer confidence. In the feel-good fifties, fashion was all about looking and achieving your best. Whether she was heading off to the office or driving the kids to school, every woman wanted to look good and feel comfortable. Despite the ongoing threats of the Cold War, there was also a newfound sense of personal freedom—a feeling of prosperity and optimism.

By now, Koret of California had become a trusted name in the women's fashion market. Millions of loyal customers counted on the company to be on the forefront of the latest trends, or at least first-to-market with the newest look. While Detroit automakers were adding chrome grilles and massive fins in an attempt to make last year's models visually obsolete, Koret of California could be counted on to provide new, seasonal designs that worked beautifully with whatever a woman already might have in her closet.

There was no need to worry about mixing and matching last year's style to next year's line; everything was designed to work together. A new lightly boned "weskit" with an off-the-shoulder cape collar was designed to fit right in alongside a new line of Koradenim skirts and slacks. Same thing with a new multi-pleat skirt based on the old Trikskirt concept that was designed to be tossed into the washing machine, with no ironing needed. Cotton or rayon, nylon or denim, flannel or wool—Koret of California had become the "go-to" fashion house for the on-the-go woman of the fifties.

By 1955, Koret of California's sales were growing steadily year-over-year, and the company was thriving. This success was illustrated in a media statement released in June of that year, noting that "what is believed to be the first full carload of woolen piece goods shipped to an individual California manufacturer will be received here Thursday by Koret of California." The car contained more than fifty-five thousand yards of wool flannel fabric from Deering Milliken Mills, and was to be used for Koret's fall line of flannel separates. The news was deemed so spectacular that the car's arrival was greeted by a reception committee consisting of Joseph and Stephanie Koret, civic officials, union representatives, and retail store executives.

Even with double-digit annual growth, Joe felt stymied by what he called "butterfly buying." Because of the explosion of advertising and capricious purchasing habits, he claimed many retailers flitted from one craze to the next, fixing momentarily on one fad and then quickly moving on to the next.

"Stores don't light on any one thing, nor do they get much out of anything, just like a butterfly," he explained in an interview with *Women's Wear Daily*. While participating in an Amos Parish fashion clinic in Manhattan, he told the publication that buyers often were instructed to devote major attention to hot, trendy items, sacrificing the chance to build repeat business and consumer acceptance of a line. In this quest for "faddish" items that typically had a short rack life, retailers were at great risk of taking markdowns on all the items that did not produce substantial sales. "These markdowns on unsuccessful items more than offset their profits on the things which sell well," he pointed out.[14]

Ultimately, retailer obsession with immediate gratification led to starved in-store stock conditions. As businesses chased the latest cultural fad, they overlooked the importance of maintaining a full assortment of merchandise that turned loyal shoppers into repeat customers. Joe Koret never allowed himself to fall into the cult craze, and never chased that one "smash" item that could prove to be an over-night sensation but leave the manufacturer with a one-hit wonder.

A surge in advertising budgets and marketing programs, driven largely by the massive amount of dollars being poured into tele-vision and other media, made many customers suspicious of Madison Avenue hyperbole. Never before in American culture had people been exposed to so many competing messages and exaggerated promises. As a result, the trust that once existed between a store and its customers began to fade. The idea of just "making the sale" was quickly replacing the notion that the customer is always right, as many businesses simply chased the fast buck.

This wariness bridged the sales chain from the consumer level all the way up to the long-valued relationship between a manufacturer's salespeople and retail buyers. A new "hard-sell" business approach began to chisel away the confidence many store buyers once had in a clothing firm's sales reps, who now came pounding at their doors in increasing numbers. It seemed everyone was trying to sell some-thing, and it was hard to know whom you could trust.

From his early days as a traveling sweater salesman, Joe always viewed his role as multifaceted. He wore the hat of sales rep, researcher, marketer, merchandiser, and quite often business counselor. His personal success was only as strong as that of his retail customers, and he believed it was his job to make sure everyone profited. Simply put, long-term success was forged through genuine relationships built on confidence and trust.

"The buyer-salesman relationship should be one fostered by loyalty," he said in the *WWD* interview. "The salesman can be invaluable to a buyer in telling her where to put emphasis when buying a line. He knows which styles are good and will sell well, and [because he] is working on a commission he is interested primarily in reorders. He can get these only by working closely with the buyer."[15]

This trust extended well beyond simply "getting the order." Joe believed retailers who followed the "butterfly" method of buying small quantities of items from a variety of uncertain or problematic suppliers ran a great risk that their orders either would be delivered well past a fad's peak, or not at all. Furthermore—in the understandable spirit of self-interest—he suggested that buyers should stock entire coordinated lines from a single manufacturer rather than assembling "mix-and-match" inventories on their own. "Too many buyers too frequently try to do their own coordinating, when manufacturers have put a lot of thought, time, and effort into this point," he explained.

To Joe Koret, that meant trusting Koret of California to provide attractive, comfortable fashions that consistently attracted customers who had come to depend on the company name that was sewn into every garment. No imitations, no gimmicks. Just comfortable sportswear that screamed "style" and "fit," all at a reasonable price.

AT THE SAME TIME JOE WAS SPEAKING WITH *Women's Wear Daily* on that balmy New York afternoon, he was sitting on an innovation that, within a few years, would revolutionize the global garment industry. Far removed from the rest of the team at 611 Mission Street, a small cadre of Koret of California researchers was secretly conducting experiments with chemicals, fibers, and heat in a small laboratory tucked away in an undisclosed location. After considerable trial and error—including skin rashes and burned fingers—they developed a process that, given the right conditions, would solve a problem as old as clothing itself.

Joe and Stephanie's decades-long obsession with pleats and wrinkle-free designs was about to pay off.

Joe and Stephanie Koret hosted large family dinners almost every Saturday evening. Seated at the front end of the table on the right in this photo from the early 1950s is Joe's mother, Sarah Koret; sitting next to her is Stephanie and, to her right, Joe.
[Koret private collection]

6

The Fifties:
A New Generation

BY THE MIDDLE OF THE 1950S, SAN FRANCISCO
was experiencing a demographic, cultural, and economic evolution.

The postwar population explosion altered not only the city's sto-
ried skyline, but also transformed many of the neighborhoods scattered
from the beach to the bay. The influx of young G.I.s and their families
prompted the build-out of the entire city, and the housing boom that
followed unleashed hungry developers on various sections of the city
that previously had been only sparsely populated. Within just a few
years, thousands of new homes were being hammered together, often
in just a few short weeks. Tens of thousands of new families settled up
and down the San Francisco Peninsula in cookie-cutter shoeboxes that
differed only by color and street number.

At the same time, San Francisco mayor George Christopher
embarked on a crusade to rid the city of what he considered to be urban
blight. A disproportionate number of targeted residential pockets were
working class, largely non-white neighborhoods, and the people who
lived there were no match for Christopher's push for eminent domain.
As a result, many black, Latino, and Asian residents were forced to

relocate to new housing projects in more undesirable areas of the city that already were rife with crime. Rather than expose themselves and their families to those deplorable conditions, many moved out of San Francisco altogether. While this may have been the mayor's plan all along, it also served to displace hundreds of Koret factory workers throughout the city.

AS KORET OF CALIFORNIA CONTINUED TO flourish, Joe and Stephanie realized that the business was consuming almost every second of their lives. In the early years, they had grown accustomed to working six- and sometimes seven-day weeks, but Joe had hoped that moving to the "wilds" of Marin could provide the peace and tranquility they needed when they weren't toiling away at 611 Mission Street. This planned serenity worked for a while, but commuting from their bay-front estate in Tiburon was proving to be more of a nuisance than they had anticipated. Whether traveling by car over the Golden Gate Bridge or by ferry to the terminal at the end of Market Street, the door-to-door trip took at least an hour, and usually much longer. Plus, Joe's income tax problems were costing thousands of dollars a month in legal fees, and there was a strong likelihood that he would end up owing the IRS hundreds of thousands more.

Eventually, he decided it was time to leave Paradise Cove. This was not a hard sell to Stephanie, who had never been fond of boats and rarely drove a car. In fact, she greatly enjoyed the solitude of her fifth-floor downtown studio, and when her husband suggested they go house-hunting back in the city, she eagerly agreed. Neither of them liked the sterile environs of high-rise apartments or the city's fabled Victorian houses, so they focused their search on the more sheltered and exclusive Sea Cliff neighborhood bordering the Pacific Ocean just south of the Golden Gate Bridge. In due time, they signed a purchase agreement for a large house plus the vacant lot in front of it. The new home was nestled among oceanfront mansions and was just a short walk to a beautiful and secluded stretch of Pacific sand. Its location shaved half the time off the commute downtown to Mission Street, and it also was just a couple of miles from the Marin Headlands and the pristine fishing streams that initially led Joe to fall in love with that part of the Bay Area.

The Paradise Cove property actually was owned by a corporation named GEM Realty, a partnership formed by Joe and several close friends and family members. Joe served as GEM's chairman, and he enlisted the company to find a reputable firm that would subdivide and then sell the Paradise Cove estate. This process took several years, but by the summer of 1954 the exclusive new Seafirth neighborhood was ready for building. Water, gas, electricity, and sewer lines had been installed, roads had been graded and paved, and twenty-eight home sites ranging in size from one-fourth to one full acre had been staked out.

The larger and more exclusive of these lots were right on the water and afforded breathtaking views of the bay to the east. The hillside sites were planted with a variety of "rare trees and shrubs," with improvements totaling a whopping half million dollars. As an advertisement in the *Chronicle* boasted, "Seafirth has been designed and restricted with a private road system and a recorded agreement to deed over to the property owners the $20,000 swimming pool, the beach, seven acres of tidelands, and the boat dock. Each lot buyer will own his own pro-rata share of these recreational facilities."[1]

Lot sales were brisk. Within a few months, one speculator snapped up several home sites and brought in a developer from Beverly Hills to custom-design homes for select clients. Some buyers built small weekender "cottages" to serve as an escape from the city, while others erected massive residences that have been updated and expanded over the years. Today, the Seafirth neighborhood remains one of the most exclusive areas in Tiburon, and virtually all the houses have stunning water views that extend across the water to the East Bay.

BY THE MID-FIFTIES, KORET OF CALIFORNIA employed hundreds of workers in its headquarters and manufacturing plants scattered around the Bay Area. From the very beginning, Joe had been a hands-on entrepreneur who oversaw all sales and merchandising aspects of the company, but rapid growth and anticipated expansion necessitated the addition of a fulltime sales director. For this role Joe tapped Walter Rubin, a trusted employee who had served as Koret's acting administrative sales manager for a number of years. The move allowed Joe to delegate many of the company's daily responsibilities to a growing team of managers while he increasingly focused on executive operations.

Meanwhile, Stephanie continued to exhibit an uncanny ability to predict, if not lead, the fashion trends of the day. She and her creative team regularly experimented with new designs and fabrics, while newspaper ads touted "crisp wool flannel skirts and shorts and jackets," "natty striped wool pants," and "a new bulky class of sweaters called Heather Isle Wools, in a soft easy-wash Orlon sweater." She was awarded numerous gold medals and blue ribbons at various fashion events and state fairs, each one of them further cementing Koret of California's reputation as the top-of-the-line women's sportswear.

Both at home and in the office, Stephanie was considered the queen, while Joe was the king. They had known each other for so long they seemed to possess an ability to read each other's minds. As Merv Brown recalls, "Stephanie would be designing the clothes upstairs in her office, and Joe would be working on the merchandising angle. She came up with the designs and he saw the potential in it when he started to sell it. It was a good relationship that way."

Whether in the office or at home, or riding in the car from one to the other, their conversation inevitably drifted to business—and usually the latest of Stephanie's designs.

"I like how it looks, but what is there for me to sell?" Joe would ask her.

Stephanie would explain how her new skirt incorporated slightly larger pleats or was just a bit more conforming to the latest fashion trend. "Women will really go for it," she assured him.

"Yes . . . I'm sure they will," he would say. "But what's my angle for selling it?"

"You don't need an angle. Women will buy it."

"I know, Stephy," Joe would agree. "But everyone out there has something to sell. If I'm a salesman, I need something to really hook the customer."

She would look at him then, trapping him with her Bette Davis eyes. "Well, you are a salesman, so find a hook."

Essentially, Stephanie designed clothes that she liked. When she was in her late twenties and thirties, she created skirts and dresses that women her age would feel comfortable wearing. Later, when she was in her forties and the nation was at war, her designs pivoted to items that working women could wear after they left the office or the factory. "That's how they filled their niche for so many years," Merv Brown points out. "They stayed away from being too young. Young women could wear Koret of California garments, but it was all made for an older, more mature customer."

Despite her creative aptitude and design genius, Stephanie was a reluctant virtuoso. She shied away from public events and participated in fashion shows only under duress. By all accounts, she was a stunning beauty who dressed with a natural, fresh elegance. "Stephanie loved fashion, and she loved to create," Brown remembers.

But she did not want to go out and meet with the press and other people. She was great when she did meet them; she could have a great conversation and keep them engaged. Some people walk into a room and instantly cause all eyes to shift to them. Stephanie was one of them. She was so dynamic that the room came to her, and she liked it. But most of the time she really didn't want to be there. She was a very private person.

Her insecurity was always unfounded, since fashion reviewers heaped endless accolades on her and her creations. Not much for promotional junkets, Stephanie was fascinated by Hollywood, and with some gentle prodding she could be enticed into attending the annual press week festivities held in Beverly Hills. Once she was comfortably ensconced in her corner of the ballroom she held court like the queen of style she was, causing reporters to gush over her latest line and her creative principles. An example, as reported by the *San Francisco Chronicle*:

> Stephanie Koret was down from San Francisco for the premiere of her Spring Koret of California line. Her fashion credo is ably expressed in her own words—"It must walk well, sit well, feel comfortable, and look pretty." This season Mrs. Koret added boating to her fashion preoccupation, showing functional clothes for every boating need from a weekend ride in the family motor boat to international sailing and relaxing ashore. . . . Also in the Koret collection are cotton knits in wicker and jacquard patterns for travel and spectator sportswear; popcorn knits in dramatic ombré stripes in play clothes and separates; gossamer lace cotton knit frocks and waist length jackets that are washable and shrug off wrinkles.[2]

Shrug off wrinkles.

Perhaps more than anything else, Stephanie and Joe were obsessed—almost to the level of fanatical zeal—with wrinkles and pleats. In early 1956, Koret of California filed an application for a patent that would change the global garment industry. Working secretly in a small laboratory in San Francisco, a team led by company executives William Warnock and Frank Hubener had perfected a process for manufacturing permanent-press garments. The system improved on previous methods to produce clothing that would be "free from wrinkles, retain all pleating and creases made therein during manufacture, and require no pressing to afford presentable, attractive, and neat-appearing apparel."[3]

According to the original patent application, other firms in recent years had developed various systems by which select fabrics could

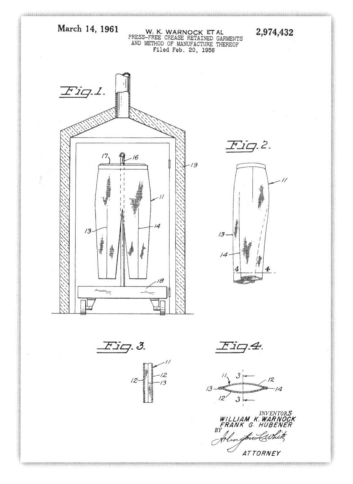

March 14, 1961   W. K. WARNOCK ET AL   2,974,432
PRESS–FREE CREASE RETAINED GARMENTS
AND METHOD OF MANUFACTURE THEREOF
Filed Feb. 20, 1956

Fig.1.

Fig.2.

Fig.3.   *Fig.4.*

INVENTORS
WILLIAM K. WARNOCK
FRANK G. HUBENER
BY
ATTORNEY

Patent drawing of original "Koraset" permanent press process, issued 1961.
[U.S. Patent Office]

be treated to "impart durable crease resistance to the fabrics." The majority of these methods involved the use of thermo-setting chemicals, and in the early stages of these processes, the fabric was infused with an aqueous solution of a specific resin. The fabric subsequently was dried at a temperature "sufficiently high enough to effect polymerization of the resin or setting thereof in the fabric." However, due to the "harsh effects of the resins on the fibers, which were rendered unduly brittle, the tensile strength as well as tear strength of the fabric suffered considerably and garments made therefrom had but little life and durability."

Koret of California's new permanent-press process changed all that. The objective of this new system was threefold: First, it provided a method of manufacturing iron-free crease-retained garments that were completely finished and ready to wear. Second, it permitted press-free garments to withstand numerous washings without loss of creases or pleats, and to be free from wrinkles after drying and while being worn. Third—and no less important for the apparel manufacturer—the new process allowed fabrics to be easily cut, sewn, and pressed before the introduction of the polymer resins.

The Koret invention improved on or obviated a number of other processes dating back as far as 1888. The company's patent attorneys described it as such a radical advancement in the manufacturing of clothing that the U.S. Patent Office took five years to review the application and weigh its merits against those of other processes that preceded it. The government's own researchers and lawyers had to satisfy themselves that the innovation was, indeed, a "new and improved" system that could stand up to the competitive and legal scrutiny that almost certainly would arise once it hit the marketplace. Joe and his team had complete faith in their innovation, and the patent finally was granted in March 1961. As a sign of internal confidence, Koret of California began using the new Koraset process on some of its own garments three years earlier, in 1958, but Joe and his team deliberately played down its significance in advertising and marketing materials.

Armed with the knowledge that his pending patent could secure Koret of California's financial future, Joe implemented several executive moves intended to position the company as a global competitor. He began by naming Koret of California veteran sales rep Charles Cain to the new position of administrative sales manager, then scheduled a series of regional meetings in New Orleans, White Sulphur Springs, and Palm Springs. While regional meetings were not uncommon events, these gatherings, scheduled for the spring of 1958—were perfectly timed to coincide with the release of the firm's first Koraset-treated clothing line.

BUOYED BY THE SUCCESS OF HIS INITIAL licensing forays into Canada and Australia, as well as the chaotic and highly controversial South African market, Joe set his sights on Europe. Long intrigued by the Paris fashion scene, he viewed the continent as a major target for the company's increasingly popular sportswear. In the spring of 1959, he and Stephanie set off for England, France, and Italy to explore manufacturing and distribution opportunities. "An industrialized Europe will provide a tremendous and growing market for middle-price-range sportswear," Joe said at the time.[4] Accompanied by vice president Leo Brown, Joe and Stephanie were impressed by both the demand for Koret of California clothing and the large labor force available in southern Italy. "We should have gone sooner," he told his executive team when he returned, noting that he was already planning a return visit.

Lest anyone think Koret of California might start incorporating French design elements in its clothing lines, Stephanie assured her staff that California styling would remain the backbone of the company's creations. Still, she did point out that, "There is so much inspiration in seeing things in different settings."[5]

While Joe considered Europe a solid foothold in his global expansion plans, he also viewed America's neighbor to the north as the next logical step for expansion. Within a week of returning from his trip across the pond, he signed an agreement to establish a new company—Koret of California-Canada—that would manufacture and sell sportswear throughout the country. According to company documents, the new corporation was owned jointly by Koret of California and Aljean Sportswear of Vancouver, BC. Both companies were quick to point out that, despite climate differences between Canada and the States, the new venture's styles would be duplicates of those of Koret of California. Some garments were manufactured in Koret's American plants and some in the Canadian firm's facilities.

AT THIS POINT, KORET OF CALIFORNIA WAS A major fixture in the California garment industry. "Today, Koret of California is the largest manufacturer of its kind in [the state]," Joe wrote in an article published in the *San Francisco Chronicle* and later reprinted in the *Christian Science Monitor*. "It ships two million garments annually to thousands of retailers throughout the U.S., and to many in foreign countries."[6]

Additionally, the company maintained several manufacturing plants in the Bay Area and had branch offices in New York, Dallas, Los Angeles, and Honolulu. Koret purchased over three million yards of fabric a year, along with millions of buttons and zippers and hundreds of millions of yards of thread. It employed over eleven hundred workers with an annual payroll exceeding $2.5 million, and had a personnel program that included health insurance, vacation funds, and profit-sharing trusts. Quite a difference from the mom-and-pop venture that began many years before in Joe and Stephanie's apartment near Alamo Square.

By now, Joe Koret was considered an icon of the women's apparel business. But his rags-to-riches story was far from over, and many major successes still lay on the distant horizon. Captains of industry probed him for advice, trade reporters pestered him for interviews, and young entrepreneurs hounded him for guidance and insight. Displaying nowhere near the reclusive tendencies of his wife, Joe had a commanding approach to all things business. His word was always final, but he was confident enough to delegate much of the day-to-day decision-making to his trusted managers.

Joe's career had always been confined to fashion, which he firmly believed was a pervasive influence throughout all facets of American industry. "There is no business in the United States today that can afford to ignore fashion," he wrote in a subsequent essay in the *Christian Science Monitor*. "Every manufacturer and every consumer is affected by [it]."[7]

Invoking memories of his first automobile, Joe recalled that Henry Ford had proudly boasted that a customer could buy a Model T in any color he wanted, as long as it was black. "Fashion has changed all of this," he said. "Now you can buy Fords in every color of the rainbow—and in several hues no rainbow ever contained. You can buy many different models of Fords. . . . In order to hold the market, automobile manufacturers have had to adapt to fashion trends, color demands, fads, and fancies. Whether it's cars or can openers, skirts or shirts, the trend is the same. Fashion is queen. It rules—with an elegantly gloved but strong hand—every manufacturing industry today."[8]

Joe knew that many business executives had an almost irrational fear of change, but not so the fashion industry. He believed that fashion creativity thrived on change, and that a good manufacturer never let down his or her guard. "Designers are always on the alert," he observed. "The world is their scouting ground. No one knows the source of the next good idea."

The 1950s retail market was inflated by promotional hyperbole and word-of-mouth exaggeration that often led to "flash fads." The inside back covers of comic books were cluttered with ads for everything from miniature spy cameras to X-ray specs. Almost out of nowhere, hula hoops, fuzzy dice, and carhops were all the rage. Poodle skirts, saddle shoes, cigarette jeans, and sailor hats all made their brief appearance as cult fads, but none had the "legs" to keep going.

"There is an important difference between fashion trends and fads," Joe observed in the *Christian Science Monitor* multipart essay. "Contrary to popular belief, fashion trends are not capricious or illogical, although fads often are. Trends result inevitably from changing patterns of living. Experienced students of fashion learn to separate the inexorable slow rolling of a major fashion trend from the flash explosion of a fad. The wise ready-to-wear manufacturer with a large organization avoids fads. Once [a manufacturer] begins to follow fads, his percentage of successes will be disproportionately low to those of his failures."[9]

Guided by this philosophy, Joe and Stephanie largely ignored the crazes of the day. Instead, Koret of California used grassroots give-and-take with retailers and consumers to intelligently assess any new trend in the making. This way, they were able to get in early, design a new line, purchase fabrics, and manufacture goods before a trend peaked. The key, Joe said, was to plan manufacturing and shipments long in advance, schedule inventories appropriately, then phase them out so as to be out of the trend at the proper time. As a result, no store would be left with unmovable overstock merchandise once the trend ran its natural course.

Fabrics also were critical to the success or failure of a new fashion line. By the late fifties, virtually all of Koret of California planning meetings began with an assessment of the latest materials and weaves. The planning team went to great lengths to determine those that would remain popular and those that had already run their course. Viable fabrics for the next season's line were then listed on a large blackboard in the company's fifth-floor conference room, where a frank and energized discussion would occur. Stephanie's team knew that not all fabrics were suitable for relaxed-fit trousers or comfortable skirts and blouses, and this vetting process was mandatory. "A fabric may be in great demand, but if it is too dressy for our type of styling or too expensive to fit our price range, it is not suitable," Joe explained.

At the end of every Koret design session, a list of fabric categories would emerge that the entire team agreed would meet the expectations of retailers and consumers. A team of merchandising executives led by Joe and Stephanie then would travel to New York to meet with each supplier to work out these particular fabric categories in textures, patterns, and coloring created exclusively for Koret of California. Once these specifics were worked out, sample yardage was rushed to San Francisco headquarters for final approval. Stephanie and her staff then would work the fabric into "test" garments, just as in the early days, to make sure they met the team's beauty, touch, color, and performance standards.

At this point, the planning committee was granted full autonomy to decide the number of garments that would fall into the coming season's collection and, even further, into each coordinated group of sportswear. Once the number of garments was set, Stephanie and her staff determined the color and basic styling for each group. Finally, working both from sketches and by draping on live models, they created the new Koret collection.

That was just the beginning. Once the planning team confirmed the various garments that were going to be manufactured in that season's "cycle," the sales and manufacturing departments drew up a "dollar plan" for each fabric. "If we [expect] large consumer demand, we may set a dollar plan of $800,000 to $1 million on the group," Joe said. "On the other hand, we know a novelty plaid fabric does not have as large a consumer demand as flannel. So, if we have a novelty plaid group, we set a smaller dollar plan for it. When the dollar plans are totaled, we have a pretty clear knowledge of our overall volume for the coming season."

These dollar plans guided the merchandising department in the purchase of fabrics, and similarly assisted the promotion department in strategizing, advertising, and marketing. A fabric group with a hefty plan would call for heavy promotion, while a group with a smaller plan called for a more targeted approach. "Promotion and distribution policies are entwined with styling and merchandising policies like a pretzel," Joe said. "Your market must be clearly defined, and your promotion and product must be aimed squarely at the target. It's the promotion, advertising, and publicizing of our product that tells our consumers what we have to offer."[10]

Once the factories began manufacturing the new fashion lines, the Koret advertising and promotion departments got to work. Guided by years of experience and accumulated know-how, the company employed a variety of methods to get out the word on Stephanie's new creations. New seasonal lines primarily were advertised in leading fashion magazines and industry trade publications, while retailers were provided with specialized materials for window and interior displays, newspaper ads, and radio "co-op" commercials for local advertising. Additionally, a series of "selling facts" were provided to all retailers' salesmen and saleswomen.

An example of this deliberate research, manufacturing, and promotion process was the final line Stephanie and her team designed in the fifties. Looking ahead to spring of 1960, the company unveiled the largest line in its history—mostly in cotton and cotton blends. The heavy emphasis on cotton in the woven fabrics division was largely because of the company's patent-pending Koraset process, which worked extremely well with that type of organic material. Strong sales projections and a bifurcated focus on woven-fabric sportswear and knits led Joe to split the sales team into two divisions. Both lines would be handled by the current sales staff, but each would now have its own advertising and promotional campaigns.

AS THE FINAL MONTHS OF 1959 TICKED DOWN, Joe made the painful decision to shutter the doors of his late brother's business. Following Al's death in 1944, the Koret Manufacturing Company had continued to roll out a dependable line of men's clothing that was popular in the western United States. Now Joe arranged for Koret of California to acquire the company's name, while all of the firm's assets would be purchased by the GEM Realty Corporation. Ronald McClennan, who served as Koret of California's secretary-treasurer as well as president of GEM Realty, said GEM would use the equipment to manufacture women's sportswear under a contract with Koret. All Koret's menswear lines would cease to exist, since Koret of California at that time had no interest in entering the men's clothing field.[11]

As champagne corks popped on New Year's Eve, no one at Koret headquarters could have possibly foreseen the momentous changes that were about to hit America head-on. Not only was the world of fashion about to be spun off its axis, but San Francisco was set to bear witness to a social and cultural evolution unparalleled in the nation's history. Hippies, Haight-Ashbury, and the Summer of Love weren't yet part of the American lexicon, but the seeds of change were being sown by what was to be one of the closest presidential elections ever held. A virtual tinderbox of disparate people, places, and events was about to detonate. Vietnam, assassination, the space race, civil rights, the British invasion—all would contribute in some way to the pulsing backdrop and vibrant soundtrack of the new decade.

Like it or not, America was about to come of age.

Joe hands a coffee pot to the winner of a Koret of California sales promotion in the early 1960s. Also pictured are (l to r) Henry Weil, Ronald McClennan, Bernard Worth, and Joyce Bickel. [Bancroft Library collection]

7

The Sixties:
A Decade of Turmoil

SAN FRANCISCO'S GROWING REPUTATION AS A progressive-minded Shangri-La served as a magnet for an emerging American counterculture.

Artists, poets, musicians, and writers flocked to the increasingly enlightened city because of its cultural liberalism and its purported acceptance of a nascent "alternative existentialism." In the 1950s, the City Lights Bookstore in North Beach had emerged as a friendly haven for the "beat generation," and as that underground movement took hold, it attracted even more proponents of unconventional lifestyles. These social alchemists rejected the traditional establishment narrative while searching for a deeper kind of universal meaning. Increasingly permissive elements of a "free society" enthusiastically invited personal experimentation, the more mind-bending the better. Individual and collective journeys into Eastern religion, new-age spirituality, altered states of psychedelic awareness, and sexual exploration were encouraged and applauded.

Interwoven with this social renaissance was a growing, but still largely discreet, homosexual population. Even after the fall of the

Barbary Coast and the demise of its reputed leniency, pockets of sexual nuance had remained throughout the city. During the war years, American military men and women had shipped out through the Golden Gate and returned to a city that was exceptionally accepting of almost everyone. Many of those who had remained closeted during their service either remained in San Francisco after being discharged by Uncle Sam, or returned to the city over the ensuing years.

Despite the previous decade's relative consumer contentment—some might say complacency—not everything was right in many corners of American society. In the 1940s and fifties, a few African Americans had successfully chiseled away at the Jim Crow laws; Jackie Robinson's debut with the Brooklyn Dodgers in 1947 was perhaps the most notable of these advancements. The 1950s saw increased violence amid forced integration, as Rosa Parks took her seat in the front of a bus in Montgomery, Alabama, and the city of Little Rock was forced to open its high school doors to students of all races.

On January 2, 1960, Massachusetts Senator John F. Kennedy declared his candidacy for president. During the subsequent campaign, he promised American voters an ambitious domestic agenda known as the "New Frontier," which included a package of reforms intended to eliminate injustice and inequality throughout the country. His controversial ideas met with great resistance among politicians and voters who liked things the way they were—*thank you very much*—and regarded him as a northern liberal interventionist.

That said, from the moment Kennedy announced his candidacy, American fashion had its new trendsetter. Even before he won the election by one of the narrowest margins ever in American politics, his wife had captured the hearts and fashion sense of American women. From the moment she walked onto the political stage, Jackie Kennedy was the embodiment of American class, which she carried with ease and confidence. Designers and fashionistas alike were enthralled by a consummate sense of style that was reflected in her tailored suit dresses, pearl necklaces, pillbox hats, and oversized sunglasses.

As *Vogue* contributor Hamish Bowles wrote in a 2013 essay:

> Even on the presidential campaign trail, Jacqueline Kennedy's elegance—focusing on impeccably made clothes of simple lines—drew all eyes. . . . [Her] impact was profound—a visual metaphor for the President's youthful, internationally minded administration. For her formal daytime ensembles, she took a leaf from Britain's royal dressmakers and their clients, avoiding prints and instead using brilliant solid colors and bold lines that marked her in a crowd. Off duty, Jacqueline Kennedy was every inch the liberated sixties woman, barefoot in capri pants and sportif tops that were always chosen with an eye to simplicity of line.[1]

Essentially, Jackie's style was clean, simple, well-fitted, and perfectly matched. She preferred dresses and skirts, with jackets that often fastened only with one large top button. She put a lot of care into her unique look, and women in the United States and overseas admired her style with affection and enthusiasm.[2]

None of this was lost on Joe or Stephanie. As the Kennedy campaign took hold in the summer of 1960, they both realized Jackie's sense of style made her a serious trendsetter, not a flash fad. She had poise and elegance, and possessed a fashion flair that was enhanced by such French designers as Christian Dior, Balenciaga, and Givenchy, although her favorite was the American couturier Oleg Cassini. Jackie had the panache to actually *lower* the bar from the accustomed fashion trends of high society and instead dress like the everyday woman would like to dress, while still giving her devotees just enough to strive for.

In the fall of 1960, Koret of California released its first clothing line of the Jackie era. Not every item was inspired by the soon-to-be first lady, but her influence was felt in the feminine styling and bold, clear modern colors. The company's design team focused on "lush, glowing pastels, cotton knits with a flat, almost satiny, finish called Alpine Knit in solid colors . . . used for skirts, shorts, slim pants and a variety of tops and jackets."[3] The line also included "spectacular separates" in three multicolor versions of scarf prints on a cotton-and-viscose-rayon-blend broadcloth, focusing on full skirts with long- or short-sleeved shirts.

By this point, Stephanie Koret had become a women's fashion maven herself. In a move that was both practical and promotional, Koret of California created a "personalized fashion advisory service" to assist women with their wardrobe challenges. This service was high-lighted by a booklet titled *How, When and Where to Wear Sportswear*, which contained a number of tips helpful to any woman who was trying to make sense of what was in her closet. These booklets were available at many stores that carried Koret fashions, or by writing to the company's Mission Street headquarters. It was free, as long as the customer paid the postage.

Joe and Stephanie also led a small Koret of California delegation on a fact-finding mission to Europe in the summer of 1960. Accompanied by Director of Merchandising Henry Weil, they toured production facilities in the Netherlands, West Germany, and England as part of a follow-up investigation initiated during Joe's visit a year earlier. His objective was to engage in future corporate affiliations with as-yet-unnamed European firms to produce and distribute sportswear under the original Koret of California name. "With the advent of the European Common Market, distribution in the European area is the third logical step in the foreign expansion of our company," Joe explained.[4]

JFK'S INAUGURATION IN JANUARY 1961 USHERED in a new era in American self-awareness. Despite deep political divisions, the country was imbued with a new sense of youth. At just forty-three years of age, Kennedy was the second-youngest man to be sworn in as president, and Jackie was just thirty-one when the couple moved into the White House. They had two young children—Caroline and John—and the news media instantly fell in love with the entire family.

Almost overnight, America seemed to grow *younger*. The post-war baby boom showed no signs of slowing down, and young parents rejected the trappings and sensibilities of their parents. Such television programs as *Leave It to Beaver* and *The Donna Reed Show* emphasized the trials and tribulations of parenthood, while musical tastes shifted from Patti Page and Perry Como to Chuck Berry and Bill Haley. Despite Ed Sullivan's refusal to show him from the waist down, Elvis Presley became an American phenomenon. Pat Boone and Rudy Vallee fans soon began to realize with utter horror that rock and roll truly was here to stay.

Even with the Kennedys in the White House, the early stretch of the 1960s seemed to be a sequel to the fifties. When the Soviets launched their Sputnik satellite into orbit in 1957, Americans became obsessed with space. Automotive engineers began designing new cars with ever-larger rocket fins each year, creating some of the most elegant and ludicrous machinery to ever hit American highways. While most fashion designers did not follow suit by creating wild collar fins or space-suit-like accessories, a new generation of consumers definitely was taking root.

Ever mindful of fads that would not last, Joe and Stephanie made slight "architectural" adaptations to the company's fashions each year but remained true to their centrist sportswear designs. In fact, while Stephanie and her team sketched out the new seasonal fashion lines, Joe and his executive staff were waiting for approval of the Koraset patent they'd applied for in 1956. The company had already used the innovative permanent press-process for some of its own garments since 1958, but Joe knew that when the patent was granted it would open up countless licensing opportunities with other apparel firms. By all accounts, Joe expected Koraset to be the company's biggest breakthrough since the Trikskirt was introduced in 1946.

As 1962 was drawing to a close, the Korets were planning their company Christmas party when Joe received the heartbreaking news that his mother had passed away. At the age of eighty-four, her death was not unexpected; over the ten years since her husband died she had become increasingly frail. The former Sarah Gorewitz, who had followed her husband, Abram, to America in 1902, had been the glue that held the Koret family together while her husband toiled ten- and twelve-hour days. As was the role of many immigrant women in the early 1900s, she endured hard times with a tight smile, rarely doubting her own resolve or the choices of her husband, trying her best to conceal any dismay or disappointment with life. Devastated by the death of her son Harold at the age of fifteen, Sarah Koret went on to endure the passing of two more sons in the 1940s and the death of her husband in 1952. Still, she never looked at the past with contempt, always focusing on the many riches God had bestowed on her and her family.

Following a service officiated by Rabbi Saul White, Sarah Koret was buried alongside her husband, Abram, at the Eternal Home Cemetery in Colma.

THE NEW YEAR BEGAN COLD AND DRY. SAN Francisco was in the middle of a winter drought, but neither Joe nor his staff paid the weather any mind. The Koraset patent had been granted the year before, and almost immediately it began to draw the interest of fabric mills and other apparel manufacturers who were both dubious and intrigued that this California-based sportswear company had apparently found a solution to the age-old permanent press challenge.

To prepare for the anticipated onslaught of wrinkle-free garments, the company soon would be manufacturing, Joe bought a four-story building on Seventeenth Street in San Francisco. Without revealing his Koraset growth plans, Joe said the company was remodeling the 130,000 square feet to accommodate expanded production and distribution operations. At a cost of $1 million, the new structure was well suited to handle the volume of business he knew would be coming his way.

Koraset quickly became synonymous with permanent-press clothing, and by early 1963 Koret of California was using the brand to market its new sportswear line to retailers and the public. As *San Francisco Chronicle* fashion reporter Evelyn Hannay wrote, "Koraset is Koret's patented process that assures never-iron and non-wrinkling performance in cotton. Mix them or match them. Toss them into the washer-dryer and back onto the body without touching an iron to them. In other words, set sail for summer in Koret of California Koraset Rancheros, and give dull care the old heave-ho."[5]

By the fall of 1963, Koraset had begun to attract acquisition offers from other garment manufacturers interested in purchasing either the patent or the company. Joe examined all offers but never actually toyed with the notion of selling. None of the dollar amounts came close to what he knew the firm was worth, and Koret of California was the child he and Stephanie never had. Neither of them was about to kick it out of the nest.

In fact, Joe was more attuned to the acquisition side of the business. He and his management team had been impressed with the success of Koret of California-Canada, the joint venture he had formed with Aljean Sportswear in Vancouver. Over the three years of their fifty-fifty partnership, the Canadian manufacturing plant had expanded to cover more than half an acre, production had shown imposing growth, and cash flow was robust. Acting on the recommendation of a study conducted by Jere Helfat Associates in Cleveland, Joe arranged to acquire all outstanding shares of the firm and fold it into Koret of California's overall operations. Koret executives Ronald McClennan and Henry Weil were appointed directors of the Canadian branch, while Stephanie Koret was named vice president in charge of styling. In that role she worked closely with William Warnock, fresh off the Koraset patent, on seasonal planning and long-range trends.

ON NOVEMBER 22, 1963, AN ASSASSIN'S BULLET
rocked the United States and the entire world. The new hope that had
been fostered by the Kennedy White House was shattered in an instant,
and a nation that had fallen in love with JFK and his young family suddenly was thrust into mourning. Americans that had recently been
laughing at the *Beverly Hillbillies* and *My Favorite Martian* now were
watching as the late president's horse-drawn caisson slowly rolled up
Pennsylvania Avenue and young John-John saluted his fallen father's
casket near St. Matthew's Cathedral.

The shockwaves that followed were immediate and intense and
rocked the nation for years to come. Kennedy had stood up to Soviet
Premiere Nikita Krushchev, endorsed the burgeoning civil rights movement, and taken the initial steps to get America's military advisers out
of Vietnam. Suddenly, all of that seemed in doubt. Lyndon Johnson
was now at the helm of a country that had been plunged into a
spiritual blackout. People felt uncertain about their futures. There was
no focal point, no cultural center, no national sense of self or social
bearing. The Beatles had yet to touch American soil, and draft cards
and bras had yet to be viewed as flammable objects. Timothy Leary's
experiments with hallucinogens notwithstanding, drugs remained the
guarded province of doctors and pharmacists. Men's hair was short,
women's hemlines were long, and American society was, by and large,
middle class.

With her husband gone and her own life in turmoil, Jackie Kennedy
retreated from public view. Now just thirty-four, she was the widow of
America's fallen and much-adored former president. It was an identity
she shunned, and she understandably refused to speak with reporters.
Eventually, she was approached by Pulitzer Prize-winning journalist
Theodore White, to whom she opened her soul for a special *Life* magazine introspective. "There will be great presidents again, but there
will never be another Camelot," she told him.[6] The parallel between
the Kennedy White House and the legendary King Arthur's round table

had become a staple of American political commentary, but the former first lady was right. The comforting notion of Camelot faded into memory, never to appear again. With Jackie's departure from the front pages, the fashion scene was forced into a major reboot. Gone was the subtle elegance of the first lady's tailored dresses and the casual Hyannis playwear. No more pillbox hats or simple white pearls.

Winter was cold and empty that year, and as spring approached many Americans were looking for a distraction from their lingering grief. Four young musicians named John, Paul, George, and Ringo provided the diversion the nation sorely needed, and within weeks all eyes were focused on what was happening "across the pond." Suddenly, all things British were in vogue, with the Beatles leading the charge. They were followed soon by the Rolling Stones, Dave Clark Five, Dusty Springfield, Petula Clark, the Kinks, and a hit parade of countless others. Fad or trend, craze or movement, Americans fell in love with the United Kingdom, giving rise to a generational "counterculture" on both sides of the Atlantic.

The British invasion had begun.

Almost overnight, the casual grace of Camelot gave way to styles that were more driven by experimentation and whimsy. Such designers as Mary Quant, Kiki Byrne, and John Bates pushed hemlines upward and ultimately gave the world the miniskirt. Quant's dresses and skirts had been daringly short in early 1960s London, and her bold prints and loud colors helped to usher in the eye-popping "mod" look. As one fashion historian wrote of the time, "It was the whole idea of a return to youth that drove most of the fashion in the 1960s. Oversize collars, bows, and delicate trim miniaturized women and made them appear smaller. Shapeless mini dresses de-emphasized a woman's natural form."[7]

At the same time, the American "youth set" fell in love with Twiggy, a diminutive London model who became a global cultural icon almost overnight. Known for her stick-figure build, large eyes, long lashes, and overall androgynous look, Twiggy (born Lesley Hornby) embodied everything British. While she spent only a mere six weeks in the United States during the sixties fashion heyday, she became the universal idol of teenagers from sea to shining sea. She embodied everything many young women aspired to: personal freedom, an individual sense of self, sexual innocence, and the anti-perfection of fashion.[8] As fashion editor Diana Vreeland stated in a *Newsweek* article, "She's no flash in the pan. She is the mini-girl in the mini-era. She's delicious looking."[9]

Delicious nor not, Joe and Stephanie viewed the mod look—indeed, many of the styles coming out of Great Britain—as faddish. While the Korets were too savvy to totally ignore the bright colors, large polka dots, and microscopic hemlines that were changing the American "dress-scape," Koret of California was not about to retool just to meet the demands of this craze. As Joe had observed several years earlier, fashion trends were neither capricious nor illogical. They resulted inevitably from changing patterns of living, and experienced students of fashion learned to distinguish between gradual social evolution and the flash explosion of a craze. He was betting on the long-term mindset of the American woman who might consider purchasing a miniskirt for fun, but was more comfortable with the style and panache of coordinated sportswear.

BY EARLY 1964, KORET OF CALIFORNIA'S NEW Koraset process—now known as Koratron—snared the interest of major U.S. textile mills and other apparel manufacturers. In short order, Joe signed licensing agreements with McCampbell-Graniteville, M. Lowenstein and Sons, and Erwin Mills, and also was working on a deal with San Francisco–based Levi Strauss & Company. Anticipating significant sales growth, he also expanded his agreement with Alamac Knitting Mills in New York, projecting a million-dollar volume increase in fabric purchases over the next three years. Additionally, the company named McCann-Erickson as the firm's advertising agency, overseeing the media elements of Koret's fall promotion plans.

"Our continued rapid growth, particularly international expansion, led us to seek the counsel of an international agency," Joyce Bickel, sales promotion manager and director of advertising, observed at the time.[10]

A somewhat quiet force inside Koret of California, Bickel possessed a creative mind and an imagination that naturally dovetailed with the expectations of the company's customers. In a multifaceted promotional excursion designed to highlight the benefits of Koraset, and to play into fantasies of overseas travel, she orchestrated a week-long fashion tour "down under" in Sydney and Melbourne. Working with the entire Koret of California marketing department, she arranged a seven-day cruise on the *Oronsay*, a luxurious passenger ship owned and operated by the Orient Line. One of the ships used in the 1958 British comedy film *The Captain's Table*, the *Oronsay* was a well-known trans-Pacific ocean liner, and Bickel viewed it as the perfect stage on which to unveil Stephanie's latest spring line.

To highlight the promotion, Bickel lined up four "representatives of the U.S.A." to wear Koret of California designs exclusively on the cruise. These four models—described by *Chronicle* financial editor Sidney Allen as "quite articulate and each charmingly personable in her individual way"—held impromptu on-board fashion shows and mingled with the twelve-hundred-plus passengers. Additionally, Bickel—billed as the "ambassadress" of the excursion—conducted fashion clinics for *Oronsay* passengers to brief them on the newest Koret fabrics, finishes, and fashion needs. "The California Look, with emphasis on our mode of outdoor living and dressing, is sure to find ready acceptance in Australia, where climates are similar," she said.[11]

When the ship docked in Sydney, the Koret entourage staged a half-dozen benefit fashion shows. They again modeled the cruise/holiday and resort clothes that had been featured onboard, as well as additional fashions from the spring 1966 Koret collection. The entire event was designed not only to showcase Stephanie's latest designs, but also to

illustrate how the new Koratron process made traveling both anxiety-
and wrinkle-free.

ONE OF THE EARLY ISSUES WITH KORATRON WAS
that it initially worked well only with cotton. Koret of California at
first incorporated the process into the manufacture of its own cotton
garments, but with so many clothes being made from rayon, nylon,
polyester, wool, and other fabrics, its use was highly limited. As the
Chronicle's Karola Saekel observed, "Koratron was great, but the kind
of sturdy cotton it appeared in was hardly what a lady could wear on a
hot day in town, taking the kids for a ride, or serving a special dinner.
No question about it: you had to choose between practicality and
feminine allure."[12]

Other critics gave Koratron mixed reviews. It was a great start as
far as "wash and wear" was concerned, but it was far from perfect.
Designers could not live by permanent-press cotton alone. The Koret of
California research engineers were working overtime to adapt the process to other fabrics, and Joe was growing anxious. He had predicted
that all garments would be permanent press within just a few years,
and he needed to have something positive to announce.

Enter—*Shalimar*.

This sturdy fabric historically was a 75 percent rayon, 25 percent polyester blend, but it had difficulty holding a Koratron crease.
After considerable trial and error, the Koret engineers came up with a
composition that was 65 percent Dacron and 35 percent cotton. This
ratio felt much more relaxed than regular cotton fabric, which was
important to Stephanie's sense of comfort. Better yet, it adapted well
to the chemical impregnation and intense heat used in the baking
process. After cutting, sewing, and fitting, Shalimar garments held
their creases and eliminated wrinkles. It was less crisp than heavier
cottons, considerably more comfortable on the human body, and
it breathed in the summer heat. As the *Chronicle* reported, the new

Koratron Shalimar had "all the machine-wash and machine-dry, never-iron handiness of its durable country cousin, but it's as soft and feminine as can be."[13]

BY THE START OF 1966, THE UNITED STATES WAS fully enmeshed in Vietnam. Death and dying was a regular fixture on the nightly news, and viewers were becoming increasingly outraged at the almost-daily bloodshed. More and more, young Americans were coming home in flag-draped caskets, and protests began to erupt from coast to coast. As battle scenes were broadcast into living rooms on a nightly basis, people saw first-hand the atrocities being inflicted on— and by—their sons and husbands.

When they weren't glued to the blood and gore, Americans were watching *Batman* and *Star Trek*, in living color. Children were fascinated by a new building toy known as Lego, and grown-ups were standing in line to purchase the novel *Valley of the Dolls*. Cigarettes began carrying health warnings, *Thunderball* and *Dr. Zhivago* hit the silver screen, the Beatles continued their reign at the top of the charts, and NASA launched the very first spacecraft into orbit around the moon.

Meanwhile, hemlines continued to levitate. The first full-fledged miniskirt arguably had been modeled by fashion superstar Jean Shrimpton in October 1965, and the garment that was little more than a strip of fabric instantly became an overnight craze. For most of the twentieth century, women's clothes had obscured the upper part of a woman's legs, but a new sense of personal empowerment and sexual liberation opened the door to self-realization and awareness. In one of the first signs of anti-parental rebellion, the miniskirt made the highly vocal rebellious statement that "we are not our mothers." Interestingly, many older women—a good number of them mothers themselves— also felt a need to liberate themselves from the "couture" of yesterday. They didn't abandon their entire wardrobes in search of a new fashion elixir, but the new freedoms that were extending throughout American youth culture began to dissolve generational barriers and ease social boundaries.

While not a fan of the miniskirt, Stephanie realized she needed to jump on board before the train left the station. Koret of California hemlines already had crept up incrementally during the early sixties, and she now took a leap of faith and announced her first mini-creation. As noted in an advertisement that appeared in *Vogue*, she urged customers to "follow the sun in the tiniest T—a skimp of pale-blue knitted cotton, snugged into a short mini-skirt, with one inverted pleat in front."[14] Yes, even during the height of the miniskirt craze, Stephanie had to include a pleat!

Plus, it was Koratron, so it never wrinkled, and never needed ironing.

Several months later, Koret of California introduced a new line of sportswear featuring separate slacks, blouses, and skirts that seemed to eschew the mod and mini craze. In a deliberately contrarian move, hemlines were kept right at the knees, and there wasn't an oversized brightly colored polka dot in sight. By this time, Kotratron had been adapted to work with Fortrel polyester-cotton, and an advertisement for the Emporium department store chain promised that "seams don't pucker, pants and skirts keep their shape. No more wilting, either— these skirts and pants will be as fresh at night as they were in the morning. Beautifully tailored with all the detail you expect to find in a skirt or pant with a Koret label." [15]

The explosion of business stemming from Kotratron, as well continued growth from its fashion lines, finally allowed Joe to realize one of his grandest dreams. In early 1966, he announced that Koret of California had registered an initial public offering with the U.S. Securities and Exchange Commission, giving investors the opportunity to buy 497,200 of the company's 2,023,971 outstanding common shares. The bulk of those shares being sold—352,000—were owned by Joe and Stephanie, and at the proposed sales price of $25 they stood to take home a little more than $8 million. The IPO valued the remainder of the Korets' personal shares at approximately $20 million, while the balance of the stock sold in the initial offering—benefitting two other shareholders and the company's stock bonus trust—yielded just over $3.6 million.[16]

The actual IPO was delayed a few days because the company and its stock underwriters were compelled to comply with SEC disclosure regulations. Koret of California was freshly engaged in a lawsuit with Burlington Industries, stemming from the apparel giant's licensing of the patented Koratron process. The commission's rules required Koret to issue a new prospectus explaining the litigation, and Joe readily complied. Koret of California officially went public on May 2 at $24.75 per share, and the underwriters—Glore Forgan, Wm. R. Staats Inc.—announced that late in the day it was oversubscribed at "$34 bid, $37 asked."

In early July, Koret of California reported sharp gains in operating results for the first six months of the calendar year. Profits through June 30 were a record $2,267,170, which translated to $1.12 for each share of stock—almost double the $1,147,662, or 57 cents a share earned in the same period the previous year. Net sales of apparel were $11.9 million, up 31 percent from the first six months of 1965, and Koratron net royalty licensing income was $3.1 million, up 90 percent.

This bright financial picture—and an infusion of cash from the public offering—allowed Joe to expand the company's distribution plant. The Mission Street space was bursting at the seams and even the newly expanded operation on Seventeenth Street was filled to capacity. To alleviate this problem and plan for the future, Joe and his executive team embarked on an extensive search for enough space to house additional facilities. After a months-long inspection of dozens of buildings and lots within a ten-mile radius of its headquarters, he settled on a ten-acre parcel in the new Cabot, Cabot and Forbes Industrial Park in South San Francisco.

Still largely undeveloped, South San Francisco for decades had identified itself—in massive white letters seemingly embossed in a hillside overlooking the airport—as "The Industrial City." Just a few miles south of San Francisco proper, the location provided convenient commutes for workers and easy access on and off the 101 Bayshore Freeway for delivery trucks. It was an ideal site to build the new 160,000-square-foot, $3 million facility, which Joe predicted would be completed by early 1967. The new plant would house an automated distribution center, with computerized inventory control and new packaging systems designed to minimize any re-pressing after a shipment was received by the local retailer. Additionally, a new $1 million electronic data-processing system—already in use at the Koret offices—was being expanded to meet the needs of the automated center.

Stephanie commemorated the groundbreaking by cracking a bottle of champagne against a bulldozer, with Joe and two models dressed in Koret's latest fashions looking on. "The new plant will be capable of handling one million garments, and could be expanded in capability to handle an additional 65 percent of the volume," he said during the ceremony.

Money in the bank also caused Joe to consider the acquisition of other garment manufacturers. He had already dabbled with licensing in South Africa and Australia, and the company now wholly owned Koret of California-Canada. The availability of ready cash in a tight money market allowed Joe to think outside the packing box and study other areas of the apparel industry, including men's and children's wear.

One of the first targeted acquisitions Joe approved was Broadway Knitting Mills Ltd., a Montreal-based producer of women's fashion sweaters and knitted skirts. On announcing the $300,000 deal, Joe said Broadway's existing product lines would be expanded and the newly acquired firm would serve as a supplier to Koret of California-Canada. "This acquisition is a major step forward in our participation in the vigorous and growing economy of Canada," he said in a statement.

To assist with the anticipated acquisition process and to take over day-to-day management responsibilities, Joe tapped Jere Helfat to serve as the company's first president not to bear the Koret name. Helfat had served as consultant to Koret of California since 1962, when he developed the long-range plan that recommended that Joe buy out the remaining shares of Koret of California-Canada. Long a proponent of aggressive acquisitions, Helfat believed a broad range of expansion opportunities lay ahead of the new public company, and he convinced Joe that the sky was the limit.

"The election of Helfat broadens and further strengthens our top management organization to enable us to maintain our rapid growth," Joe said at the time. "His duties will involve overall direction of operations, organization development, and long-range planning." This move would allow Joe, who was stepping up to serve as chairman of the board, to "concentrate on the vitally important areas of product development and merchandising."[17]

Ambitious and determined, Helfat jumped into the new job with both feet. Within weeks, he had identified a number of attractive acquisitions targets, both within and outside the apparel industry. Koret of California was set to embark on a multiyear buying spree that consumed an immense amount of cash in exchange for companies of uncertain value. To use a term coined years later by Federal Reserve Alan Greenspan, it was a period of "irrational exuberance."

And in just a few short years it would nearly kill the company.

SAN FRANCISCO IN 1967 WAS A MICROCOSM OF the self-awareness that was shape-shifting the national psyche. America's role in Vietnam continued to expand, and antiwar sentiment intensified. Race relations—or the lack thereof—exploded like a powder keg. A simmering drug counterculture driven by an antiestablishment idealism took root from one coast to the other. And a music scene that just a few years earlier had lamented that "Daddy took the T-bird away" now was engaging with hookah-smoking caterpillars and pills that made you feel ten feet tall.

Long a haven of free speech and even freer behavior, San Francisco naturally emerged as the epicenter of the Utopian experience known as the Summer of Love. The Beatles had played their final U.S. concert at the city's Candlestick Park in the waning months of 1966, leaving a void that quickly was filled with the psychedelic riffs of Jimi Hendrix, Jefferson Airplane, and Big Brother and the Holding Company. Blotter acid and mushrooms embodied a new spiritual awareness, and relaxed sexual mores encouraged men and women of all ages and gender identities to "make love, not war." The confluence of sex, drugs, and rock and roll created a perfect storm that within weeks transformed San Francisco into a cauldron of expressive freedom and existential conflict.

During this brief and possibly over-romanticized period (except, perhaps, for those who think they remember being there), the hippie with long hair in a tie-dyed shirt, grooving to the new alternative sound of the Grateful Dead and Country Joe and the Fish, epitomized the experience. The Summer of Love was neither a conscious movement nor a flash fad; in the end it was approximately 100,000 young people who gathered in a certain place at a certain time with the Leary-esque idea to "tune in, turn on, and drop out."

For Joe Koret, it was anything but. In fact, 1967 turned out to be an epic year in the history of the company. In early February, newly appointed Koret of California President Jere Helfat announced almost unprecedented corporate earnings. Apparel sales and licensing income both showed healthy double-digit quarterly gains year-over-year, although royalty revenue from Koratron experienced an alarming decline in the final quarter of the year. Downplaying this marked decrease in licensing income, Helfat told investors it primarily was due to a seasonal pattern among fabric mills and manufacturers of men's and boys' permanent-press trousers. This category had accounted for a majority of Koratron sales, but profits had begun to decline steadily over the past year. Helfat purposely did not mention the growing number of lawsuits filed against Koret of California, which threatened future earnings from the permanent-press division.

A company earnings statement released in March 1967 included a brief announcement that Stephanie Koret was retiring after twenty-nine years with the company. The official reason for her departure was that the company had implemented a mandatory retirement age of sixty-five, and therefore she was required to step down. This condition clearly didn't apply to her husband, who—three years her senior—was the company's board chairman. In fact, what was little known outside the fifth-floor office was that Stephanie, whose hard work and innovative creative sense had propelled the company's designs since the 1930s, was beginning to exhibit serious symptoms of memory loss. Joe and his colleagues had begun to see warning signs around the home and office, and there was growing concern that she no longer could perform her duties on a day-to-day basis.

THE ALARMING SLIDE IN KORATRON REVENUE that appeared in late 1966 continued through the first quarter of '67. Jere Helfat, not accustomed to communicating bad news, encouraged investors to remain optimistic about Koret of California's financial potential. "We are confident our apparel earnings for the full year will be substantially ahead of last year," he predicted, stressing that the company would be seeing an increase in Koratron royalties even though that income had yet to appear in quarterly earnings.

Helfat also was forced to address an unexpected drop in the company's apparel sales. He blamed this slide on losses from the Sue J. division, a company Koret of California had acquired several years before. Also at fault, he insisted, were seasonal first-quarter losses of the recently acquired Broadway Knitting Mills, as well as unusually heavy markdowns in some fashion-coordinated merchandise. He attributed both declines to poor apparel retail sales throughout the country.

Despite the overall dip in revenue and earnings, Koret of California continued its buying spree. Led by Helfat's nearly unchecked zeal for deal-making, the company purchased New York-based Blairmoor Knitwear Corp., which was known nationally for its fashionable women's sweaters. The firm was founded in 1941 by Leon Messing, who, after the merger, was retained by Koret in a consulting capacity. With reported sales of more than $3 million in 1967, Helfat believed it was an intelligent purchase that should drive cash flow to the bottom line almost immediately. Half of Blairmoor's manufacturing occurred in Puerto Rico, where Helfat intended to almost double capacity in the coming year.[18]

Koret of California allocated approximately $1.2 million for the Blairmoor acquisition and the initial expansion of the plant. The deal was timed so the firm's traditionally strong second half would be reflected in Koret's earnings, contributing at least $100,000 to the bottom line.

The ink on the Blairmoor contract was barely dry when Helfat announced Koret of California's next acquisition. This time he struck a deal to purchase Byer-Rolnick Corporation, marking the firm's entry into the menswear industry. The Dallas-based company for years had been a leading producer of men's felt, straw, and casual headwear, and primarily was known as the manufacturer of the highly popular Resistol brand of western hats. Over the years, the line had expanded from its utilitarian cowboy roots to produce fashionable wardrobe accessories of such actors as John Wayne and Henry Fonda, as well as President Lyndon Johnson and then California Governor Ronald Reagan. The Byer-Rolnick deal also included the acquisition of wholly owned subsidiary Weinberg Corporation, which manufactured the exclusive high-end Oxxford clothing line. Founded in 1916 by Jacob and Louis Weinberg, Oxxford proudly proclaimed that it dressed such notable celebrities as Clark Gable, Cary Grant, Walt Disney, and Joe DiMaggio.

Although Joe and Stephanie had always adhered to their plan to keep Koret of California in its established niche of women's sportswear, Joe gave the Byer-Rolnick deal the green light. "This acquisition will give Koret a menswear base from which to move into the medium-priced fields, especially in apparel with a sportswear feeling, such as sport coats, slacks, and sweaters," Helfat said. Despite the depressed business in the hat field, he said he was optimistic about Byer-Rolnick's prospects because of its brand reputation and its position in the casual hat business. According to a jointly issued news release, the price of the deal was just under $5.7 million cash, or about nine times annual earnings.[19]

With his acquisition plan well underway, Helfat established an aggressive revenue program that he insisted could propel apparel sales to over $100 million by the end of 1971. Joe Koret typically shied away from exaggerated projections that could fall short, and therefore underplayed his hand in public. A lifelong fan of business aphorisms—he always had a number of them posted around his office—Joe particularly adhered to the adage "under-promise and over-deliver." Jere Helfat seemed to be doing just the opposite. Koret of California now was a public company that was expected to provide industry analysts with forward-looking guidance, and Helfat appeared to be promising the moon and the stars.

This made Joe nervous, but he gave Helfat considerable latitude to pursue acquisitions he believed would grow the company.

Speaking at a meeting of the New York Society of Security Analysts in the summer of 1967, Helfat stood by his revenue projection, noting that the $100 million number did not include any royalty income from licensing the Koratron process. Revenues from that Koret subsidiary were just under $5 million in 1966, and he again insisted: "The sky is the limit." In fact, he predicted that the future success of Koratron rested on breakthroughs the company had recently made with garments manufactured from wool. "Washable, permanent press wool is now being delivered to retail stores across the country," he explained.

"The Koret apparel group has sold over $1.5 million in Koratron wool pants and skirts at the wholesale level in five weeks."[20]

Helfat justified his ambitious projections by providing a mathematical overview of the industry. Citing a variety of sources, he predicted that worldwide women's sportswear sales would hit $840 million by 1970, which translated to a total of 350 million units. Of that number, 40 percent would be permanent-press garments, which Helfat believed would realistically give Koret of California around 12 percent of the market total. Based on this arithmetic, he insisted, his projection of $100 million in sales by 1971 was reasonable—and achievable.

AS SOCIAL AND CULTURAL TRENDS OF THE 1960s evolved, America was facing a fashion divide. Bellbottoms coexisted with miniskirts, fishnet stockings mixed with thigh-high boots. Bright colors were just about everywhere, clashing loudly with the drab-colored Cossack blouses and dull safari suits that also were popular at the time. Fabrics ran the full spectrum of practical to oddity, from polyester to sheer nylon to metallic vinyl. Waistlines all but disappeared. Oddly, a faux-military style had become fashionable, in direct contrast to the garish colors and mod dots and stripes that still were all the rage. It was a time of "anything goes," and the free-for-all that followed was the direct result of a new independence and an anti-establishment boldness that clearly stated: "In your face."

During the Summer of Love, Koret of California released its first fashion line since Stephanie's retirement. Her absence from the design meetings at first created internal apprehension, but the creative team—primarily overseen by Koret veteran Warren Logan—soon realized the transition was nothing to dread. The fundamental challenge was to create a line of apparel that did not depart too much from the firm's traditional designs, while adapting to the cultural free-styling of the times.

Seeking to assure retailers that Koret of California had not wavered in its goal of producing apparel for every woman seeking an "active, happy way of life," Charles Sommer, sportswear merchandiser for Koret, said the company had something for everyone. "This means the young woman on the go, the college girl, the career girl, the young homemaker, and the matron who is still going someplace," he said in a marketing sheet.

As *San Francisco Chronicle* contributor Blake Green wrote in June 1967,

> The Koret styles never dynamite the fashion world with any drastic changes. They incorporate already-acceptable but still up-to-date designs with the easy-to-care-for fabrics that have made the line an answer to the busy women's prayers. There is a wide variety of women in the 18-to-30-year age bracket, and Koret of California has managed to include fashions to please a large segment of them in its fall collection.[21]

In a move away from the traditional skirt and dress line, the fall styles were centered on pants. These included pant-dresses, culottes, and pantsuits, many with the counterintuitive military look that curiously had become popular with both women and men. The highlight of the fall collection, however, was the introduction of Koratron Durawool, a blend of 50 percent wool, 40 percent rayon, and 10 percent nylon. "At the press showing last week, a pair of dark green slacks made of Durawool . . . had been machine washed and dried five times with a minimum of shrinkage," Green wrote in the *Chronicle*.

AS THE SUMMER OF LOVE EDGED INTO AUTUMN, Joe Koret became focused on two fronts. First, Jere Helfat's buying spree was just beginning to yield financial results, and Koret of California was morphing into the major corporation that its listing on the New York Stock Exchange connoted. Second, as the firm moved into new, untapped industries, its internal management structure was being tested. Joe had refrained from entering the men's apparel business for a number of reasons, not the least of which was that his brother Al's Koret Manufacturing Company had operated successfully in that realm. Also, he and Stephanie had cut their teeth on women's clothing, and he firmly believed in the saying, "Stick with what you know best."

This all changed with the Byer-Rolnick acquisition, as well as Helfat's planned purchases of other menswear firms. To accommodate these anticipated changes, Joe engineered an internal realignment that, in his mind, would allow the company to remain highly competitive and minimize any potential management chaos. This reshuffling resulted in the promotion of William Warnock, who had spearheaded the creation of the Koratron process, to the newly created post of group vice president of the new Koret Apparel division. At the same time Richard Wrobbel was named diversification and acquisition planning manager, while Stanley Herzstein was promoted to the position of vice president in charge of the new menswear division. Herzstein had joined Koret of California decades before as a stock boy and Joe's personal driver, and shortly thereafter was named the company's first salesman. All told, his relationship with Joe and the Koret family would span sixty years, including many years of service as a member of the Koret Foundation board of directors.

The realignment satisfied only half of the challenge Joe anticipated for the coming years. For decades, Koret of California had been known solely for its women's sportswear, and there was some concern that the introduction of men's apparel could confuse—if not sully—the Koret image. Additionally, revenue generated through the licensing of the Koratron patent was being squeezed by ongoing litigation, exposing the company to unwanted headlines and investor criticism. Each new lawsuit or revised claim caused the company's share price to slip another notch, and analysts were growing uneasy. Koret of California had become a crowded umbrella that was aggregating companies but losing its identity, and Joe feared that it was betraying its hard-earned character and reputation.

As the year drew to a close, Joe Koret sat down with his board of directors and proposed what was perceived as a bold, yet obvious, move: change the name of the company. The idea was a simple solution to a growing identity crisis, and after robust debate the name change was approved. Koret of California would become Koracorp Industries, Inc., while the women's apparel division would retain the Koret of California label. Koratron would become a separate rib of the overall corporate umbrella, covering all permanent press licensing business.

Since Koret of California was a public company, the proposal had to be accepted by the firm's shareholders. A majority of stock was still owned by Joe and Stephanie, as well as a few other key executives, but a legal vote was required. A proxy statement sent to shareholders in early 1968 informed them that a formal vote would be held to approve the corporate name change, as well as other proposals related to the company's "planned growth as a fashion-oriented consumer products firm."

Shareholders also were asked to increase the number of authorized common shares from 4 million to 6 million, and to approve a class of preferred stock, without par value, consisting of 2 million shares. These additional common shares and the new preferred issue would be available to the public to provide funds for additional acquisitions, although Helfat maintained that the new Koracorp entity had "nothing on fire and nothing pending that would account for stronger price action in Koret stock."[22]

That said, the coming twenty-four months would see a flurry of acquisition activity. The idea was to drive as much cash flow to the bottom line as possible, even as the company was servicing and adding debt. On paper, the plan appeared to be a sound business strategy, but in a few short years, Koracorp would come close to crumbling from its mounting debt-to-earnings ratio—and from gross mismanagement by several of its key executives.

In this photo from the mid-1960s, Koret of California executives
examine bolts of new fabrics with Joe (right).

[Bancroft Library collection]

8

Koratron: Hold the Press

JUST AS THE 1960s SERVED AS A CATALYST for cultural change, the decade also provided an abundance of break-throughs on the technological front.

Ramped-up competition between the United States and the Soviet Union focused America's attention on space and all things related to it. It also led to a course of rapid technological innovation that would spill over from the scientific realm into the mainstream consumer market-place. The need for small onboard computers led NASA scientists not only to devise methods to shrink processors and memory-storage drives, but also to come up with new languages to run them. State-of-the-art solid-state electronics quickly replaced the old vacuum tubes found in radios and televisions. Other innovations followed quickly. The first compact disc (CD) debuted in 1965, while hand-held calcu-lators and the computer mouse followed two years later. By the end of the 1960s, the world had been exposed to the first RAM computer chip, the first supermarket barcode, the first ATM, and the first artificial heart. Technology was expanding at a rapidly compounding rate, and it was affecting the everyday life of virtually all Americans.

Such was the case in 1962 when the U.S. Patent Office approved the application for Koret of California's "process for creating permanent press garments." While there was nothing bright or shiny about the Koraset innovation, it had the power to transform the entire clothing industry almost overnight. The introduction of no-iron, wrinkle-free garments was a game-changer for millions of American housewives.

Koret of California had used the Koraset process in limited garment-production runs soon after it was developed, but Joe didn't want to show his royal flush too soon. Once the patent was official, however, the gloves came off. The new invention gave Joe a two-pronged attack: he could incorporate the Koraset process into all phases of his own manufacturing, and he also could license the invention to any and all interested takers. Not only would his own clothing line carry the Koraset—soon to be Koratron—seal of permanent-press perfection, but if he played his cards right, other manufacturers would gladly pony up for the privilege.

One of Koratron's first garment licensees was San Francisco's own Levi Strauss & Company, which manufactured a line of permanent press "Sta-Prest" slacks in 1964. That year alone, the company sold 165 million pairs of permanent-press men's trousers, and the following year the figure topped 300 million. It certainly helped that the slacks were manufactured from a heavy cotton material that was well-suited to the then-limited Koratron process, and customers were thrilled that these garments could go right from the dryer to the closet.

Just as Henry Ford had told car buyers they could have a new Model T in any color as long as it was black, Koraset initially worked on any fabric as long as it was cotton. In the early years this proved to be highly restrictive to many manufacturers, but Joe plunged head-first into the new world of permanent press. As the *San Francisco Chronicle* reported in late 1964,

These days the clothing industry is all excited about a new process called permanent press, [which] makes a garment truly wash-and-wear. Creases are absolutely permanent, and the garment will keep its shape and freshness through countless machine washings and dryings. Ironing is completely unnecessary, even to touch up the costume. . . . At the moment, the available materials are heavy and the colors are limited. By spring we should be seeing a greater variety of fabrics (including stretch) and a wide spectrum of colors.

Joe Koret was said to be "bubbling with enthusiasm" over the future of permanent press, and boasted that "in five or six years there will be no garments that are not self-ironing."[1]

Levi Strauss's near-instant success with Koratron served to ease the lingering suspicions of wary manufacturers. So did the introduction of minor modifications that allowed Koratron to be used with other fabrics and blends. While permanent-press wool materials still proved elusive, by the end of 1965 Koratron was licensed to 149 clothing companies that made men's and boys' casual pants; 29 that made men's and boys' shirts; 77 that produced women's and girls' blouses, dresses, shifts, skirts, and slacks; and 10 that manufactured such products as rainwear, zipper jackets, uniforms, and neckties. As the *Chronicle* reported, this added up to 180 individual firms, "not counting overlaps, and they turn out more than 300 brands of merchandise, each with its own trade name." In just a few short years, Koraset had become what many industry analysts termed "unquestionably the single most revolutionary manufacturing concept since the sewing machine."[2]

Since Koret of California had created the Koratron process, it was easy to implement throughout its own production line. The company ordered chemicals by the carload and designed ovens large enough to heat multiple garments at a time. The addition of these new systems during the manufacturing stage was not an issue; garments just took a little longer to finish and pack for distribution than they had previously.

Many firms that licensed the Koratron process found it tedious and cumbersome to use. While the chemical "impregnation" stage was neither complicated nor lengthy, it did require precise calculations. Too much or too little of the aqueous solution and the thermosetting resins wouldn't work properly. An even bigger problem, however, came during the heating stage. Koret archives are littered with copies of instructional letters sent by William Warnock to licensees who complained that their garments had become scorched or dried-out while they were in the oven.

Some clothing manufacturers didn't even bother to license Koratron before using it. The original patent application specifically detailed every step of the process, and within months of its public debut a number of companies began treating their garments with the same (or similar) chemicals used by Koratron, and then heating them.

Joe viewed this as a blatant patent violation, and sought the advice of Herman Greenberg, a Washington, DC, attorney who had guided Koret of California through the Koratron patent-application process. A savvy business lawyer, Greenberg had served a five-year stint as enforcement director of the Office of Price Administration during World War II and knew his way around the nation's capital. He also apparently knew his way around the Federal District Court in Southern California, which entered a consent decree against Swede Company and ten other defendants for infringing on the Koratron patent.

The consent decree was only a temporary victory for Joe and his company. Within months, Koratron decided to take on one of the giants in the textile industry—Burlington Mills—which had licensed the patent but allegedly was not adhering to the requirements stipulated in the agreement. Specifically, the license required that all garments that incorporated the process must include a Koratron label. Koret's lawyers claimed that Burlington was willfully ignoring that licensing condition.

As the lawsuit ran its natural course, Joe invited Greenberg to join Koratron as executive vice president; less than six weeks later he had replaced Henry Weil as president of the division. At fifty-seven years of age, Greenberg's youthful appearance belied his age, and he grabbed the reins of the company with the same confidence he had exhibited in his previous legal dealings. Insisting that tremendous expansion lay ahead for Koratron and its parent company, Greenberg believed the permanent-press patent would open Koret of California to revenue streams that had not existed previously. "What about the compatible zipper, and pocket?" he rhetorically asked the *Chronicle*. "What about the potential in neckties, uniforms of all kinds, raincoats, and suits? And what about the enormous men's white shirt market, that's still seeking the perfect process?"[3]

Joe naturally believed that the true value of Koratron was to indelibly imprint in the consumer's mind that the name *Koratron* was synonymous with p*ermanent press* and *wrinkle-free*. As the *Chronicle*'s financial editor Sidney Allen wrote, "[Mr. Koret] wants every garment, or piece of fabric, treated with the 'Koratron' process to be so labeled, just as the 'Sanforized' label has come to mean pre-shrunk."[4]

In early January 1966, a panel of arbitrators sided with Koret. The judges ruled that Burlington had knowingly agreed to all the stipulations contained in the Koratron license agreement, and used the know-how and processes identified in the patent to manufacture wrinkle-free and permanent-press garments. The panel's ruling ordered Burlington to place the Koratron trademark on all "goods processed in accordance with the formulations and applications methods specified by the Koratron Co."

Any sense of victory Joe and his management team might have felt was short-lived. As the *Chronicle*'s Allen observed, "While Koratron naturally feels its position is unassailable, it knows full well that Burlington—one of the largest real heavyweights in the whole world of textiles—is not given to shooting from the hip aimlessly. A tremendous volume of business would be at stake."[5]

Indeed, just days after the arbitration judges issued their ruling, Burlington countersued Koratron on allegations of restraint of trade. In a claim filed in Federal Court in San Francisco, Burlington alleged that Koret of California "controls all phases of the durable press industry." Burlington attorneys claimed that Koret of California and Koratron had violated Sections 1 and 2 of the Sherman Act "with respect to patents, trademarks, and license agreements relating to the durable press processing of fabrics and garments." Furthermore, the company charged that the "restrictive Koratron licensing system" involved false representation concerning Koret/Koratron know-how and durable-press technology, as well as the overall scope of the Koratron patent.

"By the leverage of the patent and by misrepresentation of its scope, Koratron has been able to obtain combination license agreements with more than 330 garment manufacturers," the counterclaim said. "[This includes] a large number of Burlington customers representing a substantial segment of the textile mills' market for chemically treated fabrics to be used in manufacture of durable press garments."[6]

Burlington requested that the court set aside the arbitration panel's finding of its license violations, grant an injunction against further findings of violations, and issue a denial of all stipulated damages. Additionally—and this arguably was the crux of its fight—Burlington asked that the court force Koret and Koratron to "issue licenses to use Patent No. 2,974,432 to all reasonably qualified applicants," without any further conditions other than the payment of "reasonable royalties."

Joe was outraged.

His company had signed a deal with Burlington, fair and square, and now their lawyers were refusing to comply with the license and the decision of the arbitration panel. His attorney, Moses Lasky—with the law firm Brobeck, Phleger & Harrison—emphatically refuted the charges set forth in Burlington's counterclaim. Koratron previously had conceded that it licensed the formula and process to some apparel manufacturers but not to others, but insisted it did not monopolize the "processing, manufacture, and sale" of durable press fabric and apparel.

In its rebuttal, Koratron denied that its operating procedures were an "unlawful extension of the patent process," and further refuted all charges alleged by Burlington in its counterclaim.

The following month, New York–based J.E.Z. Textile Corporation filed a $19.5 million lawsuit against Koret of California, charging the company with infringing on a patent J.E.Z. had received in November 1956. That patent, identified as No. 2,769,584, had been issued to Martin Zinamon and Edward Semlitz, who subsequently assigned it to J.E.Z. On the surface, there appeared to be several strong similarities between the two patents. For starters, they both required that fabrics be impregnated with a crease-resistant chemical, such as urea formaldehyde. As noted in the J.E.Z. patent application, "excellent results were obtained with melamine formaldehyde textile resins mixed with a suitable catalyst, the purpose of which is to assure a rapid cure of the resin." The application went on to outline the actual chemical "recipe" to be used, including the precise ratio of water to catalyst, as well as the recommended temperature of the "bath" itself.

The J.E.Z. patent identified how the material was to be fed through a "mangler" to remove excess moisture and to further dry it at a heat of no more than 280°F, below the fabric's actual curing temperature. After the preliminary heating operation, the fabric was introduced into a standard pleating machine, which shaped and pressed the pleat and fixed it firmly in place throughout an entire roll of fabric. After this stage, the entire roll was to be cured for a precise length of time at a temperature around 300°F. Once an additional pleating process was completed, the fabric then was heated again, to around 350°F.

"Practical experience has shown that a fabric treated in accordance with this process maintains permanent pleats which do not disappear and are not affected after extensive washing," the application stated.[7]

While the chemical "bath" and heating processes for both patents were similar, Koret argued that Koratron was created with the J.E.Z. innovation fully in mind. In fact, the Koratron application cited "Zinamon et al." as one of the patents it sought to improve on. The primary difference, which Joe and his attorneys stressed when they filed their application in 1956, was that Koret's process was designed to be used directly in the creation of permanent-press garments themselves, not entire bolts of pleated fabric. "Wash-and-wear" had been an elusive goal for a number of textile companies for decades, but the ongoing problem was the difficulty in manufacturing actual skirts or trousers from pre-creased fabrics. Pleats that were set into a roll of fabric at the textile mill could not be cut by the manufacturer in such a way that those pleats fell precisely where the designer wanted them.

Koratron was designed to change that. The Koret application offered "a method of manufacturing ready-to-wear press-free garments unrestricted as to size, shape, style or design, and possessing crease-retention properties." This process would result in "washable, ready-to-wear press-free garments . . . provided with the imparted crease or creases retained therein after repeated washings of the garments."[8]

IN THE MIDST OF ALL THIS LEGAL WRANGLING, Koratron engineers continued in their quest to solve one major problem: wash-and-wear wool. Wool was notorious both for rejecting processed creases and for shrinking drastically when run through the washing machine. The challenge was two-fold: find a way to use the Koratron formula to pleat and crease wool garments so they remained wrinkle-free, and do so while minimizing shrinkage during the wash cycle. This had been the ultimate prize since Warnock and company began experimenting with formaldehyde and ovens in the fifties, yet the brass ring remained elusive.

The way Joe saw it, Koratron could not be considered a total success unless—and until—a solution was found for both problems. While the lawyers continued to hurl accusations back and forth in the courtroom, the Koratron researchers worked diligently in the laboratory. Finally, in the fall of 1966, they hit pay dirt.

To produce a truly permanent-press wool fabric, Koratron partnered with engineers at the U.S. Department of Agriculture Western Regional Research Center in Albany, California. Combining a stabilization process known as "Wurlan," developed by Dr. Harold Lundgren of the U.S. Department of Agriculture wool laboratories, Koratron was able to produce wool-blend garments with less than "8/10 of 1 percent" residual shrinkage. This meant they could withstand the wash process and come out of the Maytag with little change to their preexisting condition.

Once this challenge was solved, application of the Koratron process could proceed. The first wool garments created as a result of this breakthrough were wool/mohair blends in men's and women's slacks, men's shirts, and ladies' skirts—ranging in textures from lightweight broadcloth to heavier tweeds and heathers. As the *Chronicle*'s Sidney Allen wrote, "Garments with 15 to 80 percent wool were 'Koratronized' and the results reportedly are dramatic. . . .The sheep and goat people have cause to cheer."[9]

BY EARLY 1967, BOTH THE BURLINGTON AND J.E.Z. lawsuits against Koratron were slogging through the courts. Burlington was throwing its legal and financial might around, racking up tens of thousands of dollars in legal fees. Koratron attorneys also were amassing a similar number of billing hours as claims and counterclaims were volleyed back and forth like a high-pitched Wimbledon final.

In early February, the Federal Court in San Francisco ruled in favor of Koratron and ordered Burlington to pay up. Specifically, the court said Burlington owed Koratron a "considerable, but yet undetermined, sum of money" for the use of the Koratron method of applying permanent press to fabrics. The ruling reinforced the arbitration panel's decision of a year earlier, but Burlington's lawyers—seemingly indifferent to the outcome—reportedly left the courtroom unmoved.

As Koratron President Herman Greenberg observed, "It seems to please Burlington to believe that nothing in Koratron's litigation is important to them. They treated the announcement of the arbitrator's award (a year ago) in the same way. They were poorly advised then and are now."

The indifference of the Burlington attorneys suggested that the company could not be trusted to voluntarily pay up per the judge's decision. Further litigation would be necessary to collect, so the following week Joe elected to pursue "legal remedies" to enforce the court's decision. The original Arbitration Board ordered Burlington to place the Koratron trademark on all goods processed "in accordance with the formulations and applications methods specified by Koratron," which Burlington had not done. He also sought to collect royalties due his company, and he also wanted to send a powerful "David and Goliath" message that Koret of California was not an entity to mess with.

Joe instructed Moses Lasky to file a claim in U.S. District Court in San Francisco, seeking an accounting and full payment of all royalties due for the nineteen-month period from June 1964 to January 1966. Lasky charged that Burlington already had admitted, through previous legal proceedings, that it had prepared and sold apparel using the Koratron process but without the Koratron trademark soon after it had signed its license agreement.[10]

In any event, the triumph against Burlington was reason to celebrate. Not only had Joe and company taken on the big dog and won; the victory also would reverberate throughout the apparel and financial communities. Indeed, the Monday after the court's decision was announced, Koret of California stock skyrocketed from $20.50 to $27.50. As the company's two largest shareholders, Joe and Stephanie found themselves several million dollars richer, literally overnight. The share price had finally closed above the initial offering when the stock was issued nine months earlier.

At this point, Koratron was the tail that was wagging the dog. As Sidney Allen wrote in the Business Trends column of the *Chronicle* the day after the court ruling, "[The company] now is drawing royalties from more than 750 users of its permanent press process and its trademark. The list includes 250 or more foreign producers and processors of fabrics and clothing."[11]

Less than a week after the Burlington decision was handed down, J.E.Z. Textiles announced it was discontinuing its $19 million damage suit against Koret of California. Their patent infringement claim had been filed the previous May, the day after Koret's first public offering hit the New York Stock Exchange. While terms of the lawsuit's discontinuance were kept private, Koret of California President Jere Helfat hinted that J.E.Z. could never renew or reopen it under any circumstances.[12]

The lawsuits didn't stop with the resolution of the Burlington or J.E.Z. cases. Despite the successful litigation against both firms, some textile manufacturers still believed the Koratron process didn't apply to certain fabrics that already had been treated with a wrinkle-resistant formula. One of these firms was Deering Milliken, whose alleged violation of the Koratron license had come to Joe Koret's attention during the J.E.Z. proceedings.

Deering Milliken was a South Carolina–based textile and chemical firm that got its start in Portland, Maine, in 1865. Entrepreneur Seth Milliken and his brother-in-law Dan Trune formed a partnership with William Deering, the owner of a dry goods store who became wealthy selling wool uniforms to the Union Army during the Civil War. The company moved to Spartanburg, South Carolina, in the late 1800s, and it grew to become one of the nation's largest textile producers. In 1945, the firm established a research division that developed and patented a number of innovations, including Agilon, a stretch nylon for women's stockings; Belfast self-ironing cotton fabrics; and Visa, a washable polyester fabric.

It was the washability of some of its fabrics that led Deering Milliken's executives to believe that garments manufactured with the Koratron process did not need to be labeled as such. They contended that three of their fabrics—Visa, Milstar, and Milliset—already possessed permanent-press characteristics, and therefore were outside the scope of the Koratron license.

Despite the mounting legal bills and the drain on Koratron's quarterly revenues, Joe told Moses Lasky to go back to the courtroom to initiate fresh litigation. In June of 1967, Lasky filed a $5 million lawsuit against Deering Milliken, once again in U.S. District Court in San Francisco. Not only did the suit claim that the company had refused to pay royalties for the Koratron license, but that it also had threatened to publicly advise more than two hundred current Koratron licensees that they could use Deering fabrics without running afoul of the Koratron patent. In his filing, Lasky asked the court to declare "the Deering Milliken claim erroneous, to compel Deering Milliken to announce publicly that it used the Koratron patent, and to call for an accounting of unpaid royalties."[13]

To no one's surprise, Deering Milliken launched an offensive against Koratron and its parent company, Koracorp. Within a week of Koratron's filing, the textile firm filed a countersuit in Federal Court in New York, claiming that the original Koratron patent and a subsequent improvement (U.S. Patents No. 2,974,432 and No. 3,268,915) were invalid because they were "obvious in the trade; an aggregate of old elements governed by 20 American and two British patents; not precise; and failed to point out improvements which constitute discovery."

The counterclaim went on to state that Deering Milliken already sold chemically treated fabrics, which its garment-manufacturing customers then heat-cured for use in "press-free and shape-retaining washable apparel."[14]

As the legal proceedings wore on, Joe became increasingly frustrated with the entire course of events. The invention that had been developed in the Koret of California lab over ten years ago was expected to provide a substantial revenue stream once the patent was approved. While the process had, indeed, generated millions of dollars in cash flow in the three years since Koret of California began licensing it, Joe believed those dollars were being nibbled to death by ducks. Legal fees, loss of revenue from suspended licenses, reputed use of the Koratron process by firms that were not paying royalties, and misgivings on the part of other clothing companies contributed to diminished income.

Caught in the crosshairs of this frustration was Herman Greenberg, the Koratron president who had been brought on board amid much fanfare in 1965. Mounting friction between him and Koret President Jere Helfat led to heated discussions about the company's future. In November 1967, Greenberg became convinced that it would be in everyone's best interest to tender his resignation.

"Policy differences have developed between the present management of Koret of California and myself, which necessitated my leaving," Greenberg said in a statement. While declining to elaborate on these differences, he vowed to continue to serve on the Koret board of directors. "I was elected by the stockholders—all 6500 of them—and I feel I owe them a duty," he explained.[15]

In the reshuffling that followed, Arthur Cunningham was named Koratron executive vice president, and he also assumed the duties of the division's chief executive officer. One of his first moves in this new role was to implement stronger quality controls over the entire permanent-press process. Some apparel companies either had mis-understood the step-by-step impregnation and heating stages, or had intentionally skipped or eliminated them entirely. In order to ensure that the Koratron trademark became synonymous with qual-ity, Cunningham instituted new systems to standardize consistency across the board. All newspaper and magazine advertising now was required to include a new and improved Koratron trademark design, while in-store marketing plans emphasized the Koratron name to con-sumers. In short, any garment manufactured by any company using the Koratron process had to be identified and marketed as such.

IN MOST INSTANCES, THE LICENSE REVISION WAS respected and honored by Koratron customers. Occasionally, however, corporate attorneys would find what they believed was probable cause to call into question the validity of the Koratron patent, and up would pop another lawsuit.

One of these was filed by Levi Strauss & Company, one of Koratron's first garment licensees back in late 1964 and still one of its biggest customers. In October 1968, the clothing giant sued Koratron and the newly renamed Koracorp Industries, alleging various violations of anti-trust acts. In its filing, the company's lawyers requested that Koracorp's permanent-press patent be declared invalid.

Joe was livid. Over the preceding five years, Levi Strauss & Company had licensed Koratron to churn out hundreds of millions of pairs of durable-press slacks and jeans. To suddenly turn around and bite the company that helped make that possible was unreasonable and outrageous.

Infuriated by their gall, Joe requested that all steps be taken to immediately revoke Levi Strauss's license. "Our licensees should realize that they should not have the protection of the license while at the same time attempting to dispute the validity thereof," he stated bluntly.[16]

While the legal hassles continued, the Koratron researchers never gave up their ultimate goal: knock out all the wrinkles from wool fabric. Despite the development of "Koratronized" Wurlan several years earlier, many fabrics made primarily from wool, mohair, and other "protein" fibers remained difficult—and expensive—to make wrinkle-free. A discovery by researchers at American Cyanamid changed all that by creating a new formulation of chemical agents that, when used in two separate applications, worked on fabric containing as much as 65 percent wool. In late 1968, Koratron applied for a patent covering the process, although by that time Joe Koret had grown wary of the durable-press legal battles.

Those issues continued several more years as additional charges were piled on top of the originals. This frustration culminated with the opening of joint proceedings in U.S. District Court in San Francisco, tying together the claims of seventeen separate litigants. These included Jack Winter; Armory Garment Company; Haggar Company; Blue Bell; W. Koury Company; Salant & Salant; Standard Romper Company; Henry I. Siegel Company; Metro Pants Company; Bayly Corporation; Cowden Manufacturing Company; Deering Milliken; Oxford Industries; Wright Manufacturing Company; Lion Uniform; Defiance Manufacturing Company; and Levi Strauss & Company.

On April 28, 1972, twenty-three lawyers filed into Judge Charles Renfrew's courtroom, alleging various claims and antitrust violations against Koratron. In multiple briefs filed with the court, the seventeen litigants cited numerous reasons why Koratron's patent was invalid, and therefore they should not be required to pay royalties. The parties also charged that Koratron had violated U.S. antitrust laws in attempting to restrain and monopolize the permanent press trade.

Moses Lasky argued that the Koratron patent was 100 percent valid, and insisted that anyone using the process must pay up. It was that simple.

The case was expected to last two months, but a series of motions and delays filed by the various parties caused the final ruling to be delayed two additional years. From the initial filing of the Deering Milliken lawsuit in 1967 through the judge's final decision, humans traveled to the moon nine times, and landed six. The Watergate scandal erupted in Washington, and President Nixon was just a few months short of resigning. The twin towers of the World Trade Center were completed, Secretariat won the Triple Crown, and *The Godfather* and *The Exorcist* stunned moviegoers.

On March 6, 1974, District Court Judge Renfrew handed down a 111-page opinion in which he ruled that Koratron had misused its patented process for making permanent-press clothing. He ruled that Koratron's patent, referred to during trial as "432"—an abbreviation of Patent No. 2,974,432—was valid, but also said the company had violated the Sherman Antitrust Act by attempting to monopolize trade and commerce. Furthermore, Renfrew ruled that Koratron had set up illegal "tying arrangements" by which it required its licensed textile mills and manufacturers of accessories to sell Koratron-labeled products only to its licensed garment makers. Because of these violations. Judge Renfrew ruled that the Koratron patent could not be enforced until all illegal practices were eradicated.[17]

"A court of equity can deny the enforcement of the patent which has been misused until the abusive practices are terminated and the effects of those practices dissipated," he observed. "Once the practices and their effects are purged, the patent once again is enforceable."

Much of the lengthy opinion—which Renfrew read in its entirety in court—recapped Koratron's history from its inception. "The licensing of the patented process was a phenomenal commercial success," he stated. "From the date of the first license in 1963 through June 30, 1971, 281 garment makers had taken licenses with Koratron and paid it over $30 million in royalties." Ultimately, in declaring the Koratron patent valid but the company's actions in violation of antitrust laws, both sides were able to declare a victory, of sorts.

As Joe Koret told his friend and Terok Properties chief financial officer Ken Moline long after the dust settled, "It would have been nice to win, but the judge made the right decision. No company should have the control we had."

Joe Koret with (left) William Warnock and Charles Cain, commemorating Koret of California's $50 million dollar sales milestone in the 1960s. [Bancroft Library collection]

9

Koracorp:
In the Public Eye

WHEN KORACORP WENT PUBLIC ON MAY 2, 1966, Joe Koret's role in the company he'd founded twenty-eight years before transformed almost overnight. Previously. he answered only to himself and a small team of executives, many of whom also were shareholders in the privately held firm. Together, they would review last year's sales or losses; discuss current social trends and how they might affect apparel sales; and assess certain strengths and weaknesses within the corporate structure. They would make minor adjustments here or there, weigh expansion and acquisition opportunities, and contemplate the future without the specter of a government watchdog looming over their collective shoulders.

All that changed when the company went public. From that first day when Koret of California was listed on the New York Stock Exchange (with the symbol KOR), Joe and his team were placed under a financial microscope. Every t had to be crossed, every i dotted. Koret of California had always maintained complete ledgers of all transactions, and no government attorney or IRS auditor ever had an issue with the company (Joe's personal tax-evasion case notwithstanding). But the new scrutiny still created a palpable shift in the way business was conducted, as every note and journal now were part of the public record.

It didn't help matters that J.E.Z. Textiles had filed its patent infringement lawsuit the day after Koret of California went public. The volley of briefs, depositions, and accusations created considerable internal strain and cost a lot of money. Investors had not been prepared for the legal hassles, and within days of the initial offering the company's share price sank well below its opening price. Not good for a company that just months before had shown double-digit sales growth and solid earnings.

Throughout this process. Koret president Jere Helfat remained the company's ultimate cheerleader. The Cleveland-based business leader had staked his corporate reputation on the study he had developed in 1962, and he was optimistic about the apparel firm's future. In that report he identified significant growth areas for Koret of California, exhibiting a sense of confidence that within several years had elevated him to the top job. He was a strong believer in the "expansion through acquisition" philosophy that was becoming increasingly popular during the 1960s, and he insisted that carefully managed growth could raise Koret's corporate stature from mid-level to top tier.

Joe Koret trusted Helfat implicitly. After all, everything he had projected for the company thus far had materialized. Within his soul, however, Joe was still very much the hard-working entrepreneur who, with Stephanie's immeasurable support and assistance, had built Koret of California from the ground up. He was a seasoned merchandiser and marketer and possessed an intuitive sense that drove his business instinct and ultimate decisions. Imbued with street smarts at an early age, Joe had earned more than a small fortune through years of trial and error. Now in his late sixties, his self-esteem largely was shaped by how he believed other people perceived him. As he was heard to say more than once, "If I'm not making money, people won't respect me anymore."

As chairman of the board, he viewed everything from the captain's bridge. He was very much a hands-on executive, and everyone within the company was well aware of it. One day, Joe Koret, Jere Helfat, and William Warnock sat down at the table in the Mission Street conference room to discuss the future. Joe always looked at the business in rolling five-year chunks, and this meeting was convened to do just that. After several solid acquisitions, Helfat had been making noises about expanding into realms outside the apparel industry, and he'd worked up a report to show what kind of growth Koret of California could reasonably expect in the future. Joe had asked Helfat to generate some realistic projections for that five-year timeframe, and Helfat placed a folder on the table in front of him and opened it to reveal a stack of papers inside.

"Let's cut right to the chase," Joe said. "What sort of growth are we looking at?"[1]

Helfat knew his boss didn't appreciate a lot of hype or accounting mumbo-jumbo. Ever the optimist, he quickly glanced at Warnock, then looked back to Joe. "In all reality I think we're looking at 20 percent growth year-over-year for the entire five years," he said.

"You're talking about doubling our revenues," Joe pointed out. "Do you really think we can do that?"

"I see no reason why not," Helfat replied, confident in his projections. "Our core businesses are performing exceptionally well, and the new acquisitions are growing as expected. We have a lot of opportunities ahead of us, and if we time and plan them properly, we should be able to out-perform expectations."

"What about Koratron?" Warnock inquired. "Revenues there are slipping every month."

"The losses have stabilized and there's no reason to believe they won't turn around. The lawsuits have to end at some point. Meanwhile, I'm confident our existing divisions will continue to perform well, and if we purchase strong companies with solid upside, we definitely can achieve these numbers."

Joe studied the top sheet intently, then looked up and fixed Helfat with his dark, penetrating eyes. Well," he said after a moment's hesitation. "If you don't think that's 'pie in the sky,' I'm in. Just don't tell anyone, because it will scare the hell out of them."

The three men, with subsequent input and approval of the board, went on to develop a growth program that divided the company into three business segments. Joe insisted that the women's sportswear line be considered the engine that propelled the entire company; by far it was generating most of the firm's sales revenue. "You gotta dance with the girl that brung you," Joe liked to say. That "girl" now consisted of the original Koret of California line; the recently acquired Sue J; and the Canadian firms, including the recently acquired Broadway Knitting Mills.

The second of the three segments was Koratron, which Helfat steadfastly believed would reverse its decline once the lawyers ran out of things to bill for. The third division would absorb all future acquisitions, of which Helfat was planning a good number. The cash generated by the IPO made it possible to examine a number of mid-sized companies, and he believed Koret of California could expand significantly.

Several months later, Koret of California shareholders overwhelmingly approved the new, all-encompassing Koracorp Industries name. Helfat maintained that the change not only would allow for sales growth but also for *sound* growth, both organically and through acquisition. Following the plan that he, Joe Koret, and William Warnock had laid out previously, all business operations would fit into one of the company's three "unicenters."

In a notable departure from Joe's decades-long focus on women's sportswear, Helfat told shareholders that the company was primarily interested in acquiring menswear firms. The goal, he explained, was to accelerate sales of men's apparel—less than $15 million in 1967—to a point where eventually it would rival the women's apparel division. That division in 1967 reported sales of about $32.5 million, up from

$27 million the previous year, and Helfat predicted sales would jump almost 14 percent to $37 million in 1968.

Part of this planned escalation would come from diversification outside the apparel industry. After considerable discussion, Helfat convinced Joe that a natural extension of Koret of California was the home-furnishings industry.

"We can do the same thing for draperies and upholstery that we did for dresses and skirts," he insisted. "It's a natural fit."

Joe was skeptical of the proposal and ran his corporate president through his myriad concerns. "How do we know there's a market for Koret designs in furniture and window shades? Who is our target consumer? What retailers will we sell through? What kind of manufacturing facilities are we looking at?" And, ultimately, "How much will it cost?"

They were all reasonable questions, and Helfat had done his homework. Eventually, he convinced Joe that a line of home furnishings would give Koret of California the stimulus it needed to push toward his goal of $100 million in sales by 1971. As *The New York Times* reported in September 1967, "In a move unusual for the apparel industry, Koracorp plans to enter the field of home furnishings, with a coordinated line of furniture, carpets, and draperies. In preparation for this program, [the company] has been discussing acquisitions with several companies in the home furnishings industry."[2]

"We don't plan to be a conglomerate company," Helfat told *The Times*. "But we are convinced that we have skills in management, marketing, and merchandising that can be applied to other fields, as well as to women's apparel. Yet, even in doing this, we want to stay with the common denominator of fashion."

Joe Koret had made it clear that Koracorp's ongoing reputation among women stemmed from its unyielding focus on quality and comfort. The company always paid strict attention to its core customer, and any move into home furnishings had to emphasize these same commitments. Helfat agreed, insisting that the shift was neither compulsive nor capricious. "Our plan is to eventually have a full complex of home furnishings subsidiaries, producing wood and upholstered furniture, floor coverings, wall coverings, draperies, and bedspreads," he told *The Times*. "With our experience and reputation, we believe we have a sound concept to enter the home furnishings field with a similarly coordinated line of products."

Focusing on his $100 million revenue goal, Helfat accelerated his already-aggressive program of growth through acquisition. Over the next twenty-four months, he engineered the purchase of a number of small and mid-sized companies covering a broad spectrum of business. This buying spree was not abnormal for public companies "on the come," and Helfat vigorously chased every opportunity that seemed to fit his growth plan. "Our objective is to achieve as much diversity as we can effectively control, but the common denominator will be consumer-oriented products and services," he said.[3]

NINETEEN SIXTY-EIGHT WAS A YEAR THAT STARTED badly and worsened rapidly. Less than a month into the new year, North Vietnam launched the Tet Offensive, a deadly "wake-up" call for Americans who already had begun to turn against the war.[4] Adding tragedy to calamity, in April Rev. Martin Luther King, Jr., was killed by an assassin's bullet while standing on the balcony of the Lorraine Motel in Memphis. Two months later, presidential candidate Robert F. Kennedy was gunned down in the Ambassador Hotel in Los Angeles, just hours after winning the California Democratic primary.

In San Francisco, the Haight-Ashbury District continued to attract denizens of the counterculture and disaffected runaways from across the country. Many were homeless and penniless and either slept outside in parks or crashed in pads of people they barely knew. Haight Street quickly devolved into a near-anarchic haven for an increasingly dazed and confused population. Tempers flared and violence erupted. During one thirty-day period, at least one riot a day blew up somewhere in "the Haight," as people were gassed, heads were busted, and blood was spilled. Meanwhile, just a couple miles away, a student-led strike all but crippled the campus of San Francisco State University. The five-month event—still the longest strike of its kind in the United States—was sparked by mounting racial and anti-war tensions. These conflicts led to classroom sit-ins, threats by and against students and faculty, and violent clashes between protestors and police. Hundreds of sympathizers were arrested, many of them beaten, and one student was wounded while trying to set off a homemade bomb. Another explosive device was found outside the office of the university's chairman of political science, but it was defused without injury.

Race relations, anti-war protests, and a growing "generational divide" had taken hold. The daily spectacle of combat on the evening news and the arrival of body bags accelerated tensions between order and ideology. Flash zones were just about everywhere, and small clashes easily exploded into all-out conflagration. San Francisco was like a stack of kindling just ready for a splash of gasoline and a match.

Women's and men's fashion also was becoming divided over style and substance, although without all the violence. Revolution was in the air, and "do your own thing" became the refrain of the times. The mod period of the mid-sixties had already begun to shift, and by 1968 the top fashion houses were designing styles that were both "geometrically precise and soft and romantic."[5] Any defined sense of style had become blurred, with the fashion scene an imprecise mix of competing influences. Carnaby Street's look of hot pants over patterned tights clashed with Pierre Cardin's vinyl and plastics, which in turn competed with Yves Saint Laurent's safari jackets, tunics, and daring see-through blouses. Peasant shirts and long, cotton bohemian dresses could be found alongside miniskirts, tie-dyed T-shirts, and frayed knee-hole denims.

Each of these styles helped to inspire Koret of California's sportswear, and always in a way designed to assure the firm's regular customers that "all was right with the world." For example, in the spring of 1968—amidst all the crop tops and bellbottoms—the company introduced a line of "Golf Greats" characterized by "great form, great follow-through in crisp Dacron polyester and cotton sports." Of course, the look was highlighted by "Koratron permanent press fabrics that keep their good looks for keeps, through a full agenda of wearings and washings. Koratron sportswear never needs pressing!"[6]

As fashions of the late 1960s became more diverse and disparate, a growing number of businesses began to institute dress codes designed to equate quality service with a reliable, professional look. Most popular women's uniforms at that time included dress-and-jacket combinations or three-piece blazer, skirt and blouse combos. Men's uniforms typically consisted of a two-or three-piece suit with a complementary shirt (typically white or a light, muted color) and coordinating tie.

Koret of California had always focused on the individual woman customer, but Joe now realized the company could drive additional dollars to the bottom line through the simple adaptation of its fashion lines. He engaged the fifth-floor design team to create several looks that could be purchased "off the rack" by smaller business clients or customized for larger firms. As noted by the *San Francisco Chronicle* in 1969, "Koret has put together some snappy combinations like a pleated skirt, a sleeveless vest, and a long-sleeved, stick-tie shirt."[7]

In an era of newfound freedom and personal liberties, the notion of a mandated workplace outfit easily could be met with contempt and resistance. While uniforms were commonplace at hospitals and airline counters, introducing new policies at retail businesses required diplomacy. "Presenting the idea of a uniform program must be done tactfully, although once employees try it they generally like it," the company's sales and promotion manager Joyce Bickel observed. "Many employers pay for all or a part of required uniforms, and many women are delighted not to have to invest a lot of time or money on a new office wardrobe."

Koret's new "identity designs" were launched at a media event in June 1969, highlighted by the introduction of new flight-attendant uniforms for a regional West Coast airline. "The Air California girls will soon be wearing simple orange knit dresses with sombreros and fringed ponchos that were designed to reinforce [its] Spanish motif," Bickel said.

Aside from identity-dependent airlines and other high-profile companies, she was quick to discourage companies from placing any permanent identifying mark on their uniforms, for several reasons. "Does a girl really want the dirty old man to learn where she works?" she rhetorically asked the *Chronicle*. "And does a company want everyone to know that the drunken girl in the bar is its employee?"[8]

Besides Air California, early customers for Koret's uniforms were tour guides at central California's Hearst Castle, a traveling women's badminton team, and some Southern California municipal meter maids.

DURING MORE THAN THIRTY YEARS IN BUSINESS, Koret's basic process of designing, manufacturing, and distributing its apparel had remained unchanged. From its early years of turning out just hundreds of garments each season to millions of them, one thing Joe always insisted on was quality. He believed that a company was only as good as its latest products, and as long as his name hung on the door, quality was of paramount importance.

Closing in on seventy, Joe delegated much of that responsibility to William Warnock, who ran the entire Koret of California unit as well as Koracorp's women's division. Warnock had joined Koret in the early 1950s, and the Koratron endeavor had taught him the importance of getting a garment right every time. He and Joe consistently emphasized quality control, and both men placed unyielding trust in the styling and design of Koret's garments. They also knew that those styles would only work if the fabric from which they were made was of superior quality.

"Fabric is a major factor in determining the quality of the item you are shipping to the customer," Warnock told *Women's Wear Daily*'s in 1969. "Fabric is alive. It's not a piece of metal; it reacts, very often inconsistently. Only after we are satisfied that we are working with a quality piece of fabric will we place a duplication order with the mill." All Koret of California fabric was subjected to rigorous testing to ascertain "dimensional stability, crocking, washing performance, dry cleaning, and tensile strength."[9]

The Koret quality-control department conducted random checks on samples from each incoming fabric delivery during the entire life of the production run. They looked relentlessly for minuscule flaws, weight, and finish, as well as color and pattern reproduction. They did the same with the individual garments as they came off the manufacturing line.

Joe also placed exceptional value on the concept of "human touch." Stephanie's insistence on hands-on styling and design had carried through to the personal comfort and fit of every garment she created. Despite her rapidly failing health and the fact that she no longer worked for the company, her philosophy that every woman was singularly important continued to prevail within the walls of her design studio. She had always treated each customer as one of a circle of friends, and that approach never wavered. Meanwhile, Joe's face-to-face discussions with retailers and their salespeople had helped him to understand not just local-level merchandising concerns, but also customer motivation and incentive. Each person, no matter his or her role along the manufacturing cycle, had something to contribute to the company.

From the time he was a small boy, Joe believed people were inherently good. The concept of trust extended beyond his family and friends to his thousands of employees. While he had passed the daily operations of the company on to other trusted colleagues, he took great pride in his workforce and typically paid them more than his competitors paid. He repeatedly negotiated with the city's garment unions and promoted from within whenever possible. Largely because of the nature of garment manufacturing, and the available workforce in San Francisco, Joe also made major strides in minority employment. "These are federally defined minorities," William Warnock said in 1969, noting that more than half of the firm's overall workforce came from minority ethnic groups. "They're represented at all levels of the firm, from management to factory floor."[10]

BY THE SUMMER OF 1969, HELFAT HAD ACHIEVED his diversification goals. In addition to being the parent company of the long-standing Koret of California women's apparel firm, Koracorp Industries offered a full line of menswear, operated its own advertising agency, and had a fledgling home-furnishings business. The firm also was involved with an outside company that conducted medical research on such items as artificial arteries and the new pacemaker heart-stimulant device. Among its highly publicized contributions was the gold-plated fabric—at a cost of $3,500 a yard—that was used in manufacturing an antenna placed on the moon by Apollo astronauts.

Addressing a meeting of the Security Analysts of San Francisco, Helfat said these assorted and far-flung businesses were expected to deliver combined sales of $70 million in 1969 and—sticking to his projection of three years earlier—a minimum of $100 million by 1971. He explained that Koratron-based lawsuits were not expected to be settled until 1970 (he missed the mark by four years), but stressed that the downside risk in these legal actions was "negligible," while the possibility of upside potential was "tremendous."[11]

One of these "upsides" that Helfat had absorbed into the Koracorp family was a coupon publication known as *Homemaking with a Flair*. This home-shopping guide was distributed to approximately 20 million U.S. households each month, and served as a direct-mail marketing tool that incorporated attractive graphics and informative articles considered of interest to middle-income housewives. Much of this editorial content focused on food preparation, and included quick-and-easy recipes whose ingredients often were the products featured in the "cents-off" coupons.

Homemaking with a Flair was the brainchild of Phillip Weil, an advertising executive who spent almost seven years developing the innovative marketing enterprise. Jere Helfat saw a natural tie-in between the publication and Koracorp's target homemaker, and Joe readily agreed. Not only would the publication provide another avenue of communication to Koret of California customers, it would be an ideal environment to advertise the company's spring and fall fashions.[12] Helfat placed the publication under a new division he named Koratec Communications, which also included KCI Marketing & Advertising, the unit that handled all ad sales for *Homemaking*.[13]

Weil was brought in to run the operation, and immediately he hired a retired U.S. Postal Service superintendent whose job was to notify post office branches when the publications were being drop-shipped. Using a mailing list purchased from Metromedia—at that time a major communications firm—Weil knew exactly how-many of these coupon brochures were being sent to each of its targeted market areas.

Manufacturers paid $100,000 for a four-color full-page advertisement to be included in the publication, plus $60,000 for each coupon. Meanwhile, supermarkets in each market area were alerted to coupon values and all products represented in the booklet so they could stock them in sufficient quantities. To keep costs down and thus increase the chance of coupons being redeemed, *Homemaking* was distributed only to homes in the top 45 percent income bracket—those with a household income of at least $10,200.

The marketing opportunities presented by *Homemaking with a Flair* were tremendous, and Helfat put all of his executive might behind it. From his perspective, there was little risk and considerable upside. Housewives loved coupons and recipes, and advertisers would pay handsomely to place their products in front of an up-market target audience. The potential return on investment was impressive, and even considering printing and postage costs, the entire concept was scalable. It was a perfect "win-win" situation, long before that term ever became part of global business nomenclature.

It also was the idea that brought the entire Koracorp enterprise to its knees.

Joseph Koret in his office at the company's Mission Street headquarters.
Photo is signed at the bottom "With love to Mother, Joe."
[Koret private collection]

10

The Seventies: The End of an Era

THE TUMULT THAT DEFINED THE SECOND HALF of the 1960s readily spilled over into the next decade. The Vietnam War continued to fuel anti-war protests, while marginalized population groups increasingly took issue with what was perceived as blatant inequality. These issues gave rise to sit-ins, bra-burnings, peace protests, and race riots across the United States.

It didn't help much that the Beatles had just broken up, leaving an already-disillusioned generation feeling bereft and void of musical inspiration. A decade that had come of age with *Rubber Soul* and *Sergeant Pepper* was becoming increasingly disparate—and desperate. A previously under-appreciated radio frequency known as FM gave rise to album rock and such alternative artists as Black Sabbath, Pink Floyd, and Led Zeppelin. Meanwhile, mainstream radio began to churn out a smorgasbord of white-bread Top 40 pablum, much of which lacked any inspiration or imagination.

Typically the vanguard of American culture, San Francisco by now had become almost inured to ongoing war protests. Political and racial discord continued, with violent outbreaks alternately being blamed on the Black Panthers and the Weather Underground. The infamous "Zodiac Killer" terrorized the Bay Area, while thousands of flower children still roamed the city's streets spreading the doctrines of peace, love, and alternative consciousness. As the U.K.'s *Daily Mail* said, San Francisco in 1970 was characterized by "hippy street life when buskers, bongo players and impressive bouffants thronged the city by the bay."[1]

It also was a year of unrestrained expansion for Koracorp Industries. Intent on transforming the company into the major conglomerate he dreamed of, Jere Helfat continued his buying spree. After acquiring an 80 percent interest in Establissments Fra-For—France's largest producer of children's and infants' apparel—he set his sights on the Far East. Following a series of lengthy discussions, he announced an agreement with the global corporation Mitsubishi to seek approval from the Japanese government for an agreement to license the manufacture and distribution of Koret merchandise in Asia.

Under terms of the joint agreement, Mitsubishi Rayon would gain rights to the know-how relating to "design, production, and sale of certain of the women's apparel lines of Koret of California," as well as its wholly owned Identity Designs and Blairmoor Knitwear divisions. In return, Mitsubishi was to pay Koret royalties on a graduated scale "based on sales volume of Koret-designed apparel by Mitsubishi and its manufacturing sublicenses."[2]

While specifics of the royalty arrangements were not disclosed, Helfat indicated the revenues generated would have no immediate effect on corporate earnings. He did explain, however, that the Mitsubishi deal was Koracorp's first major licensing arrangement in Asia and was part of an overall plan to build a worldwide licensing business. According to a company statement, the agreement included licensing Mitsubishi's apparel businesses in Japan, Taiwan, Korea, Singapore, Laos, South Vietnam, Thailand, and Malaysia.

The next acquisition on Helfat's list was the hat business of H.C.A. Industries, billed in a company statement as "the nation's largest men's headwear manufacturer." Through this deal, Koracorp purchased the worldwide rights to the Cavanagh, Dobbs, Knox, and Champ brands from H.C.A. (formerly known as the Hat Corporation of America), effectively shutting down the company's manufacturing operations. Koracorp had entered the hat business in 1967 with the purchase of Byer-Rolnick Corporation, and Helfat saw this as a perfect complement to H.C.A.'s strength in dress and casual hats.

The move seemed somewhat perplexing to both industry analysts and *New York Times* reporter Leonard Sloane, who pointed out that the sale by H.C.A. of its well-known brands to Koracorp came at a time when men's hat sales "have long been in a sharply declining trend."[3]

Because of—or maybe in spite of—Koracorp's flurry of acquisitions, the company beat Helfat's $100 million target in 1971. Revenue came from virtually all quarters, with the Koret of California apparel unit contributing an estimated $40 million. Much of the increase seemed to stem from the introduction of Kolortron, a new variation on the old mix-and-match theme that was expected to produce over $10 million alone in 1973.

The Kolortron plan was simple and ingenious: for decades, Koret had operated around basic spring and fall fashion lines, but this new program was intended each year to introduce a "short group" of shirts, blouses, and sweaters styled to always fit the full range of pants designed in the same "color story." That way, no matter what items were added or removed from the line, they would always coordinate with the rest of the corresponding line of pants.

While Kolortron made it easy for women to purchase, or add to, a color-coordinated wardrobe, Joe knew its real strengths were in the manufacturing process and the distribution chain. He admired the plan's simplicity when Helfat and Koret Vice President Bernard Brown explained it to him and encouraged them to roll it out quickly. As Brown told *Women's Wear Daily*, "The real strength of the plan is [that] we have a tremendous inventory of pants and tops which can be reordered by the store and delivered within two weeks. Retailers don't have to tie up a large amount of 'open-to-buy' at one shot as they normally do with coordinated sportswear collections."[4]

Another advantage was that, by constantly changing the tops (all of which could be matched to the pants in selected colors), stores didn't end up with mismatched odds and ends at the end of the season. In fact, some retailers never needed to take mark-downs on Kolortron garments. "By dropping in new tops frequently, a store can keep the department looking fresh, and it's tough for a shopper to walk out because she couldn't find something new," Brown observed.[5]

AS KORACORP INCREASINGLY BECAME A GLOBAL name in the apparel industry, company executives began to emphasize—and maximize—its worldwide appeal. The marketing department had periodically arranged fashion excursions to Australia and Hawaii, but the growing company—and an expanding customer base on every continent except Antarctica—led Koret to display its new creations in more exotic locales. Merv Brown, Stephanie's nephew, was now in charge of all advertising and sales promotion and had an almost free hand in deciding how and where to highlight the upcoming fashion line. In early 1973, he arranged for a fashion shoot in Greece, which he felt would complement the new, contemporary designs Koracorp had planned for the following spring.

A contingent of Koret executives, including Joe and Stephanie and photographer Gordon Emberly, landed on the Peloponnesian peninsula with suitcases full of cameras and clothes. As the *San Francisco Chronicle* reported, "The rocky hillsides and sparkling waters have been put to work by Koret of California to loan a little reflected glory to the San Francisco manufacturer's lines of fall sportswear. . . . The result was a spectacular slide presentation designed to fire Koret's salesmen with enthusiasm for the new designs. The slide show will also be shown to store buyers during the next four or five months, but ordinary customers, unfortunately, won't get a chance to see all the magnificent pictures of Greece."[6]

The marketing shoot in Greece spawned yet another exotic excursion, this one a contest that whisked a lucky Koret of California customer (plus one) to the tropical shores of Maui. Convinced that resort clothes always look a little better with an actual resort behind them, Brown created a marketing campaign designed to lure customers into stores with the chance to spend a week in paradise. As a department store display ad proclaimed, "The backdrop is Hawaii's Maui at the Kaanapali Beach Resort. You've just crossed the Pacific on United Air Lines. Clothes aren't a problem. You've got an entire wardrobe by Koret of California. You didn't pay a penny to be where you are or wear what you're wearing. You won it all at Macy's."[7] A second-place prize consisted of a five-piece coordinated wardrobe by Koret of California, while three third-place prizes of a three-piece Koret of California wardrobe also were given away.

The campaign proved so successful that an almost identical promotion was planned for the following year. Again, the lucky winner was presented with a week's vacation for two at the Kaanapali Resort, although this time airfare was provided by Western Airlines. While "resort wear" had been the theme of 1973's marketing plan, this time around it was "softness." As newspaper promotions proclaimed, "Sparking your evenings, shimmers of metallic wink seductively from softest-upon-soft rayon and acetate in a V-neck tank in metallic white and silver. Or putting the gleam in their eye: Qiana nylon, the sexy fabric with a sensible approach to living. It's an absolute sensation to wash!"[8]

DESPITE METICULOUS FORECASTING AND JOE'S long-time emphasis on dollar plans, not even the most astute economists could accurately predict the ups and downs of the apparel market. Sometimes, the Koret design team came within a percentage point or two of projecting actual sales volume, and sometimes a particular garment sold far fewer units than expected. It all had to do with a complex matrix of fabrics, trends, home economics, and consumer tastes. These indicators all were part of doing business, and as long as the company didn't drastically over-produce its lines, losses could be kept to a minimum.

Still, Joe abhorred the thought of wasting money. By the early seventies, Koret of California was either manufacturing or buying millions of yards of cotton, rayon, wool, and polyester every year. Again, no matter how carefully the design team calculated the amount of material required for next season's line, inevitably some of it would be left over. If that same type, color, and pattern wasn't picked up again for next season's line, the fabric would be relegated to the scrap heap. Each year, thousands of bolts of quality material piled up in warehouses, collecting dust.

To remedy that situation, Koracorp opened a fabric-surplus store on Second Street just a few doors down from Market. While Joe preferred to have his customers purchase ready-made Koret sportswear from his retail partners, a profit was a profit no matter where it came from. These fabric remnants had already been paid for, and their cost had been figured into the corporate budget. Whatever dollars they drove to the bottom line now represented additional cash flow. Any woman with a sewing machine could create her own garments that matched her coordinated Koret of California wardrobe. Furthermore, Joe theorized that if a customer could sew her own creations using Koret fabrics, she might be more prone to go to her favorite clothing store to see what she might be missing.

The new surplus outlet opened March 5, 1973, amid much fanfare and was an instant success. As one newspaper advertisement explained, "First, we manufacture some fabrics in our own mills . . . and no one can sell fabrics for less than the manufacturer. Second, when we buy fabrics for our many clothing factories, we buy them in large quantities at volume prices we can pass on to you. When our clothing fabrics have finished production, they have large quantities of first-quality fabrics left over. In our new store, we will offer these pieces to you at sacrifice prices. We will precut many fabrics to the most popular lengths in order to speed service. Finally, we will sell only first quality fabrics. And as the prices on this page indicate, we will sell them for low discounts."[9]

BY THE SUMMER OF 1973, KORACORP SEEMED headed for another record year. Jere Helfat was projecting double-digit revenue gains, with earnings to match. From all outward appearances, it seemed that his plan to diversify through acquisitions was working. Koracorp stock was performing reasonably well, although the company had amassed a sizeable debt load. While this exerted pressure on profit margins and worried some of the more anxious shareholders, sales were robust and earnings were solid. Ever the optimist, Helfat assured Joe—more than once—that "the sky is the limit."

In early August, the sky came crashing down.

The first indication of difficulties came on August 6, when Joe, who still served as chairman of the board of Koracorp Industries, was alerted to a substantial financial discrepancy detected during the company's second-quarter accounting process. Arthur Andersen & Company, Koracorp's accounting firm at the time, had discovered that "certain transactions" reported by the Koratec Communications subsidiary were of a suspicious nature and, more important, that millions of dollars in receivables could not be accounted for. The primary business conducted through the Koratec unit was the coupon publication *Homemaking with a Flair*, and Helfat told Joe that its accounts receivables appeared to be coming in much more slowly than they should have been—especially given its reported high volume of sales activity. Joe told Helfat to have Koracorp controller Raymond Kittelberger look into the matter and report back as quickly as possible.

It didn't take Kittelberger long. Just days into his investigation, he encountered an accounting category labeled "unbilled accounts receivable," a classification he had never before encountered as a corporate controller. These unbilled receivables had the effect of creating the appearance that *Homemaking with a Flair* was profitable, whereas it actually was hemorrhaging money.[10]

Since Koracorp was a public company, Joe Koret was required to report any financial irregularities to the U.S. Securities and Exchange Commission, as well as the New York Stock Exchange and the Pacific Stock Exchange. He did just that, and on August 8, the SEC suspended Koracorp's trading for ten days due to what it described as "incomplete and inadequate information." During the ten-day period that followed, government investigators spent hours poring over Koracorp's books. After confirming numerous inconsistencies, the commission slammed the company with another ten-day trading interruption. A third suspension followed, and then the SEC did the almost-unthinkable by terminating Koracorp trading indefinitely until the company was able to get its financial house in order. For a company that was already significantly overextended—long-term debt in 1973 had topped $37 million—this was almost a death knell. The stock price fell through the floor and analysts walked away, shaking their heads in disbelief at how things could have gotten so out of control.

What triggered Joe's initial suspicions was an inexplicable $10.5 million discrepancy for the first half of 1973. No one had seen this coming, and at first no one could determine what had caused it. Kittelberger's review found that almost every penny of the loss had come from the Koratec unit. That shortfall represented almost 10 percent of Koracorp's entire annual sales, and could not have been caused by misplaced digits or commas. Infuriated by the prospect of large-scale fraud being perpetrated within the Koret walls, Joe realized the multimillion-dollar business he had founded thirty-five years earlier was at serious risk of coming apart at the seams. The more the investigators from the SEC and Arthur Andersen reviewed the Koratec books, the more the pit in his stomach grew.

By the middle of August, the parallel investigations confirmed what Joe already suspected: *Homemaking with a Flair* and Koretec, its parent division, had overstated their respective accounts receivables by almost ten million dollars.[11] Jere Helfat could not explain the discrepancy, but evidence strongly suggested that someone inside Koratec was either embezzling or skimming cash directly into his or her own pockets. The formal legal term for this activity is defalcation, and Joe was determined to find out who was responsible. More immediate, however, he knew he had to excise the tumor that allowed this activity to exist in the first place. On August 24, he called an emergency board meeting and demanded Helfat's resignation. Joe was careful not to cite any wrongdoing, and even allowed Helfat to remain with the company as a "special consultant," thus allowing him to retain some of his reputation and find alternative employment. Arthur Cunningham, who had directly supervised the Koratec division, was not as fortunate; Joe terminated him without ceremony during that same meeting. Additionally, the board asked for and received the resignations of Phillip Weil and *Homemaking* associates Jay Fleischmann and Norman Pinsky.

Joe also ordered an immediate restructuring of the top officers of the board, as well as Koracorp itself. He was unanimously reelected chairman and then named himself temporary president of the company. Now almost seventy-three years old, he had not intended to step back into day-to-day operations, but at this point he had no other realistic options. His primary mission was to save Koracorp, and no one else was prepared at the time to take the helm. Despite the mounting debt load accrued from his serial acquisitions, Helfat had been a steady and reliable voice of reason—until Koratec imploded. Joe had not anticipated making a change at the top, but now his hand was forced.

Always keeping a steady eye on a five-year business cycle, Joe recommended that an outside director of the company named Thaddeus Taube be elected vice chairman of the board. He had known Taube for many years and had worked with him in the formation of Terok

Properties, an independent real estate venture Joe owned. This motion was quickly approved, as was the decision to coax long-time Koret of California executive Ronald McClennan out of early retirement to serve as executive vice president. Additionally, company treasurer Joseph Berghold was elected a vice president. No replacement for Cunningham was named, and the few remaining Koratec operations now reported directly to Taube.[12]

Because of the egregious nature of Koracorp's accounting losses, the SEC set some steep restrictions for the company to follow if it wanted its trading suspension lifted. One of these was to cease publication of *Homemaking with a Flair*, an action that already had occurred with the termination of Cunningham and Weil. The company also divested itself of several loss-leading non-apparel operations, and employed the services of Clarence Rainess & Company to recertify its 1972 and 1973 accounting statements. Satisfied that Koracorp had jumped through its flaming hoops, the SEC reinstated the trading of Koracorp stock on January 24, 1974.[13]

A 1990 petition in U.S. Federal Tax Court offers some clarity on how the *Homemaking* debacle evolved. In a proceeding titled Weil v. Commissioner and dated August 6 of that year, U.S. Tax Court Judge Edna Parker ruled that tax returns filed by Phillip Weil and his wife Beatrice Weil for 1971, 1972, and 1973 underreported income by more than $1.6 million. According to Judge Parker's ruling, Weil—listed in the tax court filing as Louis P. Weil—and his wife had established a number of shell companies designed to receive money that he was funneling to himself from various *Homemaking* ad and coupon sales. These companies—including Verve, Associated Graphics, Allison Production Affiliates, Western Gateway Corporation, Paradise Found Ltd., Gateway Foods, Rainbow Production, and Hawaiian Fragrances—served as third-party conduits through which unreported income was deposited into Weil and his wife's personal bank accounts. Norman Pinsky and Jay Fleischmann, who were terminated once the embezzlement scheme unraveled, were alleged to have assisted Weil with what Judge Carter described as "kickbacks and diversions."

In her 1990 ruling, Judge Parker stated that "The evidence in the record in this case is exceedingly detailed. Reviewing and weighing this evidence requires painstaking attention to complex banking and accounting records to trace the various funds, to unravel the convoluted money trail, and to untie the Gordian knot of petitioner's after-the-fact 'reconstruction' of accounting books and records." The judge ruled that "Petitioner [Louis P. Weil] used his shell corporations as his own deep pockets, funneling the funds to cover gambling debts at Caesar's Palace in Las Vegas. He also purchased a Maserati, acquired a home in Hawaii, paid living expenses for his entire family, hired a housekeeper, and furnished his wife's walk-in closet. Additionally, he used the unreported and untaxed income to invest in other businesses, including Hawaiian Fragrances, Paradise Found, and Gateway Foods."[14]

Seventeen years after the *Homemaking with a Flair* initial discrepancies surfaced, the IRS forced Weil to pay up.

THE $10.5 MILLION FIRST-HALF LOSS, COMBINED with the specter of corporate malfeasance, pummeled Koracorp's public image. Even though the SEC eventually re-listed the company's stock, investors who already had endured the Koratron patent-infringement lawsuits were wary of the company's perceived mismanagement. Now that *Homemaking with a Flair* was off the books, Koracorp reported a slight narrowing of losses in the third quarter and the first nine months of the year, but this was little solace to shareholders who watched the value of their stock disintegrate. Still, through the first three-quarters of 1973, the company reported a slight profit of $1.7 million on sales of $92.4 million, a figure that actually was 20 percent ahead of the $76.8 million reported for the same period a year earlier.

Much of that sales gain came from the ever-popular Koret of California division. Despite its parent company's difficulties, the women's sportswear subsidiary projected full-year sales of $52 million, and division president Charles Cain said his plans included the addition of an "entirely new merchandising category." He further pointed out that Koracorp's overall difficulties had little bearing on Koret of California, which, he said, "had its best profit year last year, and will top that significantly this year." Still, he observed that, "When a member of the family is sick, you never feel good."[15]

Still reeling from the near-catastrophe just months earlier, Joe Koret tapped Thaddeus (Tad) Taube to replace him as president of Koracorp and also serve as president of the board's executive committee. Taube was president of Taube Associates, a real estate investment and management company he had founded in Belmont, just a few miles south of San Francisco. He and Joe had been acquaintances for many years, and Taube's firm had brokered a number of his lucrative property transactions in the 1960s. Joe had recommended that Taube be elected as an outside officer to the Koracorp board in 1970, and now that the company was in crisis mode his business expertise was sorely needed fulltime.

THE LEGAL SINKHOLE THAT NEARLY SWALLOWED Koracorp in 1973 took years to repair. Despite the swift action taken by Joe Koret, the SEC still filed charges against the firm, claiming it had violated federal securities laws. Realizing that the public company's future was on the line, Tad Taube announced Koracorp would defend itself against any and all charges, noting that the individuals the Commission alleged to be responsible for the *Homemaking with a Flair* debacle no longer were associated with the company in any way.

Still, the federal charges initiated a flurry of shareholder lawsuits, further dampening Koracorp's stock price. Cash was drying up, and many of the companies acquired during Helfat's reign were struggling. Adding mayhem to that misery, ongoing lawsuits continued to loom over Koratron, whose licensing income atrophied. Earnings were stagnant and at one point it was suggested that the only way to pull out of the abyss was to file for Chapter 11 protection.

Fortunately, the Koret of California women's apparel division was still producing solid revenues and generating significant cash flow. When the idea of bankruptcy came up, Joe was unwavering in his commitment to the core business and adamant that he would never take the "easy" way out. In his mind, bankruptcy was for cowards who lacked long-term vision. Instead, he insisted—with Taube's unwavering encouragement—that the company would work its way back from the brink, no matter how long it took. Although Taube had never before run a company the size of Koracorp—with all its various financial and legal entanglements—Joe gave him virtual *carte blanche* to take whatever measures he had to in order to save it.

"We didn't want Chapter 11," Taube once told the *L.A. Times*'s Ronald Soble. "We do business with 20,000 accounts. Our commercial business would have been eroded."[16] Instead, Taube began the long and tedious task of shaking the company to its core, and then building it back up, piece by piece. He began by divesting Koracorp of virtually all the non-apparel businesses Helfat had acquired, with the goal of returning the firm to its core product lines.

It took several long years and considerable wrangling, but Koracorp eventually was able to extract itself from its financial and legal problems. Gone were the home furnishings and color-coordinated curtains, the advertising agency, and the remnants of the Koratec subsidiary that got the company into trouble in the first place. A leaner, meaner Koracorp meant annual revenues were lower than they'd been before the *Homemaking* fiasco, but the renewed focus on women's and men's sportswear returned Koret of California to profitability. In fact, Koret's unit and dollar sales had been increasing despite Koracorp's lingering issues, and Taube was able to keep the firm aloft while trying to figure out how to refuel it.

Reinvigorating the company was only part of the ultimate challenge. The charges filed by the SEC and the lawsuits filed by disgruntled shareholders were equally problematic, and they were not about to disappear just because corporate dead weight was being shed. It took three long years to wade through all the litigation, but in 1976 the Koracorp board of directors agreed to resolve the shareholder suits, per a court ruling by the U.S. District Court, Northern District of California. In that ruling, Judge William Sweigert ordered that all contending parties, as well as all individuals who had purchased Koracorp stock between January 1 and August 7, 1973, appear at a hearing to work out settlement terms. The various cases by that time had been consolidated into two class actions known, respectively, as "Edmund Prescottano and ano, et al." and "Irving Miller" and named for two of the original litigants.

The hearing was designed to solve two primary issues. The first addressed Koracorp's alleged violation of Section 10(b) of the Securities Exchange Act, and charged that the company and its executives issued and disseminated "false and misleading information which overstated Koracorp's income and financial worth." Stemming from these allegations, the suits claimed the market price of Koracorp "was artificially inflated during [the cited] period, and the actions seek recovery of alleged damages suffered by persons" who purchased it.[17]

The defendants named in these actions were Koracorp Industries and Koratec Communications, as well as executives and board members including Joseph Koret, Jere Helfat, Charles Cain, Arthur Cunningham, Howard Friedman, George Herzog, Daniel Jackson, Ronald McClennan, Stanley Morgenstern, Thaddeus Taube, and William Warnock. Accounting firm Arthur Andersen & Company, which had initially certified the *Homemaking with a Flair* figures, also was identified as partially responsible and thus became a party to the actions.

Under the terms of the Amended Stipulation of Settlement, Koracorp and all named defendants agreed to provide "a Settlement Fund of $345,000 cash and a new issue of $805,000 stated value of Koracorp's presently authorized and unissued preferred stock." The stated value of each share of the preferred stock would be 1.25 times the average last sale price of Koracorp common stock quoted on the New York Stock Exchange during the ten trading days immediately preceding the effective date of the settlement.[18]

Despite the legal aggravations and pending SEC actions, Koracorp exhibited remarkable staying power. The shareholder lawsuits eventually were disposed of for approximately $1.5 million, and $1.1 million was recovered from the company's fraud charges filed against Weil and his alleged coconspirators. Additionally, in November of 1976 Koracorp reported record sales of $107 million, and per-share earnings of $1.74, for the first nine months of the year.

One lingering issue continued to be the U.S. Securities and Exchange Commission. As Tad Taube told the *Chronicle* in November 1976, the government watchdog was still hounding Koracorp, even after all the lawsuits had been settled and the company had done everything necessary to ensure that such a problem would never occur again. "Despite the court's dismissal of all charges against us, the SEC has appealed the ruling and we will now have the specter of alleged wrongdoing hanging over us for years to come," he said. One way out would be sign a consent decree, a legal agreement designed to resolve a dispute between two parties without admission of guilt (in a criminal case) or liability (in a civil case). Taube explained that he'd been tempted to take that route, but was opposed to the option for ideological reasons. "I shudder to think what would happen to this country if everyone took that attitude," he explained.[19] In December 1978, the SEC terminated its action against Koracorp, noting the complete restructuring of the company and acknowledging that there had been no securities laws violations since late 1974. In a short statement, Taube observed that "management can now focus all its energies and resources on the continued growth of our business."[20]

By this time, Koracorp's sales were setting new records almost every quarter, and the stock had recovered from the embarrassingly low $1 price tag that hammered it when the *Homemaking* scandal broke. Eventually, as the price crept up to $5, then $9, and eventually crossed the $10 mark, analysts started to poke around under the hood again. Taube at the time had become the third-largest holder of Koracorp stock, behind Joe and Stephanie's equal number of shares, and began to woo investors as well as potential acquisition targets.

"I am one of the weirdos who believes this industry has more potential than any other in the United States," he told *San Francisco Chronicle* reporter Donald White. "We're the third largest manufacturing industry in the country and [Koracorp] has adopted sophisticated planning and efficient controls on inventory and accounts receivable. Our return on equity last year was 30 percent, one of the highest for any manufacturing company."[21]

Feeling confident about Koracorp's growth prospects and financial future, Taube convinced Joe to poke his toe back into the acquisition market. He'd identified a healthy sportswear manufacturer in the Midwest and thought it would make a good fit with the product lines Koracorp already had in place. The company, Chicago-based Robert Bruce, was a wholly owned subsidiary of Consolidated Foods Corporation, and was generating sizeable revenue and earnings. In early 1979, Taube signed an agreement to bring the firm into the Koracorp fold, pending any unexpected circumstances.

The merger was well on its way to completion in 1978 when the unexpected did come to pass. The month before the SEC settlement, Joe Koret celebrated his seventy-eighth birthday, his first since the death of his wife back in February. Stephanie had endured a lengthy battle with Alzheimer's disease that began in the mid-sixties, and she became more and more housebound as the years wore on. The daily rigors of going to the office and coming home to nurture his ailing wife took a great toll on Joe, and he had grown exhausted. The only regular activity that kept him moving forward at that time was his passion for fishing, and he found himself going out on his boat in almost any kind of weather two or three times a week.

Eventually, Joe decided it was time to get out. Koracorp's share price had reemerged from the dark hole that had almost swallowed it five years earlier, and its continual record-setting sales and earnings made it an attractive acquisition target. Taube had been quietly shopping the company to "suitable buyers," and eventually he found one just a stone's throw from Koret's Mission Street headquarters.

MORE THAN A CENTURY BEFORE, IN 1848, A young man named Loeb Strauss emigrated from Bavaria to a small community in rural Kentucky. The son of a peddler back in the old country, Strauss set about learning the dry goods business in this new "land of opportunity." He was barely making ends meet when he heard about the massive gold strike that had been discovered in the Sierra foothills. In 1853, the enterprising romantic set out across the Wild West and arrived in San Francisco, along with thousands of others whose pockets were almost empty but whose heads were filled with dreams. By that time, much of the gold had been panned out of the mountain streams, and many of those who had gambled on getting rich had gone bust. Now, they trudged up and down the muddy streets of the bustling city looking for any kind of work.

A natural-born optimist, Strauss saw opportunity where others saw despair. Even though the gold rush was waning, San Francisco remained a lively pioneer town. In 1853, he opened a dry goods store where he sold an eclectic selection of merchandise that ranged from camp stoves to saddle soap to dried beans. A couple years of hard work turned it into a modestly profitable business that catered to the city's growing cadre of working class men. One day, the young Mr. Strauss loaded a bolt of heavy fabric used to manufacture camp tents into a cart and began to push it down a crowded street. Within minutes, he came across a disheartened miner who had just come back from the hills, and tried to sell him a new tent.

"Nobody needs tents up there," the miner told Strauss. "They need pants."

As local lore has it, Loeb—now known as Levi to his friends and customers—took a piece of his tent material to a local tailor, who fashioned a pair of heavy-duty trousers from it.[22] They sold almost instantly, and within weeks he couldn't produce them as fast as he could sell them. The heavy cloth used in making the new garments—and, presumably, sturdy tents of the time—derived its name from the French town of Nimes, where it was made. Hence its name *de Nimes*—or, in its Americanized form, "denim."[23]

These sturdy new trousers seemed to last forever. They could be worn plowing a field, herding cattle atop a horse, and of course, panning for gold in a bubbling stream. The only problem was that the denim material was so durable that the pockets and button fly tended to rip before the jeans wore out. In 1872, on the advice of a tailor in Nevada named Jacob Davis, Strauss inserted metal rivets in the corners of the pockets and at the base of the fly. Everything stayed put, and the pants seemed to never grow old. Davis and Strauss patented the idea, and the following year the two men opened the company's first San Francisco manufacturing plant, on Fremont Street.

Fast forward one hundred years and Levi Strauss & Company had grown to become one of the world's largest manufacturers of men's and women's clothing. Levi Strauss had died in 1902, one year after Joe Koret sailed to America, and, lacking any children of his own, he left the company to his four nephews to run. In 1979, the chairman was Walter A. Haas, Jr., son of Walter Haas, who was the son-in-law of Strauss's nephew Sigmund Stern. From the very beginning the business was kept very much "all in the family."

Walter Haas, Jr., had been president/CEO and chairman of the rapidly growing company during the 1960s when it signed the licensing deal with Koratron, enabling it to manufacture a new line of permanent-press slacks. He also backed the decision to file the lawsuit against Koratron, an action that so angered Joe Koret that he immediately yanked the garment-maker's license and berated them for biting the hand that fed them.

By 1979, this acrimony had dissipated. Koracorp and Levi Strauss & Company coexisted peacefully, their San Francisco headquarters just a few blocks apart. Haas now had his sights set on rapidly expanding the business, and he was actively looking for acquisitions that could extend Levi Strauss's existing product lines. In 1978, the firm had reported revenues of around $1.6 billion, and with money in the bank, Haas had a long-range plan that would far exceed that figure.

Having just signed the papers to buy Robert Bruce, Tad Taube was of a mind to expand Koracorp rather than sell it. Total sales in 1978 topped $185 million, earnings had never been better, and the stock price was rising every month. While still far below the price at which it opened when the company went public more than ten years earlier, it was well above the $1 basement where it had crashed during the Koratec disaster. Taube saw considerable upside in the business, and the analysts he spoke with were beginning to sing Koracorp's praises again.

But Joe Koret was growing tired. The long period leading up to Stephanie's death had taken its toll, and his doctors were telling him it was time to get on with his life. From the time he arrived in San Francisco sixty-two years before, Joe had experienced success beyond his wildest dreams, and he now was one of the wealthiest men in San Francisco. He'd lived a remarkable life, built a thriving company from the ground up, and had been married for over fifty years to a beautiful and creative woman who had become his business partner, wife, and best friend.

Now that she was gone, he was ready for a change.

In early 1979, Tad Taube and Walter Haas sat down with members of their respective boards and inked an agreement that would allow

Koracorp to merge with Levi Strauss & Company. The proposed acquisition would give the clothing giant a reputable, high-profile women's sportswear company, as well as allow Haas to expand his firm's collection of menswear and clothing accessories. Plus, even though the Koratron lawsuits had been settled years before, the deal would transfer any and all proprietary knowledge of the permanent-press process to Levi Strauss.

In exchange, Joe and the rest of the Koracorp stockholders would share in the purchase price of $71 million, which translated to $18.68 per share. Joe Koret, who now served as chairman emeritus, owned 15.2 percent of the outstanding shares, which made his stake worth approximately $10.8 million. The estate of his late wife held an identical number of shares. Taube, who by now had assumed the title of chairman of the board, was the third-largest stockholder and held 9.2 percent of all outstanding shares. His net take from the merger would be just over $6.5 million.

Disclosure of the sale on May 18, 1979 caused a four-hour delay in the opening of trading of Koracorp stock on the New York Stock Exchange. It finally opened at $17 a share, up $5.25 a share from the previous close, and ended the day at that same price.[24] The merger announcement was timed to coincide with the annual meeting of Koracorp's shareholders, who were almost unanimous in approving the deal. One of the holdouts was a retired grocery clerk named Stanley Perawicki, who had been buying stock in the company since 1970. Noting that "that man [Taube] rescued this company from near-disaster," he demanded to know why the company had settled for $18.68 a share. When Taube reminded him that the price was double its book value, Perawicki remained unsatisfied.[25] One casualty of the acquisition plan was Koracorp's previously announced plan to purchase the Robert Bruce sportswear company from Consolidated Foods. Levi Strauss was not interested in pursuing that deal, and because it was not yet part of Koracorp's assets, the purchase was scrapped.

Most financial analysts considered the merger of the two clothing giants as a positive move. "I view the acquisition as merely an extension of Levi's long-term move away from being a jeans manufacturer," Kenneth Golden of Sutro & Company told the *Chronicle*. "Both firms are in separate ends of the business and really don't compete. Koracorp is more in the mainstream, while Levi is still in a specialty area."[26]

When the deal closed later that year, it marked the end of an era not just for Joe Koret, but for the thousands of employees whom he credited with building the company into the apparel megastar it had become. Many of them—including a number of top executives—followed their jobs into the much larger Levi Strauss organization, where three years later they were folded into a new unit known as Battery Street Enterprises. Named for its location in downtown San Francisco, the division was created to handle all the labels that were picked up through the Koracorp purchase, including Koret of California, Oxxford men's suits, Resistol Hats, and Rainfair rainwear.

As for Joe Koret, he went home. He went fishing. He'd already created the Koret Foundation, so he began giving away the millions of dollars he had struggled his entire life to earn. He took great satisfaction in the comfort and joy his gifts brought to those who needed help, and the process carried him full circle to those days when he would bring stale bread or a purloined fish to his hungry parents and brothers.

Most of all, Joe took his doctors' advice. Even though he only had a few more years to live, he began a new life. He embarked on new travels, started new business ventures, and fell in love with a remarkable woman who was destined to change his world. Now close to eighty, he was about to become a young man again.

(Top) Even when he was in his late 70s, Joe spent several days a week
casting for salmon at one of his secret fishing spots along the Marin coast.
(Above) Line in the water, cigar in mouth, rain or shine, Joe was at home—and
at peace—out on the open ocean. [Koret private collection]

11

The Old Man and the Sea

ONE WARM SATURDAY IN THE FALL OF 1924, young Joe Koret did what he usually did when he had a day off: he ventured north of the city to the dry hills of the Marin headlands.

In the early 1920s, the entire area north of the Golden Gate was a virtually untouched wilderness, home to a few farmers and ranchers but mostly to deer and raccoons and wild birds. The massive orange bridge that one day would frame the entrance to San Francisco Bay was not even a sketch on a drawing board, and the few roads that had been carved into the rugged terrain were barely more than two tires wide. Horses were much more common than automobiles, and the folks who lived there liked it that way. They were miles—and decades— away from the dynamic city rising out of the earthquake ashes, and to them it was a world of difference.

As summer gradually rolled into the autumn of 1923, the days began to grow short. The lack of rain had thrust the land into the seasonal drought that gave the hills the parched hue of a desert camel. The seasonal rains that would soak California throughout the winter were still a few weeks off, and the pervasive summer layer of marine fog had disappeared. Mount Tamalpais rose like a pharaoh's pyramid chiseled out of the coastal range to the north. The scent of salt and sardines and seaweed hung in the air, and Joe stood at the rail as a passenger ferry plowed through the whitecaps that churned through San Francisco Bay. Shrieking gulls circled above the boat, occasionally swooping down in search of a morsel, always seeking their next meal. Joe remembered what that felt like, and now as the pier in Sausalito grew close he imagined how his father had felt that first morning in New York Harbor more than twenty years ago.

Once the ferry was securely tied to the dock, Joe caught a ride to one of his favorite North Bay haunts. He got out at an old goat trail and trudged upstream to a quiet grove of towering coastal redwoods that commanded the sky. Over the last several years, he had explored a number of streams that trickled along the moss-covered riverbanks and sliced past slippery rocks. As was his habit on these adventurous sprees, he was traveling with a fishing pole—little more than a bamboo rod with a string and a hook attached—and a wicker basket that contained a handful of bait fish. His hosiery stall at the Crystal Palace Market in downtown San Francisco was closed for the day, which meant he had a few spare hours to disappear into the pristine wilderness and commune with nature. His new wife, Stephanie, was much more cosmopolitan in her tastes and disliked boats and fishing, so that day she opted to stay home with her family.

On this particular morning, Joe carefully picked his way along his chosen stream, watching the water cascade around roots and stones as it babbled on its way to the bay. Other than the occasional cry of a hawk overhead there was no sound to interrupt his thoughts. His mind was always a jumble of notions: the wholesale price of stockings, what his customers were saying about the latest trends, what his new wife and her mother might prepare for dinner. With any luck, it would be a few of the lovely trout that he now could see swimming through the crystal waters of this almost primeval stream. Eventually, he settled down on a mossy bank next to a placid pool and dropped his line into the water.

It was so quiet Joe could almost hear the first trout as it chomped onto the hook. Catching fish in a barrel didn't properly describe what came next, but it was close. Drop the line, wait a few minutes, pull another trout up to the bank. Drop the line, wait, haul it in. It was as if these fish couldn't wait to join Joe on the riverbank. Take a number.

All of a sudden, the quietude was disturbed by a voice that made Joe jump. It was a man's voice, and it came from behind him, near the trail that gently wound upstream into the redwood grove.

"What do you have there?" the voice asked with a thick immigrant inflection.

In New York and here in San Francisco, Joe had encountered almost every European accent there was. A number of new arrivals worked the stalls at the Crystal Palace Market, and his own parents still conversed with a noticeably Russian intonation. But this was different: probably German, or somewhere in that region of the continent. Certainly not French or Italian.

The voice stepped out of the shadows and Joe now could see a young fellow, maybe eighteen or nineteen years old, dressed in baggy trousers and an ill-fitting shirt. He appeared transfixed by the row of fish lined up on the ground next to Joe, as well as those he could see swimming in the stream.

"Mostly trout," Joe told him. "But a few sculpins and suckers. Not as good to eat, but they're just as hungry."

"How many have you got?" the young newcomer asked him.

"Not enough," Joe replied. "You have a name?"

By now the young man had joined Joe right at the edge of the riverbank and was peering into the clear water. "Sure do," he said in his thick accent. "Robert. Robert Upright."

"Joe Koret," Joe introduced himself, refusing to let go of the pole to shake hands. "I'm telling you, these things pretty near jump right onto the hook. Here—give it a try."

He handed the pole to Robert and invited him to drop the line into the cascading stream. He gave him a few tips on where to place the hook, how to tease the fish and—when one inevitably took the bait—how to haul it out of the stream carefully.

"See?" Joe said when Robert landed an exhausted trout on the river-bank. "They're just begging to come home with you. Where are you from, anyway?"

It turned out Joe was right about the accent.

Robert Aufrichtig was born on May 23, 1905 in Prague, which at the time had been a part of the vast Austro-Hungarian Empire. An intelligent and imaginative boy, he attended excellent schools that promised a lifetime of opportunities in his homeland. Any dreams he might have had, however, changed one day in June 1914 when Archduke Franz Ferdinand—the presumptive heir to the empire's throne—was fatally shot while riding in an open car in Sarajevo, Bosnia. Exactly one month later, the country declared war on Serbia, and less than a week after that Russia, Belgium, France, Great Britain, and Serbia lined up against the empire and its ally, Germany.

World War I had begun.

The conflict officially ended with the signing of the Treaty of Versailles on June 28, 1919—exactly five years after the archduke's assassination—but by then the war had torn most of Europe apart. The empire was in ruins, and most of the continent was reeling from the physical and political scars. While Prague was selected the capital of the newly formed Czechoslovakia, Mr. Aufrichtig determined that his son would do better in America than in his splintered homeland. A relative in San Francisco offered to sponsor the young man's immigration to the United States, so Mr. Aufrichtig bought Robert passage to the United States. The young man left his home in Prague in the spring of 1922 and arrived in New York two weeks later. Armed with a student visa and just enough money to make his way to California, he boarded a train and never looked back.

After his arrival in America, Robert was advised that the name Aufrichtig was a bit cumbersome to an Americanized tongue, so he became Robert Upright. Speaking only German, he made his way across the American continent in a roundabout way, going wherever his pocket change and the train tracks would carry him. For reasons that don't need much explanation, he particularly enjoyed New Orleans, which, at the height of Prohibition and social austerity, proved to be a fascinating rest stop for many young men.

Robert's uncle, Moritz Aufrichtig, lived in Richmond, a small but growing community located across the bay from San Francisco. The family was close-knit, and on weekends they enjoyed exploring the unspoiled countryside. On that particular Saturday, the family had boarded a ferry that took them to the other side of the bay, then trekked through the hilly terrain and forested streams. At one point, Robert—every bit the adventurer who enjoyed striking out on his own—wandered away from the rest of the family. He found himself poking along a footpath that wound along a stream that was wilder than anything he had ever seen. Except, perhaps, New Orleans.

Neither young man knew it then, but that chance encounter would be the start of a lifelong friendship. Joe was a twenty-three-year-old newlywed with a hosiery stall on Market Street, while Robert, who had turned nineteen in May, was engrossed in his schoolbooks and perfecting his language skills. Come rain or shine, through downpours and ocean squalls, the two men would fish, work, and generally enjoy the adventures of life together for the next sixty years.

As a young man struggling to survive in New York, Joe equated fishing with survival. The rivers around Manhattan at the time were swollen with sewage flowing from the streets and gutters, but to Joe that was hardly a deterrent. A fish meant one more day that his family had something to eat, and the fetid quality of the city's ecosystem was only a minor deterrence.

When the Korets arrived in San Francisco, the bounty of California's fertile farmlands meant there was always plenty to eat. The city was surrounded on three sides with waters that were teeming with life, and the fishmongers down on the wharf sold everything from salmon and squid, to sea bass and Dungeness crabs. The Korets seemed to be living in a horn of plenty, and Joe's clandestine forays in search of food no longer seemed necessary. Still, old habits die hard, and he never lost the desire to wander up a lazy stream in search of a tranquil pool where he could drop a line.

NO FISH AND GAME WARDEN WAS ON HAND TO check their catch that day of their chance meeting, but Joe and Robert likely exceeded their limit. It was typical of Joe to ignore the voice of authority, just as he had in Central Park as a boy when he disregarded the "No Fishing" signs. When it came to fishing, rules did not apply, and later in life he took great pains—some might even say an errant degree of delight—in circumventing regulations that got in the way of a quality fishing experience.

Robert Upright quickly became a family friend and a fixture in the Koret home. As newlyweds, Joe and Stephanie lived for a time with her parents who, like many Jewish families, were particularly welcoming to anyone who might show up at the front door. Setting one more place at the table was no big deal, especially if it included fresh-caught trout or maybe a salmon. Later, when the Korets moved into their own apartment nearby, Upright practically moved in with them. He became a regular guest at the dinner table, often after spending an entire Saturday with Joe at one of his favorite fishing haunts. Some days, they would venture down to the rocks near Crissy Field, where perch were particularly plentiful. On others, they would explore the fields and streams of Marin County, and when Robert invested in a small rowboat, they would try their hands with some of the larger fish that were abundant just a few yards from the shore.

As the years passed, the two anglers grew especially fond of Napa Val Resort, a fishing camp set along a tranquil stretch of the Napa River at the north end of San Francisco Bay. In the 1930s, the Napa Valley region was home to hundreds of fruit and nut orchards, as well as small farms and cattle ranches. Live oaks draped lazily over the pastoral hillsides and grasslands, and the intense heat of fall warmed the earth just before the winter rains blew in from the coast. Winding through this bucolic setting from its seasonal source as Kimball Canyon Creek in what today is Robert Louis Stevenson State Park, the Napa River descended the southern slope of Mount St. Helena. From there, it flowed freely from the narrow valley north of Calistoga southward for fifty-five miles to a tidal estuary at San Pablo Bay, at the very north end of San Francisco Bay.

Before a wave of extensive development swept across the region in the second half of the twentieth century, this was a prime spawning ground for numerous species of fish. Chinook salmon were particularly prevalent near the entrance to the Sacramento and San Joaquin Rivers, close to the tidal areas. Farther upstream, steelhead trout and coho salmon could be found by the thousands, while other species— including Pacific and river lamprey, hardhead, perch, flounder, and white sturgeon— were also were plentiful, and ready to jump on the hook.

In other words, it was an ideal location for two avid fishermen to cast a line. Joe would rise at the crack of dawn and be out of the house before seven o'clock. He usually would collect Bob Upright along the way, and the two of them would head northeast toward San Pablo Bay. By this time, Joe owned his own boat, which he kept at Napa Val, and as soon as the bait and daily provisions were aboard, the two anglers would set out in search of whatever was biting. While Joe typically viewed his pending catch as a hearty meal, Bob was more inclined just to enjoy any adventures the day happened to bring.

Napa Val outings were considered part of the local competitive scene, and the results of weekly fishing tournaments often could be found in the Sporting Green section of the *San Francisco Chronicle*. On February 10, 1953, the newspaper noted,

> [Napa Val Resort manager] Frank Silva reported that fishing on the Napa River was terrific all day Saturday with fish up to 25 pounds being brought in, but the big wind hit there on Sunday and was still continuing yesterday, and conditions were pretty impossible. . . . Among those who had it good on Saturday were Joe Koret and Bob Upright of San Francisco who brought in an eight-pound and 22-pounder.[1]

One month later. the two fishermen were at it again, with the *Chronicle* reporting: "We had a lot of small limits, that's from five to eight pounds," Frank Silva said. "They were mostly all taken downriver by the flour mill and at both bridges." Among those who took limits in the smaller-pound brackets that day were Joe Koret and Bob Upright.[2]

JOE'S FASCINATION WITH FISHING GREW YEAR by year and eventually turned into an obsession. One problem with heading out to Napa Val every Saturday was that it was a solid hour away, which took him away from Stephanie and limited his time on the water. On the other hand, the San Francisco Coast Guard Pier was located at the western end of Crissy Field, which had served as a military airfield during World War II. If Joe lacked the motivation to drive halfway around the bay, he would simply go to the pier, located close to the southern base of the Golden Gate Bridge, and cast his line into the water. The running of the tide, unpredictable weather, and seasonal fluctuations in the fish population caused him a good deal of frustration, but in the 1950s it proved to be a good spot to get away from the rigors of work and indulge his Number One pastime, if not passion.

In December 1957, one of Joe's relatives gave him a diary in hopes that he might begin keeping a journal. He had just turned fifty-seven years old and had committed very little of his life's endeavors to paper. The suggestion seems to have worked, at least for a time. Joe began a day-by-day accounting of the new year, beginning on January 1, 1958. This journaling lasted a total of fifty-five days, as Joe's last entry in the journal is dated February 24.

The diary provides considerable insight into what was important to Joe during this rainy five-week stretch. His entry for New Year's Day, which was a Wednesday, reveals that he and Stephanie had hosted a party for close family and friends the night before. They'd cracked bottles of twenty-five-year-old champagne and eventually went to bed at six in the morning, sleeping most of the day away. After a gap of about eight hours, the journal—really a day-planner with spaces for hour-by-hour appointment entries—shows that at 4 p.m. he was up and out of the house. In an entry that reads like a modern-day tweet, he wrote: "Went fishing. Crissy Field. Sand crab bait. Caught 35 perch, all kinds."

At that point in his life, it was rare for Joe to go fishing on a weekday, but New Year's Day was an exception. In fact, he didn't go out again until that Saturday (January 4), which he described in a much longer entry:

> Very cold. Went fishing with Bob. Fished deep water. Had tiny little bites but hooked only one legal bass. Lots of fish but almost impossible to hook. Very windy all day. Went to the "slough." "Dutchmen." No fish. Went to "Severn Flats." We killed them. Hooked large fish on outgoing tide toward the end of day. 4 o'clock. Small hooks, sardine bait. Let them bite and take it. Ended with limits. Large fish.

The following week was fraught with work challenges, ranging from difficulties involved in duplicating colors for a line of skirts and dresses, to dealing with a particular fabric that had abrasion problems. Joe appointed a quality-control director to deal with these issues. "Stephy" was not feeling well but approved sketches for "remakes" in the flannel group. By Friday, she was feeling worse and Joe wrote that some much-needed rest over the upcoming weekend would do her good.

It did Joe good, too. Saturday morning, he was up early and headed to Napa Val, where the weather was fair and 55 degrees. Despite clear skies and poor fishing, he and Bob landed one bass and twelve flounders, just to "keep active." With Stephanie still feeling tired, Joe was back at it on Sunday. He dropped off a few bags of groceries at his mother's house, then spent the afternoon at Napa Val to try his luck with slightly better weather than the day before. He caught eight perch "in low water, rocky bottom." The next day—Monday—he was back at Napa Val once more, catching two "eight-pounders" and "lots of small fish." "Beautiful, sunny day," he wrote. "Like spring."

Every Saturday and Sunday for the next month, he and Bob went fishing, almost always to Napa Val. Central California winters can be unpredictable, largely because of the storms that charge in from the Pacific Ocean and slam the coast with periods of heavy rain and wind. These fast-moving tempests race through, then clear up quickly as the front moves east over the Sierra Nevada. This was long before weather satellites were the norm; instead, Joe relied on what he read in the newspaper and heard on the radio. Even then he couldn't know whether the fish were biting or not, as his diary entries bear out:

Saturday, January 18: No bass. Too windy. Flounders only.

Saturday, January 25: Rain and wind, about 52 degrees. Went bass fishing with Bob to Vallejo. Six flounders. I caught two bass, Bob caught one.

Sunday, January 26: Beautiful day. Went fishing to Napa Val. The rain of the last three days made the water thick with mud. The fish did not feed. Did not get a bass. Caught only one flounder. But the weather was good and I enjoyed the day very much.

The following weekend was very much the same. Muddy water, few fish except flounder. Even the waters off the Crissy Field pier were lacking, and he landed nothing.

Eventually, Joe got tired of writing in the journal; it became a bit of a chore as each new entry began to sound like the day before. His last entry—again, recounting a fishing outing—reads like a *Gilligan's Island* nightmare—except to an avid fisherman like Joe: "Gale today . . . rain. Winds to 60 miles an hour. Rained all day incessantly and heavily. The wind blew and blew. I went out anyway because of south wind. Lots of bites but too much wind. Caught one 8 lb. bass . . . Home early. Rain and rain and rain."

OVER THE YEARS, JOE HAD GROWN ESPECIALLY fond of Napa Val. He knew where the fish hung out near the bridges, and he'd become familiar with the currents and the pools. He even unofficially named one favorite hideout "Koret Cove." But work pressures and mounting concerns over his mother's health caused him to look to fishing spots a little closer to home. Over time, he refocused his passion on the larger and wilder fish that could be caught out beyond the bridge, and his passion for fishing—as well as an incessant appetite for adventure—drew him to the open ocean.

Joe's jaunts up to Napa Val became fewer and fewer, and he gradually evolved into "the old man of the sea." He purchased a used thirty-six-foot cabin cruiser named *Rosica* that he kept at Clipper Yacht Harbor in Sausalito. The boat, which initially was fitted with wall-to-wall carpeting, a Naugahyde sofa, and several easy chairs, eventually went through a complete retrofit. He had the seats and bunks ripped out and installed chairs that were more suited to reeling in creatures from the deep. He also fitted several large coolers for the daily catch, which was always brought home and divided judiciously among whoever had accompanied him that day. Depending on the weather and whomever he could persuade to venture out with him, he would take the boat— renamed the *Stephanie K*—into the rolling swells beyond the bridge. From there, he would explore his "secret" fishing spots up the coastline toward Point Reyes.

Joe quickly fell in love with the ocean. His frustrated river excursions that ended in catching flounder just "to stay active" evolved into regular weekend journeys that were not for the faint of heart. Unless the weather appeared particularly hazardous, he would top off the fuel tanks, load shrimp or small sand crabs into the bait locker, and chug out to sea. Fanatic that he was, Joe was neither senseless nor death-defying; he knew what his boat was capable of, and so did Bob Upright, who often found himself at the helm.

Sometimes, if the weather was too harsh, or if Joe simply didn't have time for a full sunup-to-sundown escapade, he and that day's fishing party would troll San Francisco Bay. Over the years he'd explored all the best fishing spots, and by now he knew what species would be running and when. From Suisun Slough up in the tidal estuaries of San Pablo Bay to Paradise Beach near his old digs in Tiburon, down to Candlestick Point, Joe knew where to find them. He had a trout season, a bass season, an albacore season, and—most important—a salmon season. Joe got an almost existential thrill wrestling just about any kind of fish into his boat, but he had a special relationship with salmon.

Salmon fascinated him, for a number of reasons. First, they were smart. They weren't easily fooled. Even when they were running, they often were too wary to bite a hook. But when they did bite, they were particularly energetic once they were on the line. They were a challenge to work back to the boat, and they gave Joe a peculiar sense of accomplishment when he swept one up into the net and hauled it over the gunwale. For many sport fishermen, the fascination and challenge ended there, but Joe was no ordinary fish wrangler. To Joe, salmon embodied much more than a victory of man over beast. Each deep-sea encounter served as a reminder of earlier times when hunger was an everyday specter. For years, he displayed a popular quote on his office wall, a framed aphorism that read, "Give a man a fish, he eats for a day. Teach a man to fish and he eats for a lifetime."

For Joe Koret, no words were ever truer.

When Joe bought his first oceangoing vessel, the world of salmon opened up to him. The Northern California coastline just outside the Golden Gate was a prime salmon-fishing area, and Joe quickly learned that if he headed north after venturing out past the bridge he would find more fish than he could dream of. He particularly liked the waters south of Bolinas, although he could almost always count on Duxbury Reef near Point Reyes. If the season was right, salmon would swim in through the Golden Gate and head up to Raccoon Strait, between Tiburon and Angel Island, on their way to their spawning grounds in the upper reaches of the bay.

For Joe, fishing was not a solitary pursuit. He enjoyed inviting his friends along for the experience, but only if they really wanted to work. Fishing with Joe Koret was an all-day exercise of grueling stamina and willpower. Anyone who expected a pleasure cruise with pink champagne and finger sandwiches was on the wrong boat. It was an endurance mission that began at seven o'clock sharp and some-times ended only when there wasn't a sliver of light in the western sky. Joe welcomed almost anybody on board at least once, but whether they ever came back a second time generally was a mutual decision. Those who were considered too nonchalant or too lazy were summarily checked off the list, as were those who became seasick or overly fearful for their safety.

Using the above criteria to cull the herd, Joe and Bob developed a list of loyal regulars who could always be counted on for their camaraderie and hard work. One of these was Benjamin Kline, a former purchasing officer for the city of San Francisco. Kline had spent twenty years in the newspaper business, including a lengthy stint as the *Chronicle's* City Hall reporter. One Saturday morning just before Thanksgiving in 1968, Kline joined Joe, Bob, and several other friends on board the *Stephanie K,* and they headed out on what was expected to be a typically challenging fishing expedition. After exploring several trusted spots with no real luck, they ventured up the coast to Muir Beach, a little over sixteen miles north of the bridge on the Marin shoreline. There, the party found the salmon ready and waiting, and they settled in for the day.

The fishermen had already landed several large specimens when Kline hooked a particularly spirited salmon. He began working the line and playing the fish in, when he suddenly dropped to one knee, breathing hard and struggling to maintain his balance. He kept working the rod, trying to bring the powerful salmon to the boat, but then buckled face first on the boat deck. Joe and Bob Upright at first thought Kline was just fighting a particularly feisty fish, then figured he had simply given up. Joe rushed to his side and yelled, "Ben—get up. What are you doing?"

But Ben Kline didn't answer, nor did he get up. The seventy-four-year-old retired city worker had suffered a massive heart attack reeling in that salmon and collapsed. Joe and Bob and the other anglers worked feverishly to revive him, but their efforts were too late. Benjamin Kline died on the boat, and he was officially pronounced dead at Letterman General Hospital after a fast but grim boat ride back to San Francisco.[3] Joe was understandably horrified by his friend's death, but managed to find some consolation in the fact that Kline had passed away pursuing what he considered one of life's great pastimes.

FOR ALL HIS LOVE OF SALMON AND THE OPEN ocean, Joe's biggest catch ever was the one-hundred-pound sturgeon he reeled in while trolling the waters in Richardson Bay. An urban estuary now under the protection of a Joint Powers Agency of four Northern California cities, Richardson Bay is located just a stone's throw from Raccoon Strait near Tiburon. Even today, it's considered one of the most pristine estuaries on the Pacific Coast.[4] It also was right around the point from the old Koret home at Paradise Cove, which had been subdivided into the upscale Seafirth Estates years before. Joe knew the water there was teeming with fish, and when sturgeon were in season he often would motor around the point from his berth in Sausalito and cast his line.

"One spring day they hooked this huge fish that began fighting the boat," recalls Paul Bernstein, Bob Upright's son-in-law.

> It was a forty-two-foot boat, but this sturgeon began towing it backwards. They took turns playing the fish because they were three old guys, and it was hard work. It took them a few hours to get the fish up alongside the boat, where they gaffed it. Then all of a sudden there were four weary creatures on the deck of that boat: the three men, exhausted from the struggle, and the fish. They kept it, of course. They smoked it.

As Joe grew older, he entrusted more and more of the day-to-day Koracorp operations to his department heads. This freed up even more time to spend out on the water. What began as a Saturday hobby evolved into a two- and, eventually, three-day-a-week compulsion. He became so preoccupied with fishing that it haunted him day and night. He obsessed about salmon at home and in the office, and studied the ocean currents and bird patterns and wave ripples so he could determine where they might be lurking. Joe served as "spotter" and would guide Bob Upright, who almost always was at the wheel, where to go.

"They all had their assigned positions on the fishing boat," recalls Ken Moline, who in the late 1970s served as chief financial officer of Terok Properties, Joe's real estate investment firm. "Mr. Koret had his spot, and the other guys had their spots. These guys were serious fishermen. If you were going to go you'd better be on that boat by seven. If you were five minutes late they would take off without you. And if you did go, you needed to plan to be out virtually all day."

Moline never accompanied the aging die-hards on these excursions, partly because he wasn't into fishing, but mostly because he didn't want to endure the punishing rigors that a Koret fishing expedition entailed. "They would go way, way out, well past the bridge, but Mr. Koret never told anyone where his fishing spots were," he says. "He had certain places he liked, and they were a secret. The other guys could not invite anyone else to go without first clearing it through him."

Even when Joe was out on the water, he didn't leave the office far behind. He always had a cigar in his mouth, and as the boat pounded outward in pursuit of his prized salmon he would sit and ruminate about yesterday's work events. Even though Koracorp was operating efficiently without him, he still spent four days a week in the office, and when he arrived at the fishing grounds and began casting his line, work wasn't far away. "This was a perfect way for him to concentrate," says his second wife, Susan Koret, whom he married in 1980. Joe had hired her as a fulltime home caregiver for Stephanie in 1976 (See Chapter 12), and over the ensuing years she came to know him better than anyone in his close circle of family and friends. "Catch a fish, think about business. Catch a fish, think about business. These were the two things that totally occupied his mind." No matter who was aboard on any particular day, Joe would always find time to sit by himself, smoke his cigar, and think.

"It was a good place to concentrate on other things," Susan says. "When he was fishing the line would be out, and when fish finally found it Joe would know. His mind was always working, working, working."

THOSE LONG, SEAFARING OUTINGS INFLICTED considerable wear and tear on the old boat's engine and other moving parts. The rough-and-tumble thrashing of the waves and the cruel salt air took their toll, and every few months the vessel had to go into dry dock to be fixed. "We dreaded those times," Ken Moline remembers. "If Mr. Koret couldn't go out he would come in to the office five days a week and drive everyone nuts. He literally was on the go all the time, while what he really wanted was to be out on the water with a fishing rod. After a while we finally convinced him he could afford to buy a new boat."

Joe conducted an exhaustive search and eventually found a new forty-two-foot Grand Banks cruiser with twin diesel engines that was equipped to accommodate eight overnight guests, which he named for his second wife. Since Joe's seafaring ventures never included sleepovers, he had no use for fancy berths and luxurious accoutrements, so he had all the custom fittings torn out. In their place, he installed professional cutting tables on which to carve up the day's catch, and lockers in which to store it all. According to the original bill of sale, the *Susan K* was docked in berth 408 at the Clipper Yacht Harbor in Sausalito.

Most of the intrepid fishermen who ventured out with Joe were male friends and acquaintances, but occasionally a woman would be invited aboard. One of these was Bob Upright's daughter Arlene, who grew up around Joe and Stephanie and was treated like the daughter they never had. As a young girl, she would explore the rocks along the shoreline of the Koret estate at Paradise Cove, and when she grew older she was permitted to go out on the boat—as long as she didn't get in the way. Occasionally, her father would put a rod in her hand, but most of the time she chose to watch from an inconspicuous corner of the boat. A self-described tomboy, Arlene never got seasick and always enjoyed the excitement of a Koret sea hunt. "Uncle Joe" was especially entertaining to watch, even though he often was so preoccupied with his rod and reel that he would forget she was on board.

Some years later, when Arlene fell in love with her future husband, Paul, he inevitably was invited to accompany Joe and his pals on one of their excursions. The trip was one part fishing expedition and one part test: any man who was likely to become part of Joe's extended family—which encompasses all of Bob Upright's world—had to prove his mettle. And his seaworthiness.

Since Arlene had already endured a number of these breathtaking experiences, she knew what her young beau was getting himself into. In fact, she personally asked Joe if she could accompany them, a gesture of genuine adoration that Paul had yet to comprehend. In his mind, Joe was simply the best friend of the man who would become his father-in-law—two kind gentlemen who shared a maniacal love of fishing. The two old chums were now in their sixties and showing signs of slowing down, so what kind of trouble could they possibly get into?

On the appointed Saturday, Paul and Arlene arrived at the dock in Sausalito right on time. They helped load the mounds of gear onto the *Stephanie K*, and Paul was anticipating a relaxing day on the water. As soon as everything was properly stowed, Bob Upright started the engine and nudged the boat out of its slip. He was at the wheel that day, and wanted to show a thing or two about navigation to this young man who had struck his daughter's fancy. The old boat began churning through the ragged waters of San Francisco Bay and eventually made its way under the Golden Gate Bridge. The water was especially rough that day, and the boat was bucking up and down like a bull rider at the state fair. Joe paid neither the seas nor the weather any mind as he directed Bob to his favorite fishing spots, one after the other. None of them seemed encouraging, so they kept pushing on.

Eventually, they encountered a run of salmon near Duxbury Reef, where they hauled out the rods and settled in for the day. For the next six hours, they would cast and reel, cast and reel. There was a quick break for a power lunch, and then the lines were back in the water. Paul masterfully held his own and reeled in a couple of fish, only to watch them get whisked off to the cutting tables down below.

As the sun began to slide toward the horizon, Joe reluctantly called it quits. The coolers were stuffed and they were at risk of running afoul of the fish-and-game warden. The thick marine layer was beginning to fold in on the shoreline, and Bob Upright started the engine just as visibility was reduced to less than zero. Somewhere off in the distance, breakers could be heard crashing on the rocks, and the heavy curtain of fog landed with a resounding thud. Bob was an exceptional captain and could pilot a boat in almost any kind of weather, but that afternoon he couldn't even see past the windshield. Nor did he have any experience with the boat's electronic gear; he'd never had to use it before. So much for showing his future son-in-law a thing or two about nautical navigation.

"We almost didn't make it back," Paul Bernstein recalls a half-century later. "We were enveloped by this thick fog, and Bob had no idea how to work the electronics. We got back to shore by zigzagging, listening to the waves on the rocks, not by using the sonar."

The fact was, while Bob Upright was Joe's fishing buddy, many of these rough weather expeditions terrified him. "Joe is crazy," Bob would tell anyone who might listen. "He'll go out in any kind of weather, and one of these days that boat is going to capsize." Skilled sailor that he was, Bob knew his limitations, and eventually he told Joe that he couldn't drive the boat under those conditions anymore. He hoped that might cause Joe to rethink some of these more dangerous voyages, but instead Joe simply hired a licensed skipper and went out anyway.

"No matter how bad the weather was, he would still go out," Susan Koret recalls. "I felt so sorry for Bob because he had no choice."

IT MAY SEEM LIKE A FINE DISTINCTION, BUT JOE and his friends were meat fisherman, not sport fishermen. Their fanatical zeal came from imagining all those fish they would bring home and stuff into their freezers. No such thing as catch-and-release or stuffed trophies on the wall for these seafaring anglers.

"I shouldn't say this, but they frequently disobeyed the wildlife rules," Paul Bernstein remembers. "They kept undersized fish instead of throwing them back. They cooked them right there on the boat and threw the bones overboard so when they got back to shore there wouldn't be a trace. One day, my father joined us and we were out there catching these undersized salmon, which by law you must throw back. There's a huge fine if you don't. Joe and Bob and the others kept running around with these small fish as they caught them, and my father asked me, 'Where are they going with all those little ones?' Turns out they were hiding them in the shower. When we got back to shore they left them there, then came back after dark to get them."

For all his passion for fishing, Joe was intelligent enough to know that on really dismal days he shouldn't venture out on the rolling ocean. Instead, he would drive the short distance down to the Coast Guard pier, near the Golden Gate Bridge. Problem was, by now all fishing at that spot was strictly forbidden, and there were big signs everywhere warning: "U.S. Government Property—No Fishing."

One day, Paul Bernstein accompanied Joe and his buddies to the pier anyway, and they cast their lines within clear view of those signs. Paul edged over to Joe and cautiously asked him, "Do you have permission to be here?"

"I don't need permission," Joe replied.

"We really shouldn't be doing this—"

"Relax," Joe said, trying to reassure him. "It's actually not a problem. Every few years, I learn the name of the new captain stationed here. I find out his wife's dress size, and then I show up on their doorstep with a box of clothes. It's worked for every captain so far."

AT THE END OF EVERY FISHING EXPEDITION, JOE and his friends would divide up that day's catch and take their shares home. Most of them would slice it into thick steaks, which they would either grill that night or freeze for a future date. Whatever was left over often would be given away to any willing takers who desired a chunk of fresh salmon.

Not Joe. While he definitely enjoyed a salmon fillet, he particularly savored it when it was properly smoked. In the early years, he paid someone to smoke them, but soon figured he could save a few dollars if he bought his own equipment and smoked them himself.

"Uncle Joe smoked just about all the salmon he caught," says Arlene Bernstein. "He enjoyed it so much that he would buy the latest smoker each year and try it out. Some of them would work better than others, and each one would create an entirely different taste. In the early days, he did most of his smoking outdoors, but when they moved into the new house they built in Sea Cliff he relocated the smokers indoors."

As Joe quickly learned, there are several ways to smoke fish, each of which produces a different taste and texture. Most salmon is "cold smoked," employing a temperature that hovers right around 100°F. The process requires the use of aromatic wood chips—usually a variety of oak—that is burned in such a way as to produce a large amount of smoke while keeping the heat low enough to as not to actually cook the meat. By contrast, "hot smoking" is intended to actually cook the salmon, which tends to make it drier and somewhat less tender. This process also requires a sufficient amount of brine and periodic drying of the skin to remove globs of unsightly "ooze" as it heats. Joe preferred the "cold smoked" method, and often visitors to the Koret house were greeted not only with a welcoming smile, but also with the aroma of salmon being smoked in the basement.

"No one could smoke lox like Joe," says Merv Brown, who for years oversaw Koret of California's advertising and promotion department. "The Korets had the only house I knew where there were freezers lined up to put it in. No one ever knew what his formula was, but we loved having him over for dinner, because he'd always bring a package of lox."

IN THE LAST YEARS OF HIS LIFE, JOE BEGAN TO suffer periodic health issues that would slow down almost any man. Most of his friends thought this would curtail his fishing activities, or at least dampen them more than the fog and rain ever might achieve. Joe was tenacious and obstinate to a fault, however, and he stubbornly refused to let anything or anyone get in the way of his lifelong passion. Even his doctors couldn't deter him from his quest. As Susan Koret affectionately recounts, "He was a very determined guy and didn't listen to anyone. He had a female doctor who had been Stephanie's doctor for a long, long time. She was afraid Joe would catch pneumonia from all this fishing. He actually did go in and out of the hospital a few times, and more than once the doctor gave him clear instructions not to go fishing until he was completely well."

Susan gently but repeatedly reminded him that cold weather could make him very sick, but he refused to pay attention. One day, he forgot to go to a scheduled doctor's appointment, and Susan found him putting on his fishing boots and clothes.

"What do you think you're doing?" she demanded.

"I'm going fishing," he replied with a shrug.

"Oh my God—do you remember what the doctor said?" she pressed him.

"Forget the doctor," he told her. "The fish are biting."

Ignoring the words of perhaps the two most important women in his life—his wife and his doctor—he threw his fishing gear into his car and asked Susan if she wanted to go with him. Fearing for his health, she jumped in and accompanied him down to the pier—but not without first calling the doctor.

"That's it. I quit," she told Susan. "Joe can find himself someone else not to listen to."

That day was particularly cold and windy. A "pineapple express" storm was battering the Pacific Coast, and the only fish that were biting were small perch that Joe ended up throwing back. "My hair was wet and dripping, but he just stood there, casting his line out and reeling them in," Susan recalls. "Over and over and over again. I watched him, shaking my head at his stubbornness. I ended up talking to the swans that were swimming around. 'Do you understand what's going on here?' I asked them. 'This man is crazy.'"

JOE'S ADDICTION CARRIED WELL OUTSIDE THE country. In the 1950s and sixties, he and Stephanie often flew down to Mexico, where he would charter a boat and spend a day in the sun. He'd smoke his cigar, cast his line, and think about business. Cast and think. Stephanie accompanied him as far as the dock, but she never ventured out on the water with him. The only thing she liked less than fishing was boating, and the confluence of the two events was enough to make her physically ill. In the latter years of Joe's life, Susan joined him on these expeditions south of the border and would join him on whatever deep sea vessel her new husband chartered.

Not even the occasional ocean cruise could dampen Joe's obsession. As Stephanie's mental health issues became noticeably worse, Joe occasionally took her on a European cruise, often with an entourage of Koret compadres and household help. These seafaring journeys were easier for everyone involved because, rather than hopping around from one hotel to the next, they could remain in comfort on the boat during the entire trip. Stephanie was confined to a wheelchair, and the ship's dining room was right down the hallway from the luxurious suite Joe would book. A beautiful promenade area offered panoramic vistas of the ocean or whatever port they were in, and Joe would spend hours slowly pushing her chair around the deck. When they ventured ashore, he would personally guide her wherever they went, and when they were sailing on to the next city he would stand at the rail and inhale the salt spray into his lungs.

Even though these vessels were considerably larger than his own refitted cabin cruiser, they provided him the same sense of independence and freedom he always felt when he was out on the open ocean. The only thing missing was a fishing rod and reel, and some bait.

That gave him an idea. The ocean was the ocean, no matter where on the planet you happened to be. The water temperature might be a little cooler or warmer, but beneath the surface, the sea was packed with fish. Not necessarily the same kind of fish that ran in the waters outside the Golden Gate, but they were fish nonetheless. Dropping a line off the back of a cruise ship was not much different from casting a hook off his own boat back home. All he needed was a rod long enough to extend out over the passenger decks below. And a slightly longer line, since the distance to the water from the lido deck was a bit greater.

From the moment this revelation struck, whenever Joe went on a cruise he always packed a collapsible rod and reel in his luggage. Bait shrimp were readily available from the shipboard buffet, sans the ice and cocktail sauce. Once the ship rumbled out of port, he would approach the captain and politely seek permission to cast his line off the stern.

"He didn't catch a lot of fish on those cruises, but that wasn't the point," Susan Koret observes today, many years later. "The point was there were fish in that ocean, and he had a rod in his hand. That's what made him happy; it's what made him whole."

Susan and Joe Koret, 1980. [Koret private collection]

═══ 12 ═══

Not Your Average Joe

BY THE MID-SEVENTIES, TAD TAUBE WAS AT THE helm of Koracorp, so Joe Koret again felt comfortable pulling back from the company's day-to-day operations.

The *Homemaking with a Flair* disaster was in the past—except for lingering SEC issues—and the Koratron lawsuits had been settled. Taube had begun to purge Koracorp of the nonessential businesses Jere Helfat had gorged on, and the balance sheet was showing more black ink than red. Joe still went to the office four days a week, sitting in on divisional meetings and fulfilling the titular duties of board chairman emeritus. That meant he could go wherever he wanted, offer his opinion on the latest apparel design or dollar plan, and still have plenty of time to go out on his boat.

Joe Koret easily could have hung up a permanent "gone fishing" sign and few people outside the executive suite would have worried. The company was functioning like a well-oiled machine, and the stock price continued to creep upward. But Koracorp was more than just a company founded in a small Sutter Street loft almost forty years before;

it was Joe's entire identity. His name was still on every piece of clothing that was loaded into the distribution trucks and delivered to the four corners of the world. Not only did he have his reputation to protect, but also his pride. In his mind, the name Joe Koret was inseparable from Koracorp; you didn't get one without the other.

Still, his largely empty mornings and afternoons left him with little to do. He occasionally scheduled appointments in his office with civic leaders, other local businessmen, or young entrepreneurs eager to learn his secrets for success. Divisional managers would involve him in critical decisions that affected corporate operations, but day-by-day functions were rightfully delegated to team leaders. Taube's remedial actions gave him comfort that his company was in good hands. Short of being bored, he filled his days any way he could.

One day, his executive assistant went AWOL. She often would slip out during the day to take care of personal errands, but on this particular day she just didn't show up. Joe was at a loss without a gatekeeper to answer the phones and greet people when they arrived, and as the minutes wore on he began to fret over her absence. Eventually, he placed a call to John Carter, an independent CPA who did some accounting work for Terok Properties, his real estate investment firm. Carter's office was located on the fifth floor, and over the past few months the two gentlemen had become fast friends. Once Joe figured out how to make the inter-office phone call. he waited for Carter to pick up.

He didn't. Instead the phone was answered by Carter's own executive assistant who had recently relocated from Los Angeles to San Francisco with her boss. Her name was JoAnne Vente, and she had come to know Joe as a likable but impatient old grump. Deep down, however, she knew he was a pleasant and agreeable gentleman, and she always treated him with the utmost respect.

"Honey, it's Joe," he said to her. "Is John in?"

"Just a moment, Mr. Koret," she replied, and forwarded the call to her boss.

Two minutes later, Carter came out to her desk and explained what was going on. Joe was all alone downstairs in his office suite, and he needed assistance. "Would you mind helping him out for the day?" he asked JoAnne.

"Not at all, sir," she replied. She knew that the relationship between Carter and Joe Koret was one of mutual interdependence, so she gladly did as her boss suggested. "It would be a pleasure."

JoAnne had spoken with Joe on numerous occasions, but rarely more than to say "hello" or exchange small talk during meetings between him and Carter. Nevertheless, she went downstairs and approached Joe's office where, on a normal day, she would have been greeted by the assistant sitting behind the desk. But, as she had been told, that person was not there, so she knocked directly on Joe's door.

"Come in, honey," he told her.

She entered his office and he motioned for her to sit down. She did as he suggested and folded her hands in her lap. "Mr. Carter said you needed a little help today," she said.

"I do," he confessed. "I need some assistance getting things done around here."

"Well, it's a little slow upstairs, so I can help with that," JoAnne told him. "What would you like me to do?"

Joe Koret scratched his head and gave this a few seconds' thought, then said, "Well, honey, I need you to fill the candy bowl."

Joe was known for having a bowl that was always filled with some of the finest chocolates from around the world. JoAnne could see that it was almost empty, so she said, "Yes, Mr. Koret. What else?"

He thought for another moment, then showed her a cupboard that held dozens of cartons of cigarettes. "We're getting low on these," he told her.

JoAnne stared at them and at first thought they were candy cigarettes. But she knew Joe Koret better than that; they were the real deal. "You want me to buy cigarettes?" she asked him.

"Yes, honey. That's part of the job."

"What kind of cigarettes?"

"All kinds. Every customer who comes in to see me knows I always have his favorite brand. I need you to keep that cabinet full."

Even though the surgeon general had recently warned that cigarettes could be hazardous to one's health, smoking was still acceptable office protocol. It was common for employees to have a cigarette wedged between their fingers while typing a memo, or for desktop ashtrays to be mounded with ashes and butts.

"Yes, sir," she said, thinking this was easy. "Anything else?"

"I need you to answer the phone and screen my calls. And I need you to get to work before I do."

"Yes, sir," she said again.

None of this seemed too difficult and, since Joe's regular assistant continued her AWOL status, JoAnne showed up early the next day and went directly to Joe's suite. On Tuesday, he arrived at eight-thirty, but on Wednesday, he didn't show until ten. She made sure to beat him in, and that the candy bowl and cigarette cupboard were filled. She answered the phone, and during "down time" the two of them would chat. On Wednesday morning, not long after he settled into his chair, he thumped his desk and summoned her into his office. He waved her into the same chair, and she again sat with her hands folded in her lap.

After a long silence, she asked him, "What is it, Mr. Koret?"

"Honey?" he finally said. "Why aren't you my full-time assistant?"

"Well, *honey*," she replied, not quite holding back on the sarcasm. "You never asked me to be your assistant."

"I'm serious," he told her. "I want you to work for me."

JoAnne studied him and said, "I've been working with Mr. Carter for nine years. I'll have to think about this."

"I'll work it out with John," Joe told her, and he did.

The next day when she reported to work, she again went to Joe's office and assumed her new responsibilities as his full-time assistant.

JoAnne was smart and a quick study, and felt a natural ease when she was around her new boss. She soon learned that one of her new job requirements was to take him out to lunch every day, usually to one of his favorite neighborhood haunts. Joe particularly liked Chinese food, and this being San Francisco, he had a reasonable selection of choices within a five-block radius. He preferred inexpensive joints with paper plates and faded pictures of fried rice and egg foo yung taped to the wall. Fine dining was not his style, unless he absolutely had to entertain a high-end client.

The first day, JoAnne ate lunch with Joe they chatted over plates of sweet-and-sour chicken and chow mein. At the end of the meal, the waitress cleared their plates and brought the check, and they continued to chat. Five, ten, fifteen minutes passed, and Joe made no motion to leave. She was taking her cues from him, so she made no move to go, either.

Finally, Joe said, "Honey, pay the bill."

She stared at him and said, "Mr. Koret, I don't have any money with me."

He did a double take, as if this were the most ludicrous thing he'd ever heard. Then he replied, "What do you mean, you don't have any money?"

"I only have a couple dollars," she confessed.

Dumbfounded, he opened his wallet and handed her five twenties. "Don't you *ever* let me catch you with less than a hundred dollars in your pocket," he admonished her. "You always pay for all the meals."

"Of course," she said.

Once lunch was finished, Joe enjoyed meandering around the neighborhood to let his food settle. Since there wasn't much back at the office that needed his immediate attention, he liked to take his time. He and JoAnne would stroll down the street to Walgreens, where he bought sweets and canned goods, for which he would usually produce a coupon that he'd clipped from Sunday's *Chronicle*. But from that first lunch onward, JoAnne always paid for every bag of candy, every can of beans, every pack of cigarettes. It was always paper money—never a credit card—and she was always reimbursed. It was her job to make sure that Joe Koret never was seen in public paying for *anything*.

After leaving Walgreens, they would walk back to 611 Mission Street, window-shopping as they zigzagged block by block until they eventually arrived back at the office. Then JoAnne would return to her desk, and Joe would stretch out on the couch to take a nap.

FROM THE EARLY DAYS IN THE 1940S WHEN HE formed GEM Realty, Joe always understood the inherent value of real estate. No one was creating any more of it, and the laws of supply and demand dictated that its value could only go up. In his mind, nothing could beat it as a long-term investment, and the family estate at Paradise Cove in Tiburon was a prime example of this philosophy. This investment—facilitated through GEM—yielded a significant profit when the property eventually was sold and subdivided. Although the company had been dissolved in the 1960s after acquiring the assets of Al Koret's menswear business, Joe remained enamored of Bay Area real estate and understood the potential it had for generating serious cash flow.

By the time Joe hired JoAnne Vente as his executive assistant, he already was deeply involved in a second real estate enterprise. This venture was cleverly named "Terok Properties" (*Terok* was *Koret* spelled backward) and was an investment and management company that primarily owned and operated apartment complexes on the San Francisco Peninsula. Many of these were strategically located in Silicon Valley, and Terok invested in the area before it erupted into the high-tech megalopolis it is today. Properties were modestly priced, and the residents who rented Terok's units were average middle-class working men and women.

Just as JoAnne Vente worked for John Carter prior to joining Joe at Koracorp, her husband, Ken Moline, also was employed by his accounting firm. "We had a small office down in San Carlos for some of John's smaller clients, and I would do their accounting work," Ken explained. "Mr. Koret was really big on having someone watch over his properties, and his own CPA—a man named George Turnbull—usually made sure everything was being done correctly. At one point there was a problem with some of the Terok accounting, and Mr. Koret wanted John Carter to provide an overview of the financials. John asked me to go down there and conduct an informal audit."

The audit found some minor accounting inconsistencies, and not long afterward, JoAnne came home one evening and said to him, "Mr. Koret would like you come to the office tomorrow."

"What for?" he asked her. "Is there a problem?"

"He didn't say," JoAnne replied. "But he sounded serious."

Ken knew an invitation from Joe Koret was not optional, so the next day he drove up to 611 Mission Street and sat down in the man's richly paneled office. They chit-chatted a bit, and then Joe said to him, "I'm going to cut right to the chase. I would like to hire you."

Ken Moline had not been expecting this, especially since he didn't think Joe knew much about his background other than he was pursuing his CPA. "I'm very flattered," he said, acutely aware that Joe was accustomed to getting whatever he wanted. "And I appreciate the offer. But I'm not sure if it's the right thing for me at this time."

They talked some more, and then Joe said, "I'm serious about this, Ken. You do excellent work, and I think you'd be a good fit here. Take a few days to think it over, and then let me know your decision."

Moline did just that. He went back to work in John Carter's satellite office and thought long and hard about Joe's offer. The following week, he was summoned back to Koracorp headquarters and again sat down in Joe's office.

"What do you think?" Joe asked him.

"Well, I'm somewhat interested, but I have to be honest. I'm a bit concerned about your age." Joe had just turned seventy-seven, and

Ken and JoAnne had attended the birthday gathering at his home—complete with a take-home pack of smoked salmon.

Joe could have been upset, but he wasn't. Instead, he nodded and said, "I look at everything in five-year increments, Ken. I have to admit I don't know how long I'll be sitting here in this office. I can't promise you a job forever, but as long as you do the work I think you're capable of, there would be a possibility you would be involved in the Koret Foundation."

The Koret Foundation had been chartered in the 1960s to ensure that the couple's wealth could be used to fund local charitable causes rather than being consumed by federal and state taxes. The legal language made it clear that the foundation would remain inert until either Joe or Stephanie passed away, at which point the decedent's half of the couple's estate would be used for initial funding. At the time Joe and Ken had this conversation in November 1977, Stephanie's passing was only a matter of time, and Joe was all too aware of that eventuality.

As nebulous as Joe's pitch was, Ken ultimately accepted the job offer and went to work for Terok Properties. He quickly learned that, as obsessed as Joe was with fishing, he was equally fixated on his real estate investments. "Once a month we would go on a property tour," Ken recalls. "He had two properties that were his favorites: Lauriedale in Belmont and Valley Green in Cupertino. He loved them, and he loved to visit them. As we drove around looking at these properties, I learned that he was highly suspicious of a lot of people, and didn't know who he could trust."

"Part of your job is to watch over the people who manage my money," Joe told him one day.

Ken gave him a curious look and said, "What do you mean?"

"I've probably had more money stolen from me than I'm worth today," he replied. "So your job is to make sure we keep that loss to a minimum."

"If people are stealing from you, you should get rid of them," Ken said.

Joe lifted his shoulder in a casual shrug and said, "If I have a dollar and someone turns that into three dollars, then slips one into his pocket, I still have double what I had before."

"In his own unique way Mr. Koret could be very political," Ken recalls. "He preferred to be the good guy, so part of my job was to be the bad guy. One day I said to him, 'Mr. Koret, why are you still working? It's not like you need the money.' And he said, "Ken, people only respect me if I'm making money. So every day I'm going to make money. Otherwise they aren't going to respect me."

NEVER DURING HIS FORTY YEARS OF RUNNING the Koret of California enterprise was there any question that Joe was in charge. At five-nine he was a solid man, muscular and well built. Even with employees who were taller than he was, he seemed to tower over them. He commanded attention, and even more important, he expected allegiance. Anyone who worked for Koret of California or any of its divisions also worked for Joe personally. He placed high value on those around him, and he rewarded them with a solid paycheck and a good working environment. But those things were not gifts; they had to be earned.

Patient and inquisitive, Joe wasn't afraid to reveal his temper when he felt he was right and others were being inflexible. As a result, a number of people were intimidated by him, although he never practiced "management through fear." Quite the opposite, in fact. At times of disagreement over a style or a business plan, he would listen attentively, absorbing all sides of the discussion. He asked numerous questions and weighed all responses carefully. He rarely sought to belittle someone for his or her opinion, instead choosing to point out his own rationale for a decision that might be unpopular. He listened to opposing views and always was a consistent, logical thinker. He placed a lot of faith in common sense and, after weighing all sides of an issue, Joe usually prevailed.

"Many people were afraid of Mr. Koret," says JoAnne Vente, who perhaps spent more time with him at the office than anyone during those final years at Koracorp. "He was the boss, so they wouldn't take the time to really sit down and reason with him. They should have, because he was a very wise and prudent man. When his heart didn't get in the way, he followed his gut. He had good intuition; he just wouldn't always use it. He was a very smart man, very creative. He was an honorable, wonderful man."

Joe was well known for his eccentric behavior, and JoAnne, for her part, expected propriety and decorum in the office. Over the six years they worked together, Joe fired her three times and she quit twice. On all five occasions, he was immediately upset by the prospect of losing her, and each time he brought Ken in to serve as arbitrator. Joe trusted him implicitly, as did JoAnne.

During these arbitration meetings, she would sit in her customary chair, while Ken sat next to her and Joe occupied his usual position behind his desk. Termination or resignation, the cause at the time seemed of ultimate importance, although today—forty years after the fact—JoAnne concedes they were petty and insignificant.

"Your wife quit on me," Joe would tell Ken.

"I quit before you could fire me," she would counter.

Joe would raise his hand for silence and say, "Ken, I want to tell you my side. What *really* happened."

She would shake her head and say, "No, you need to hear my side."

Ken would sit there, watching this ping-pong exchange, and hear them out. And after each of these encounters JoAnne remained working at 611 Mission Street.

"Mr. Koret was very loyal, and he demanded loyalty," she recalls. "If he wanted something done, he would be very direct—and very steady. He was a very consistent person, and always fair. Even when he was negotiating a deal, his philosophy always was to leave something for the person on the other side of the table."

Still, Joe was known to midjudge people. Despite his many years in business, and the countless deals he'd struck, he placed a lot of trust in people who might not always have deserved it. He liked to believe that people were as straightforward and honest as he was, and he learned the hard way that sometimes what you see is not what you get. He expected friends and colleagues to believe in him as much as he believed in them, and was deceived more than once. He was generous and forgiving to a fault, but if he discovered someone had betrayed his trust the disappointment was obvious.

"Mr. Koret had a blackboard in his office behind a curtain," JoAnne says.

> He would write on that board who he was going to leave some money to. Occasionally he called me into the office and said, "Honey, erase that name. I want you to write this other name down instead. I really like that person." He would fall in love with someone—not in a romantic way, but in a business sense—and then that person would do something hurtful, and it would kind of crush him. He was kind of a mystery in that way, but the bottom line was, once he trusted you, it was very hard to lose that trust.

While Joe could be firm and impulsive in the office, Stephanie over the years was considered level-headed and fair-minded. Prior to the onset of her dementia, she was perceived as a firm voice of reason within the Koret headquarters, while exhibiting all the grace and style of the fashion queen she was. Like Mary Tyler Moore, she could light a room up with her smile, and she genuinely cared for everyone she touched—and those who touched her.

"When I was a young girl I hung out with Stephy," recalls Arlene Bernstein, Robert Upright's daughter:

Joe didn't have much use for little kids who got in the way, although I did end up going fishing with him. But I spent more time with Stephy. When I went to college she was thrilled to outfit me. I was their walking advertisement. This was the early sixties when the company was becoming more traditional. So some of the clothes worked for me, and some didn't. Stephy ran the house and Joe really liked having her in charge at home, although when she got sick and wasn't able to do it anymore he took over that role, too.

Susan Behr, Joe's grand-niece (her grandmother was Stephanie's sister Anne), has similar memories. "I often was invited to Mission Street where they worked," she says:

I was allowed up into that office, where she would be sitting behind her desk. She would come out and hug me. That's how she was: warm, loving, and always hugging. I would sit there and watch her sketch, and she would show me all the clothes hanging there—garments she was working on. She always had a hat on, and when she took me out to lunch we always wore gloves. Her hair was perfect, and she always wore a skirt. She had a dressing room in her home that seemed as big as my entire house. Everything was arranged perfectly, and I got to go in there and play. She tried to teach me the right way to do things. She taught me how to sit at a table properly and how to use a fork, knife, and spoon. She was an elegant woman, but she also was a very real, delightful person. She loved Elvis Presley, and she taught me all about music.

"As a child I was drawn to her because everyone was always moving around the room, but Stephanie had a chair," adds Ron Brown, Merv Brown's son. "It was almost like a throne. One day she was smoking a cigarette, and the ash kept getting longer and longer, and I just wanted to run over and flick it into an ashtray. But I couldn't because she was so elegant."

Stephanie considered a cigarette in her hand a valuable fashion statement, and she frequently lit up at a party or in her office. At the same time, she was extremely conscious of her weight, and as a petite size 2 she became fixated on keeping her waistline trim. *Beyond trim.* "She starved herself to stay thin, always very concerned about her figure," recalls Arlene Bernstein. "She drank those Metrecal diet drinks that were popular in the 1960s. I remember my mother saying Stephy had gotten really thin and was trying too hard to diet. She became obsessed with being thin."

Much to Stephanie's dismay, in the mid-1960s Koret of California launched the Stephanie K brand which, in addition to being the name of Joe's boat, was a line of clothing designed to fit larger-sized women. The new label was created to attract women who were beginning to shop at Lane Bryant, and Joe didn't want to give up that segment of potential customers without a fight. A size two for most of her life, Stephanie was persistent about maintaining a healthy diet and a lean figure. Over the years she'd made it clear that everything she created in her design studio was done so with her own sense of style and fit in mind, and she believed the "active sportswear" look was synonymous with the Koret of California brand. She found the notion of "large size" sportswear almost oxymoronic, and was vocal about her displeasure with the concept. Joe believed the new line would serve a lucrative and growing consumer segment, however, and after vociferous debate both in the executive suite and at home, the division was approved.

"We needed a large-size division because that's what was happening in America, and in the fashion business," says Merv Brown. "It was a successful division, but Stephanie was less than thrilled. She went along with it, but she didn't like it."

For all her proper style and fashion sense, Stephanie also had what might be considered an eccentric side. While she and Joe could afford almost anything they desired, most of Stephanie's bracelets and necklaces were of the inexpensive costume variety. The only valuable piece she owned was a diamond ring Joe had given her many years after they had become engaged, when he finally could afford it. Although she wore the ring every day, she regarded it as any other bauble on her hand. She also kept a parrot in her office. The bird's name is lost to history, but it lived on a stand in her fifth-floor suite. The parrot had free rein of the space, and often it would perch on her shoulder while she conducted design meetings. Stephanie would sit with her elbow propped on the design table, placing her hand at shoulder height, and while she spoke the parrot would peck at the diamond, sharpening its beak.

"We were always afraid the parrot would pluck that diamond right out of the ring," says Joyce Brown, Merv Brown's wife.

AFTER STEPHANIE RETIRED AND HER HEALTH continued to worsen, Joe found his life increasingly disrupted and disorganized. He had been a businessman ever since he hawked used newspapers on the streets of New York as a young boy, so staying home to care for a wife who barely recognized him was a major shift in his daily routine. He looked after Stephanie every morning before going to work, and he spent hours with her every evening, holding hands and talking to her. Sometimes he would even try to feed her, but those attempts usually were met with frustration and soiled clothing. Even though he had full-time household help, he realized he couldn't do it alone, and that's how he often felt: alone.

By 1975, Stephanie was in such ill health that Joe made the decision to add an additional employee to the Koret household staff. Stephanie had become a 'round-the-clock labor of love, and while many families today would have placed her in a care facility, Joe refused to do that. They had recently celebrated their fiftieth wedding anniversary, and she was his wife for better or for worse. She was part of his home, and at home she would stay.

Still, he needed help. So did Pausan, the Singaporean housekeeper/cook/nurse who had been a longtime employee of the Koret household.

After considerable debate and introspection, Joe made the decision to hire an additional caregiver who was willing to do everything and wasn't afraid to do anything.

WHILE JOE WAS STRUGGLING WITH THIS ISSUE, just a few miles across the bay in Oakland, a young Korean widow named Susan McClain was struggling with her own difficult decisions. She had moved to the United States with her American husband just a year before, and a few months after arriving in the Bay Area he died following a long and debilitating illness. Susan had never contemplated living in America, even when her closest girlfriends from childhood had announced their intentions to find a way to do so. When her new husband told her they would be moving to the United States, she balked at the idea; Korea was her home and her entire family lived there. She had no friends or family in America, and because her husband spoke Korean, she barely knew a word of English.

During the state of limbo that followed her husband's death, Susan returned to Korea several times, weighing whether she should remain in her native land or return to the States. She enjoyed both countries but truly felt at home in neither, and the inner conflict became a dilemma that gnawed at her through many sleepless nights. She had grown up in a traditional Korean family that held strongly to the belief that a woman's role was to love, obey, and respect her husband. Her father had died when she was very young, and her mother adhered to a strict code of social mores. She had not approved of her daughter's marriage to an American, and had rolled out the red carpet when Susan returned to Korea following his death.

Susan eventually chose to return to the Unites States, determined to make a new life for herself in a country where so many others had found opportunity. She moved in with a friend in Oakland and began to map out her next moves. She'd attended college classes in Korea but, by her own admission, was not the studious type. She was smart, she was adventurous, and she was brave. But she was practically alone in a country that, more than two decades after the conflict that separated Korea at the 38th parallel, remained largely uninformed about her homeland and its people. As a widowed housewife who had been raised to cater to her husband's needs, she had few marketable skills, but her upbringing had instilled in her a strong work ethic and an inestimable personal drive.

While crashing at her friend's small apartment, Susan devised a two-pronged plan: she would learn English, and she would find a job that would sustain her until she made enough progress to establish some solid career goals. The immediate problem, she realized, was finding a workplace where she could earn a living wage without speaking the language. Prone to looking at all sides of an issue before determining a course of action, Susan spent many hours discussing this predicament with her roommate.

One day the roommate said, "You need to go to the Korean Consulate."

"The consulate? What can they do?"

"Do you think you're the only Korean in America who has this problem? They might help you figure out what to do."

"I know what I need to do," Susan said. "I need to learn English."

"Go to the consulate."

"And I need a job."

"So go to the consulate."

Eventually, Susan decided to follow her friend's advice, and paid a visit to the Korean Consulate on Clay Street in San Francisco. There, she discovered that her roommate was right; the people who worked there dealt with this sort of challenge all the time, and they were prepared to help. A supportive employee sat down with her and inquired about her situation.

Susan explained how she had come to be alone in the United States. Although her husband had died, she had received her residency status, so she could work in the States legally. It was her English and job skills—or lack thereof—that could be problematic.

"Your situation really is not much different from a lot of other Koreans in the area," the consulate worker said, confirming what Susan's roommate had told her. "A lot of students come here to learn English."

"I'm not a student," Susan reminded him. "And I don't learn things the 'student' way."

As a Korean, he understood what she was talking about, but remained encouraging. "Some people end up finding work in restaurants or as companions for the elderly and sick. If you're willing to work hard you can learn English quite fast."

"These restaurants or elderly places—do the employees there speak Korean?"

The consulate worker shook his head. "Not as a rule," he said. "You need to speak English."

"But I don't speak English—"

"You will, and you'll learn it fast. Then you can go to a formal school."

Susan listened to what he was telling her. If she were going to remain in the United States, this would be just about the only route open for her. She weighed the pros and cons, and as the notion began to sink in, she realized she could make it work. She also realized she preferred the idea of being a home companion over a kitchen worker in a smelly restaurant downtown.

"I think I'd like to work with sick people," she finally told him. "What do I do next?"

As fate would have it, the consulate had just been contacted by an elderly retired gentleman who was seeking a caregiver who could look after his ailing wife. The woman was in the advanced stages of dementia, and while she was not yet completely infirm, she required constant assistance and companionship. The successful job applicant would bathe her and help her get dressed, provide light nursing duties, and help feed her. The household already had a full-time housekeeper and cook, but that person was unable to tend to all of the sick woman's needs in addition to a full slate of household responsibilities.

Generous and giving to a fault, Susan believed the position was just what she was looking for to jump-start her life in America. It provided the living wage she needed, and it would force her to learn the rudiments of English that she would need for her future language studies. If the elderly gentleman wished to hire her, she was eager to get started.

The consulate worker arranged a meeting between Joe Koret and Susan McClain. Joe had long respected the Asian work ethic that he'd witnessed in his clothing factories, so she already had a strong check mark in the "yes" column. She was polite, confident, shy, and possessed an air of grace that belied her genuine modesty. Additionally, she was quite a beauty, with unblemished alabaster skin framed by dark hair that fell to her shoulders. She easily could have passed for a former Miss Korea, and in Joe's eyes she was just as much a work of art as the Asian sculptures and paintings he'd begun displaying throughout his house.

Susan said very little—and understood even less—during that first meeting. She knew only a few dozen English words, and used them sparingly but intelligently. Joe asked her a lot of questions, and through an interpreter he determined she was honest, candid, and dependable. She had nothing to hide and she genuinely wanted to help this retired man and his ailing wife. Without giving it much deliberation, he told her the job was hers, if she wanted it.

She did.

Several days later, she moved into the Koret house in Sea Cliff Estates. It was a postmodern structure Joe had built on the vacant lot in front of the home he and Stephanie had purchased years before. With a modest view of the Golden Gate Bridge and just a short stroll from Baker Beach, it was an idyllic setting for a live-in caretaker still trying to find her way in America. At that time Pausan took care of the Korets' basic needs, and she set about showing Susan the ropes. Originally from Singapore, Pausan was a proficient cook and equally skilled at maintaining the daily upkeep of the home. Those responsibilities, however, made it difficult for her to also keep a constant eye on Stephanie, so many of those care-giving duties fell to Susan.

"I was more than thirty years old at the time, and Joe was a little worried because I had never worked," Susan recalls. "I had a good idea of what I had to do, and I did whatever they asked me to do: clean the house, do laundry, watch Stephanie. I wanted to work hard, and I was determined to like it. Still, my plan after six months was to leave so I could learn English at a school somewhere in the city."

During those first days in the Koret home, she quickly learned that Joe had no close family of his own. His parents and three brothers had all died years before, and a vast emptiness had set in to his daily routine. "Joe was very lonely," Susan says:

> He always, always cared about Stephanie. He always came home and sat next to her for a while each day. She always knew when it was time for Joe to come home; she would go to the window and would watch for him. Every single day. And when he came in they would sit together and hold hands. On those days he had no tears; he just sat with her and smiled. Until the end he was very good at taking care of her. A lot of men would have just put her in a home, but not Joe. At the very end when she had to go to the hospital I saw him sitting next to her, and he was crying.

The long days tumbled one into the next, like dominoes, and Susan settled into a routine that was both exhausting and engaging. While she still struggled with the language, she possessed a strong intuitive sense about people. She became quite a student of the Korets and the people who came and went, watching and listening and trying to understand what they were saying. She found the differences between her native Korean culture and what she was experiencing on a daily basis both fascinating and challenging. And she was determined to absorb all she could.

One of Joe's favorite pastimes—when he wasn't at the office or out on his boat fishing—was walking his German shepherd, Nico, down to Baker Beach. Beginning near the southern end of Golden Gate Point, this long stretch of sand extends southward along the serpentine coastline near where the Sutro Baths once stood. On most summer days, the area is engulfed by the customary marine fog, but in the winter, when a storm isn't blustering in from the ocean, the beach is a clear and pristine urban hideaway.

While Joe greatly appreciated his solitude, he was a social creature and often appreciated human company on his regular walks down to the beach. Sometimes, these excursions would involve a friend or a member of Stephanie's family, but on most occasions, he would ask either Pausan or Susan to accompany him. Susan didn't understand why he would want her along, since she barely comprehended anything he was telling her, and thus she rarely said a word. But Joe was her employer, he was a very cordial gentleman, and she enjoyed the dog. So when he asked her to go for a walk she did, as long as Stephanie didn't need anything.

One morning, they set out up the street on the way to the access trail that led down to the sand. As usual, Joe was talking and Susan was trying to keep up with what he was saying, deciphering the few words she understood. It was a casual stroll, with the dog sniffing the shrubs and trees at the edge of the sidewalk. Joe was telling Susan about his recent visit to the doctor, who was concerned for his health as well that of as his ailing wife.

"She told me Stephy is getting worse," Joe explained to her patiently, speaking slowly so she could pick up a few familiar words. "She's not going to live much longer."

Susan nodded but said nothing, indicating that she grasped what Joe was telling her. She didn't, not at the time, but she wanted to appear polite and respectful.

"She told me it won't be long," Joe continued.

Again, Susan nodded.

"Stephy is going to require a lot more help than I can provide," Joe went on.

A light clicked on in Susan's brain: now she understood what this man was telling her. His wife's condition was worsening, and she—Susan—would have to work longer hours and care for her even more. She felt a sense of triumph in figuring out what her boss was telling her, and she was more than willing to do whatever she could to help.

"Yes, sir," she replied.

"The doctor also told me I need to get a new life," Joe explained. "Even while Stephy is still with us."

Now, Susan was convinced she knew what Joe was implying. Not only did Stephanie need more assistance, but he was going to be spending more time outside the home. He intended to meet new people and forge a new life that would carry him beyond his wife's eventual passing. That meant he would have even *less* time to comfort Stephanie when he was home, and *that* meant Susan would have to pay *even more* attention to her needs. Her workload was about to get more pressured, which—translated into her immediate world—meant less opportunity to take English classes.

"That makes sense," she said.

Joe had been very casual in sharing these thoughts with her and, because of the language barrier, Susan missed almost every nuance of their lopsided conversation. This young Korean beauty didn't yet possess the vocabulary to grasp what he had tried to tell her, and that night he pondered how he could make her understand his feelings, if not his words.

The next day he asked her to go for another walk. Since this was not an unusual request she agreed, again as soon as she was certain that Stephanie was settled comfortably for the next few hours.

"My doctor says I need to get on with my life," he said, repeating almost word-for-word what he had told her the day before. "I still have a few good years left in me, and it's time for me to look to the future."

Susan understood just enough English—and enough about the male of the species—to get an idea of what he was driving at. He was contemplating life without Stephanie, which meant he was thinking about the prospect of eventually dating other women. His doctor had given him permission to entertain this prospect, and Joe wanted to alert Susan that he might go out on a date or two, even though his wife was still alive. Stephanie no longer recognized anyone when they came to visit, not even Joe, even though out of habit she would wait by the door for him to come home. Her short-term memory had disappeared months, if not years, before, and her long-term recollections were all but gone, as well.

Plain and simple, Joe didn't want Susan to think he was being cruel or callous if he went out with another woman.

"I understand, sir," she said. "Good idea."

She clearly *didn't* understand the full scope of what he was saying, not until he casually took hold of her hand and gave it a gentle squeeze. And didn't let it go.

Oh, my God, she thought as the truth finally hit her.

He said nothing more on the topic for the rest of that walk, but he held on to her hand for a good part of it. He only let go when they approached the house, where someone might be able to see them. Feeling renewed and light on his feet, he led her up the steps to the front door and unlocked the deadbolt.

"Excuse me," Susan told him politely, as she quickly disappeared into the back of the house to check on Stephanie.

As soon as she was gone, Joe sauntered into the ornate living room, decorated with Asian statues and museum-quality artwork, and collapsed on the sofa. For the first time in months, he felt young again. A mighty weight had been lifted from his heart, and he felt all the giddiness of a schoolboy who had just kissed a girl for the first time. He was floating on air, and despite a thread of lingering guilt, he could see a new future on the horizon. Joe still loved Stephanie with all his heart, but the despair that had gripped him as he'd watched her steadily decline over the years was losing its hold.

At the same time, as Susan looked in on her sleeping patient, she thought, *Oh, my God. This is horrible. What am I going to do?*

Forty years later, Susan laughs at the predicament, but at the time she was terrified. Her Asian upbringing had led her to be a dedicated caregiver to Stephanie, and she had been taught to love and respect her elders. But Joe Koret was not Asian, and in Susan's mind he had misread the signs. It was her job to be polite and deferential, to exhibit natural courtesy and a subtle submissiveness that he must have mistaken as feminine availability. Or vulnerability. He was twice her age and suffering a personal heartache, something far greater than she was prepared to deal with.

Fortunately, Susan had a good friend who lived not far away in the city. On her days off, they would often meet for tea or lunch, and the next time she got a chance she hurried over to the woman's apartment. Susan had been afraid to tell her too much on the telephone; there were two phones in the Koret house—a business line and a personal line—but neither of them was very private. Joe could pick up at any time, and even if he wouldn't understand anything she was saying, she couldn't risk him overhearing her.

As soon as Susan arrived at her friend's house she unloaded. "What is that man thinking?" she asked when she was finished with her story.

"It's obvious," the friend replied. "He's trying to make you his girlfriend."

"But . . . that's crazy," Susan said.

"Not really. He may be old, but you're pretty and smart and you're nice to him."

"But . . . I can't. *I'm taking care of his wife!*"

"Don't think about her, not right now," the friend told her.

"How can I not think of her? It's my *job* to think about her! Oh, my God. What am I going to do?"

"Stop overreacting," her friend said. "Take it one day at a time."

"I think I need to leave," Susan said abruptly. "I need to run away."

"You're not a child anymore," her friend told her. "You can't run away."

Susan didn't leave, and she didn't run away. She cared too much for Stephanie to do something that disrespectful. In fact, as shocked and confused as she was, she also cared too much for Joe to just disappear. So she returned to the house and went back to work, intending to go about her job as if nothing had happened.

That night she sat in her room, almost immobile with fear and indecision. When she had come home earlier that afternoon every-one suddenly looked different to her. Stephanie was still the same, but Joe was no longer just her boss. He was a man who definitely had romantic intentions, and she had no idea how to deal with it. Even Pausan, who had an uncanny knack for seeing everything that was going on in the house, looked different.

And looked at her differently.

She tossed and turned and barely got any sleep as she contem-plated her future. *Why me?* she thought. *He's handsome and wealthy, and there are lots of women who would be interested in him. Am I just convenient? What am I going to do?*

The next morning when Susan woke up, she again was convinced she had to quit her job and get out of the house. She needed to just pack up her things and move in temporarily with her friend. But she had not been raised to quit when the going got rough; patience was a Korean virtue, and perseverance was imperative. Indeed, Joe had given her more and more responsibility in taking care of his wife, and Susan had to weigh Stephanie's needs against her own. Other than her friend, she had no one in whom to confide, no one to help her figure this out. Her own mother and sister were an ocean away, so she was in this alone.

She couldn't stay, and she couldn't quit.

Sometimes indecision is the best decision. Susan kept her head down and poured all her energy into her job. She actually enjoyed what she was doing, and she took pride in caring for a woman in her last months of life. It was difficult work, but the emotional rewards far outweighed the downsides. She also tried to look at the entire situation from Joe's point of view. "All he wanted was to be like a normal human being, rather than being alone," she says today. "He didn't really enjoy his life at that point. He couldn't tell people what he felt, but he would always tell me. I didn't understand a fraction of what he was saying, but he told me anyway."

Eventually, Joe got up the nerve to ask her out, and she said "yes." They went to a movie, and he asked her out again. They started going to dinner, and he made no effort to keep their relationship a secret. At that point, Joe still went in to the office three days a week, and he was still active in the business and the community. He didn't seem to care that people knew he was enjoying a night on the town while his wife was home, and Susan learned not to worry what people might think when they saw Joe's hand in hers.

"Joe just wanted someone close," she recalls. "Stephanie had been ill for a long time, and he missed the companionship and communication. He could talk to me, even if I didn't have a clue what he was saying."

What worried her the most was what Stephanie's relatives might think. They still came to visit her on a weekly basis, and Susan was concerned they might view her as a Korean gold digger. Despite what might be going on in their collective heads, however, they were always polite and respectful. "Stephanie's family didn't want to make Joe angry," she explains. "I think they were all expecting something from him, so everybody was nice to me. They knew Joe was entitled to a new life. He was very happy with our relationship, and none of Stephanie's family ever said anything to me at all."

Still, Susan felt racked with guilt. She was living in the house and dating her boss, while his ailing wife was lying downstairs in her own private bedroom, unaware of anything. Not even the creators of *All My Children* could dream up a plot line like that. Despite Susan's initial concerns, their relationship grew closer, and after a while it became increasingly difficult for her to think about walking away. She spent hours wondering if Joe was just "playing" her, but she truly believed—and hoped—he wasn't that type of man. Honest and truthful to a fault, he was falling in love with her.

And, she began to realize, she was falling in love with him.

After selling Koracorp to Levi Strauss & Co. in 1979 Joe opened a high-end
Asian art emporium known as Far East Traders. Though the endeavor was short-lived,
it was his pride and joy. [Bancroft Library collection]

═══ 13 ═══

Wedding Bell Blues

IN THE YEARS BEFORE STEPHANIE BECAME ILL, she and Joe had been enthusiastic global travelers. The hard-working couple would embark on business trips to New York or seek out various locales in Europe, usually to check out manufacturing plants (for him) or fashion shows (for her). They escorted the winners of the company's promotions to Hawaii, and Stephanie accompanied her husband to Baja California when he wanted to try out some warm-water deep-sea fishing.

Eventually, Stephanie's condition grew so dire that she was confined to bed or a wheelchair every hour of the day. This didn't dissuade Joe from treating her like his wife of fifty years, and he often would be seen dining with her in local restaurants. Jet-set flights to Europe or Australia were replaced with slow cruises through the Greek Isles or the Baltic Sea. No matter what Stephanie's condition might be, the Korets always flew or sailed first class, and Joe rarely let his ailing wife out of his sight. Few people outside the family suspected that Susan's role in the Koret household had evolved into a tragicomic romance. As a result, those trips proved extremely awkward—and, at times, embarrassing.

"Every time we took a trip, our relationship would be up and down," Susan remembers. "Our lifestyles were different, and Stephanie was always there. I had to follow Joe's lead, and sometimes I didn't want to do that. While we grew closer and closer, I also learned that when you bring an old person and a young person together in a relationship, it can be very sad. No matter what I did, if he didn't see me he would get jealous. Even on a ship."

On one cruise, Joe became particularly covetous because of all the Italian men who worked as part of the crew. One young man in particular began to show an interest in Susan. He was the ultimate seventies cliché: tall, dark, rugged, with a chiseled chin and hair that was longish in a hunky sort of way. At first, Joe paid him no mind, considering him just an overly attentive steward. But as the days passed and the Italian stallion began to show up at unexpected moments, Joe grew increasingly suspicious. Some of these cruises had earned a reputation for being "love boats" for single women—married, divorced, or widowed—intent on having a sea-borne fling with a Latin lover. As a result, Joe's mind became fixated on wild images of what was going on when Susan was out of his sight.

Because she and Joe stayed in separate quarters and Joe quite obviously was married to the woman in the wheelchair, no one suspected the truth behind this peculiar love triangle. Certainly not the Italian steward, whom Susan remembers as friendly, if not overly focused on her every move. "He didn't know about Joe and me," she recalls. "He would come up to me and ask what I had done the night before, or where I had been. And Joe started wondering why the hell he was always coming around."

When the ship pulled into port, Joe and his entourage typically would disembark and go shopping. On some of these occasions, Susan would elect to remain behind, since she rarely had time off while Stephanie was in her care. By this time, Mrs. Koret was completely unaware of her surroundings and her traveling companions, but Joe wouldn't leave her behind on the ship for anything in the world. He didn't need Susan to push the chair; he was fully capable of doing it himself, or he delegated the task to Pausan. Still, on this particular cruise he hated to leave Susan behind on the ship with the Italian interloper, while he and the others roamed the streets and perused high-end gift shops.

"One day I just didn't want to go shopping, and Joe got really upset," Susan says. "He started thinking, 'Why is she not coming with us?' He demanded to know what was going on, and I told him I really didn't like to go shopping. He was very unhappy and got angry with me, but I just didn't feel like it." Throughout the day Joe's imagination grew more wild and apoplectic. He pictured the Italian man knocking on Susan's stateroom door, maybe asking her if she needed anything, and then slipping inside and making himself comfortable. Pulling off his Italian tie, kicking off his Italian shoes, maybe unbuttoning his Italian shirt . . .

"When Joe came back that afternoon the man showed up again, and Joe thought I had 'gone out' with him," Susan remembers:

> He was furious, but what could he say? His mind was filled with this jealous anger. I thought it was silly, and I eventually was able to convince him I had not "gone out" at all. I told him he was wrong in what he had been thinking. "You're crazy!" I told him. He could see I was telling the truth, and when he realized how foolish he had been he said, "Honey— come to me!" That's how he found out more and more I was not that kind of person, and I learned he was not playing a game with me. He'd run into a lot of deceitful people in his life, and he found I was not that way. Honesty was Number One to both of us. He was very smart, and he was a genuinely nice gentleman—not the crazy, fool-around type. That's how our relationship kept growing.

That cruise served to nurture the budding romance, although Susan still wasn't sure what to make of it. Her primary goal was, and always had been, to learn English. She was doing that, but it was not occurring in the structured and institutional manner she had planned. Plus, she had not anticipated that her lessons would grow into a multicultural love story—and that made her even more nervous. Still, as a popular 1970s aphorism observed, "Life is what happens when you're busy making other plans." When she had visited the Korean Consulate that fateful day more than a year before, she had had no idea that this caretaker job would lead to love.

DURING THE FINAL YEAR OF STEPHANIE'S LIFE, Joe grew less and less involved with the daily management of Koracorp Industries. The company's fortunes were improving every quarter, and Joe's personal holdings in Terok Properties were delivering substantial cash flow. The real estate was appreciating nicely every year, and he was making money without even working at it. That allowed him the freedom to do whatever he wanted—such as spend more time reeling in salmon out beyond the bridge.

As a creature of habit, however, he enjoyed going in to the office three or four days a week, and on many of those days Susan would drive him. It was on one of these morning trips that Joe began to talk about an idea that had building in the back of his mind. He had long had a strong appreciation for Asian art and, in his mind, he'd collected a number of authentic pieces, which were on display in the Koret home. "What if," he proposed, "I create a high-end store where the people of San Francisco can enjoy this wonderful art the way I do?"

On paper, it seemed like a sound financial idea. As a city of art patrons and uber-wealthy families, San Francisco for over a century had honored its Asian heritage. Chinese, Koreans, Japanese, and virtually every other ethnic group from the western edge of the Pacific Rim had made their homes here, and their cultural contributions could be found everywhere. Joe wanted to tap into that artistic and historic influence in a high-end way, and the more he thought about it, the clearer his dream became.

With one of the largest Asian populations in the United States, San Francisco was the ideal market for such a store. Chinatown was littered with outlets that sold jade trinkets and paper lanterns, but those shops mostly targeted the tourist day-trippers in search of inexpensive souvenirs. What Joe had in mind was a "real" Asian trading post, with exquisite art and valuable antiques from all over the Far East.

"I think I'll call it Far East Traders," he announced, and the idea was born.

Joe's first foray into running a retail outlet had come in late 1922, when he'd opened the hosiery stall at the Crystal Palace Market on Market Street. He'd been underwhelmed by the experience, but his venture many years later with the Koret of California remnant store had proven more lucrative. If Far East Traders was going to be a success, it needed just the right location: high traffic and high-end floor space, which translated to "high rent." In San Francisco *that* meant the Union Square area, home to Macy's, City of Paris, and the St. Francis Hotel. Joe and his close confidants scoured the neighborhood, particularly the fashionable Maiden Lane area, which today is home to top-line boutiques and galleries. Hard as they tried, nothing seemed to pop.

"The problem was, Joe didn't want to pay those rents," Ken Moline recalls. "In fact, he didn't want to pay rent at all."

Joe eventually was tipped to the availability of the old Godeau Funeral Parlor, located at the intersection of Van Ness and Market Street. The family that owned and operated the business was selling out and, when Joe first toured the building, the basement was still equipped with embalming tables and vats of fluids. Although the facility was off the beaten path and much farther down Market Street than anyone ever dared venture on foot in those days, it was the right size—and, better yet, the right price. The smell of formaldehyde, glutaraldehyde, methanol, and other solvents had to be scrubbed from the walls, and there was always the specter of some long-dead soul lingering in a dark stairwell. Still, with the vision of an Asian antiques emporium planted firmly in his mind, he bought the place and began transforming it into a true palace of Far East fine art.

Despite the looming concern about "location, location, location"— or, in this case, the lack thereof—Joe set about creating his dream. He hired Charles Chan, who had been manager of the high-end Hastings Department Store in San Francisco, to manage the new venture. He also brought in a crew of designers to give it an authentic Asian flair. Through Chan's contacts. Joe was able to line up merchants in different Asian countries from whom he would acquire his artworks, and he signed a prominent artist to paint a larger-than-life mural on one side of the nearly three-story building. The result was a lovely Japanese woman in a kimono that drew attention from all corners of the intersection.

As the store began to take shape, Stephanie's health continued to worsen, and on February 22, 1978, she died at home. Through all the years of her mental downturn, Joe had refused to place her in a nursing facility, and with two competent and compassionate around-the-clock caregivers to look after her, she had more skilled help than any hospital could have provided. Her decline had been long and worrisome to everyone in the Koret household, and when she did finally take her last breath Joe was heartbroken. The woman he had met in the Crystal Palace Market all those years ago—and who had helped him build one of the largest women's apparel companies in the United States—was gone. Because Stephanie's health had declined slowly for most of the previous decade, Joe had ample time to prepare for her passing, and had even allowed himself to engage in a romantic relationship with Susan. Still, he could not fully anticipate the grief that his wife's absence would bring, and after her entombment at the Gardens of Eternity in Colma he called for a short moratorium on developing Far East Traders.

For decades, Stephanie was the queen bee of the Koret fashion world. "Mrs. K," as she was called by her staff, exhibited an uncanny ability to predict, if not lead, the design trends of the day. She and her creative team regularly experimented with new designs and fabrics, and over the years she was awarded numerous gold medals and blue ribbons at various fashion events and state fairs. Each accolade cemented Koret of California's reputation as the top-of-the-line women's sportswear. Beautiful and stylish, she felt at home whether she was posing for a Hollywood-style publicity "head shot" (above) or enjoying a cup of coffee following a business luncheon (below). [Koret private collection]

A week or two later, Joe was back at it, directing all phases of the store's completion. Striving for authenticity, Joe also proclaimed that all the sales personnel would be Asian. While this decision might run afoul of today's equal-opportunity laws, he was adamant that Far East Traders be genuine in every way. He ran a series of ads in the local newspapers and within short order had filled his staff with attractive women to serve as "curators." Finally, to celebrate the grand opening of his new venture—and to chase away any lingering spirits from the funeral home days—he hired a Chinese firm to light up the sky with a tremendous display of pyrotechnics.

Unfortunately, Joe's fondness for Asian beauty set off some fireworks at home. As he spent more and more time putting the finishing touches on the store, his romantic eye began to roam. "When he started Far East Traders I wanted him to continue being active," Susan says. "We went to Taiwan, Thailand, and Hong Kong and bought all the goods for the store. A lot of it was cheap stuff—reproductions rather than antiques—but he was insistent. We were hiring all these Asian people, and he started to become attracted to some of the lovely Chinese saleswomen he was meeting."

One day Joe did or said something that made Susan furious. "I don't remember what it was, but it seemed significant back then," she recalls:

> He knew what he had done was wrong but he would not apologize, and I simply didn't want to be around him. I decided right then to leave and start my own life. I had always intended to learn English, and I was speaking it a lot better than when I had arrived. Certainly not perfect, but I was able to communicate. So I left, and moved into a condo on Geary Street. I was totally gone from the Koret house. Joe had tremendous pride, and that was okay with me. I was happy to get out and be on my own.

The preparations for the grand opening continued, but Joe's demeanor changed radically. Outwardly, his male pride forced him to appear stoic and indifferent, but inside he was a distraught mess. He missed Susan intensely, but was too stubborn to give her a call. He was worried she might view that as an admission of guilt, or at least fault, and he was too obstinate to let that happen. Despite his loneliness, he convinced himself that if she wanted to come back to him, she would have to make the first move. Besides, he had a new store full of beautiful saleswomen to charm and woo. His doctor had told him to make a new life for himself, and he'd planted a tree that was beginning to bear a lot of low-hanging fruit.

"Joe didn't realize how important I was to him until after I was gone," Susan says. "He thought all Asian women were pretty much the same: young women looking for money, not companionship. When I left him, he learned that money didn't matter to me as long as he was happy. If he was happy without me, I was happy without him."

Susan did her best to move on. As much as she cared for Joe, she convinced herself that leaving him was the best for everyone. The Korean Consulate worker was right: her situation as a caretaker had forced her to learn enough English that she now could enroll in a structured language program that could make her fluent. She found another job as a housekeeper and was eking out a living while she pursued the next chapter of her story in America.

One day she met up with a friend who, along with her husband, had accompanied Susan and Joe on a buying trip to Asia. Susan had done her best to avoid any connection with Joe and the pending opening of his store, and all her friends had respected her wishes. But on this day, this particular friend confided in her that Joe was not the same. Gone were the vibrancy and enthusiasm that had caused his spirit to overflow when she had been in his life. Instead, he was glum and grumpy all the time, barking orders and ignoring the sound advice of friends and colleagues. It was clear to everyone that he was unhappy, even though he was periodically occupying his time with the sales-women from the store.

"You need to call Joe," the friend, Karen, told her. "He's so sad all the time."

"How could he be sad when he's dating all those girls?" Susan replied.

"It's not the same," Karen observed. "They're just dates. They're not you."

"I wish him well, but I've moved on. So has he."

"He needs you. You have no idea what he's going through."

"I have no hard feelings toward Joe at all," Susan said, doing her best to convince her friend—and herself. "He deserves all the best in life."

"But the grand opening is this week," Karen reminded her. "It won't be the same without you."

Susan was not about to budge easily. "He has a lot of good people working with him. He'll be fine."

"No, he won't. None of them are like you."

"He should have figured that out sooner."

Sensing a touch of empathy in her stubborn Korean friend, Karen went in for the kill. "Come on, Susan. Please. Just call him and at least tell him congratulations."

Susan had no intention of doing that. She was done with Joe and the whole Koret thing. Stephanie had passed away just a couple months before, and she no longer had a legitimate reason for being in the house. Pausan was the main housekeeper and cook, so Susan's presence really wasn't required.

"I didn't feel like doing it, not at all," she says today. "But Karen kept pushing me. She saw that he needed me, and she wanted me to make that call."

Karen finally broke her. Susan agreed to phone Joe, as long as she could keep it short and sweet. Just, "Good luck with your new store, Joe," and then she would hang up.

But affairs of the heart are complicated, so anything short and sweet was highly unlikely. When she called him she said, "Hi, Joe. I just want to say congratulations. Make a lot of money, be a success, and be healthy."

At that point she was planning on hanging up, but for a man nearing eighty Joe was very quick. And shrewd. He knew Susan's weak spot had always been taking care of him when he was sick, so he pretended to be seriously ill. He could barely speak, his words coming out as if they were being dragged over sandpaper.

"I'm not feeling well," he told her, between ragged coughs.

"I'm sorry to hear that," Susan replied coolly.

"There's no one here to take care of me," he said.

"Where's Pausan?"

"She's not like you. Please, honey—I need you."

Susan knew she was being played, but she realized she also was missing him. "Okay, Joe. I'll come by and check on you."

She didn't rush right over. In fact, she wanted to draw out the suspense to let him know she was in no hurry to return. When she finally did arrive at the house, she came in the side door, just in time to hear Joe tell Pausan to cancel his dinner date for the evening. Gone were the sniffles and the scratchy voice.

"He was such a different person that day," Susan remembers. "He was so happy to see me that he didn't know what to do. It really didn't bother me that he'd had a date lined up; it was a Korean lady that we both knew. All I cared about was that he was happy. And he *was* happy, because he had learned that not all Asian women were like me."

FAR EAST TRADERS OPENED ITS DOORS IN MAY 1978 to great promotional fanfare. Large newspaper ads in the *Chronicle* and *Examiner* hyped the grand opening of Joe Koret's new venture, which was described as specializing in fine Asian art and rare antiques. A broad selection of collectibles, including handcrafted porcelain, brass, rattan furniture, rugs, wood carvings, jade, and jewelry from eleven countries was available for any budget. Rather than promote its less-than-desirable location in what was then a seedy section of Market Street, the newspaper ads listed the address as "two blocks south of the Opera House at 41 Van Ness Avenue."[1]

More than just a store, Far East Traders also served as an educational forum for Asian art. Lecturers would come in and speak about everything from Ming vases to bronze sculptures from ancient China. Would-be customers were invited to bring their own collectibles in to have them appraised—and then maybe be up-sold on another item to complement the piece. The old Koret of California mix-and-match merchandising technique was alive and well.

Unfortunately, the venture was shaky from the start. Aside from its poor location, much of the merchandise was less than desirable, let alone collectible. As the store began to take shape, Susan realized a lot of the goods they'd ordered were reproductions rather than true antiques. Some of these pieces ended up in the Koret home, and one day Joe thought it would be a good idea to have an expert come in and appraise it all.

"We hired a professor from Berkeley, a curator who was knowledgeable about Asian art," Susan recalls. "He came to the house to see what Joe was buying, and so much of it was junk. I'd already put away some of the really cheap things because I was embarrassed to have this expert see them. The poor curator didn't know what to do. He knew if he told the truth, Joe would be crushed. Sadly, a lot of people—including Joe—didn't know that so many of those things we were selling in the store were not antiques."

One of the problems was a buyer in Thailand who kept shipping goods that weren't even close to being authentic. As the store sold out of a certain kind of inexpensive carving, for instance, she would send more reproductions of the same piece. That worked for the average Joe, but *this* Joe was not average—and neither were his target customers.

They wanted genuine works of art they could display with pride in their Pacific Heights mansions.

One day about a month after the grand opening, Charles Chan—who was managing the store—approached Joe and Ken Moline. They were sitting in an upstairs office reviewing financial spreadsheets for Terok Properties when he came in.

"Your buyer wants to place an order for twenty-five thousand dollars," Chan said, waving a sheet of paper in front of him. "Twenty-five thousand!"

This was in the days when a large purchase required a letter of credit, not just a signature on a charge card receipt. Joe looked from Chan to Ken Moline and said, "What do you think?"

Moline knew which items were quality antiques and which were inexpensive knockoffs, and the store didn't need to spend another $25,000 on cheap tchotchkes. "I wouldn't do it," he said.

"Why not?" Joe asked. "She's a good buyer."

"She's buying stuff that isn't worth it," Moline insisted. "I wouldn't give her a dime more."

Joe pondered this a moment, then said to Chan, "Go ahead and give her the letter of credit."

"What are you doing?" Moline demanded. "That's crazy!"

"It's my store and I can buy what I want!" Joe snapped.

"But you're supposed to be the expert merchandiser," Moline pressed him. He was horrified that his boss was being taken for a ride and wanted to put an end to it. "You know this stuff isn't worth it, but you're going to give her more money and she's going to send you more crap."

Joe leveled him with a dark glare that meant *don't you argue with me*, and said, "You go back to Mission Street and don't ever come back here."

Ken Moline did as he was told and went back to his office at Koracorp headquarters. He knew Joe was making a mistake buying more of the same worthless junk, but it was even worse to cross him. At the end of the day Joe came back to the office and Moline, fearful for his job, went in to apologize to him.

"Mr. Koret, I was really out of line," he said. "I shouldn't have said what I said, at least not in the manner that I said it. I am sorry."

Joe mulled this over, then nodded. "I accept your apology," he said. "And I need to tell you that you were right. That stuff isn't worth it. It's junk. But we're going to send her the money anyway."

By now, Joe had been selling products of one sort or another for more most of his life. He knew what to pay for his goods, and how to price them so they would sell. Business was business, and Joe almost always was able to separate personality from commerce. His one soft spot, however, was trust. As a salesman he knew how important it was to build trust with his customers, and he returned that trust pound for pound. Even though he knew his buyer in Thailand was shipping him goods that cheapened the image of Far East Traders, he had built a balance of trust with her. He simply could not let that bond crumble.

From the very first day, sales were slower than Joe had anticipated and overhead was steep. Joe had invested hundreds of thousands of dollars in items of questionable value, and employee turnover was a challenge. The biggest setback, however, was that three months before the store opened its doors, Stephanie Koret had passed away. Aside from the grief—and yes, a guilty sense of relief—that darkened Joe's life, he also was faced with a financial issue he had not expected.

Joe had purchased the old funeral home on Van Ness with money that came out of his and Stephanie's community property. When she died, however, her half of the assets held in their irrevocable trust flowed into the newly created Koret Foundation. That meant her half of their personal fortune no longer was available for him to use on personal ventures. Far East Traders was losing money every month, and if he was going to keep it open he would have to do it by using his own holdings and monthly income. This was still months before there was any talk of a merger with Levi Strauss & Company, so funding options for what was turning out to be an expensive "hobby shop" were limited. Joe was generating solid revenue from his Terok Properties rental units, but he was loath to tap into that income to stanch the cash flow hemorrhage.

"What do you think I should do?" he asked Ken Moline one day.

"You're losing a lot of money, and I don't think business is going to improve."

"I've invested a lot of money in this place," Joe pointed out. "A lot of my own money."

"It's a great store," Moline told him, anticipating what was coming. "It's the only one of its kind in San Francisco."

"But it's in the wrong location. I should have known better, but I had a lot of fun."

"We all did," Moline said. "It was a great idea."

"Well, I have an even better one," Joe said with a sigh. "Let's close it down."

"You're serious?"

"I've made up my mind. We're going to liquidate and move on."

WITH HIS LIMITED WORK RESPONSIBILITIES AND the entire California salmon population calling to him, Joe returned to the sea. He'd never actually been very far from it; even as he was creating Far East Traders he still went out on his boat at least twice a week, rain or shine. Saturdays and Mondays were his fishing days, while Fridays and Sundays usually were his days of rest. The other three he would spend at the office, keeping JoAnne Vente busy making Koret dinner party plans, stocking the candy bowl, and taking long, leisurely lunches before his routine nap. For a man who had just celebrated his seventy-eighth birthday, life had settled into a comfortable routine.

While Joe particularly looked forward to his Saturday fishing expeditions, he also enjoyed regular dinner gatherings after he returned home from the sea. For years, he and Stephanie had entertained family and friends around a massive dining room table, and that routine did not stop with his wife's passing. One of JoAnne's weekly responsibilities was to drum up the guests for that weekly dinner—a task that, over time, proved to be more and more problematic.

"A lot of people really didn't want to come," Susan Koret remembers:

The food really wasn't very good. It was always fish of some kind, and the cook had to make it taste better than it was. The guests were expected to eat it—*all of it*. People were beginning to realize this, and they just didn't want to come. Plus, he was the boss. They knew they would have to listen to a lot of boring business conversation. It wasn't very exciting, so it got harder and harder to find people who didn't already have "other plans."

What began as Saturday events, over the years transformed into two and sometimes three nights a week. "It took a lot of time to set these things up," Susan says. "JoAnne got tired of doing it, so she turned the task over to me. It was a lot of work, especially because people were so reluctant to come. A lot of times they would eat dinner before they arrived so they had an excuse not to eat at our house."

Topping off the fish dinners and tedious office conversation was the mandatory gin rummy match. Joe Koret was an avid gin rummy player, and no evening with family and friends was complete without an hour or two of serious card-playing. The problem was that Joe was compulsive and competitive, determined to defeat every player at the table. If he didn't win everybody's money, he insisted on at least getting his own pot back by the end of the night. And it had to be the actual coins he had ponied up to start with, not just their face value.

"Joe was a tenacious player," JoAnne Vente recalls. "He had these quarters with red fingernail polish painted on them. We were not allowed to go home until he got every one of those red quarters back.

I would tell him, 'Mr. Koret —it's eleven o'clock. You have to go to bed, and we have to go to work in the morning.' But no, not Joe. 'No one's going anywhere until I get this quarter, and that one, and that one,' he would say."

"Joe was possessed by the game, and he had to win all the time," Susan adds:

> Sometimes, I would try to lose just so we could all go to bed. When we went on trips, of course he wanted to play gin rummy on the ship. Sometimes, I would be on a winning streak, and he wouldn't let me go to bed. One time I was really tired, almost asleep, and I tried to lose. But I kept winning. The more I tried to lose, the more I won. And he wouldn't let me stop. I got so mad at him and said, "You know, you are worse than Hitler." Everyone was gone except for maybe one or two tables in the ship's dining room. He needed to win that much.

One perk at the end of any dinner party—and the gin rummy marathons—was smoked salmon. Even though most guests grew tired of eating fish at a Koret gathering, they always enjoyed the "parting gift." Joe went fishing so frequently and caught so many salmon that the five freezers in the basement were always packed with fish he had smoked himself. Even after long evenings of gin rummy, Joe always had packages of salmon waiting for people as they left.

THE DAY AFTER JOE SOLD KORACORP TO LEVI Strauss, he found himself with more time on his hands than ever before. From all outward appearances he was a contented man, and many of his friends and colleagues saw a marked change in him. Gone was the tycoon who was haunted by marketing and merchandising issues at all hours of the day and night. He no longer obsessed about fabrics or styles or dollar plans. Koracorp Industries was now part of a large multinational corporation, and he had more money than he knew what to do with. His time was now completely his own, and Susan had returned to live in the house in Sea Cliff. Ever the businessman, he was anxious to find an enterprise that could keep him busy, and he occasionally entertained ideas from aspiring entrepreneurs who came seeking his advice. He generously offered his insights and shared his wisdom, enjoying the role of industry mogul and mentor.

Still, Joe needed more. He had been happily married for fifty-five of his seventy-eight years, and the concept looked good on him. He'd met Stephanie when he was just twenty-two years old and had fallen madly in love with her—and she with him. Neither had any idea what lay ahead, but both were equally committed to a partnership that ultimately carried them though a successful marriage and a thriving business. The years were fraught with challenges, and they had triumphed through a combination of hard work and perseverance.

"When I look back, some of those challenges seemed so enormous," Joe recalled in the 1979 TV interview:

> But I'm up on a mountain now, and the path really wasn't so terrible. It was all worth it. Year after year, my wife and I both worked twelve, fourteen hours a day. We didn't have any Saturdays or Sundays off. We didn't have any capital, so we put our youth into the operation. It really wasn't so terrible. We went on many trips, we enjoyed life. I was blessed with a good companion. I was blessed with a good wife.

A good marriage with a loving, comforting wife was what Joe wanted—and needed. As it does with many men, marriage had come to define who he was, and being partners with a woman made him feel whole. When Susan McClain arrived in the Koret household, she rekindled the embers that still smoldered inside, and when he began building Far East Traders he began to sow a few wild oats, time-worn as they were. The entire experience taught him that the love of one good woman was far more valuable than the attention of a dozen pretty girls, and when Susan reentered his life his heart settled into a comfortable rhythm.

Still, he liked being married. He enjoyed being a husband, and he wanted a wife by his side. One day at breakfast he simply looked at her across the table and said, "Honey—we're getting married."

"No way—we can't," she replied, worried that he might be following his late wife's decline into dementia.

"I'm serious," Joe insisted. "I've made up my mind, and I want to marry you."

In all the years Joe and Susan had known each other, the "m" word had never come up. Neither of them ever breathed one word of it, and Susan believed he had no more desire to get married than she did. In fact, she was bewildered by its unexpected mention now.

"Where did this suddenly come from?" she asked him.

"We're going to get married," he repeated, ignoring her question.

Susan stared at him, panic building in her heart. Just when she thought her life had gotten back to normal, there was that sense of anxiety again. It reminded her of the day of the beach walk, when she finally grasped that he wanted her to be more to him than just his ill wife's caretaker.

Today, almost forty years later, Susan remembers that conversation with fond amusement. "I never thought we would get married," she says. "He never mentioned it. He'd been married to Stephanie all those years, and I never expected him to want to marry me. We just had good companionship, and that was it. Looking back I think he may have been worried that I was going to leave him. I was so much younger than he was, and at the time I thought he was crazy. It wasn't normal. Today I understand, but back then I didn't."

Susan also knew what people might say about her, marrying an older man worth many millions of dollars. "Joe was a genuinely nice guy and had a lot of respect for me," she explains:

We respected each other, we loved each other, and we communicated with each other. Whether I always understood him or not, he always told me what he thought. It was a classy, clean relationship. I know a lot of people were thinking, "Oh, we know why she married the old man." They still do. People naturally think I married him for the money. I didn't care what they said, and I still don't. That's how they think, not me.

In any event, Susan said "yes."

Susan Koret, San Francisco mayor Dianne Feinstein, and Joe Koret at the opening of Cassidy's Western Outfitters in 1981. [Koret private collection]

14

Urbane Cowboy

MARRIAGE TO JOE KORET CAME WITH ONE SMALL stipulation.

Several days after he proposed to her—in his own direct and straightforward style—he told Susan, "Honey, I've been thinking. I want you to convert."

Susan's English had improved significantly since she first came to work in the Koret household, and she usually understood what he was telling her. But the word *convert* was something you did with Korean currency to U.S. dollars. Was he talking about a financial transaction, or something else?

"Excuse me?" she asked him.

"Tell me: Are you Catholic?" he inquired.

"No," she said.

"Buddhist?"

"No."

"Then what religion are you?" he inquired.

"I don't have a religion," she told him. "It's never been that important to me."

"Then you definitely need to convert," he said again. "This house can only have one religion under its roof. You need to become a Jew."

Susan still didn't know precisely what he meant, much less what "converting" entailed. She had spent enough years in the Koret house to know that Joe eagerly celebrated Passover and Yom Kippur, but Chanukah was mostly an afterthought. In fact, he and his work colleagues—even those who were Jewish—exchanged Christmas gifts every year. She knew Joe was Jewish, as were all of Stephanie's relatives. Bob Upright, too. At that point, however, she didn't come close to comprehending the deep religious convictions and cultural implications of "becoming a Jew." In her mind, it involved some deeply spiritual moments—especially on holidays—that included Hebrew prayers and a number of ceremonies that traditionally included food.

Still, she agreed. Susan was sincere in her adoration of and respect for Joe, and if this made him feel more comfortable, why not?

"If I really had known what he meant and everything it involved I probably would have been scared to death," she recalls.

During the years she had been employed in the Koret home, Susan had become acquainted with Rabbi Saul White, who lived across the street. The Korets always had several dogs in the home, and one of them—a large and commanding German shepherd—had a vicious streak. He was particularly prone to sinking his teeth into strangers who came to the front door, and on several occasions the target of those sharp fangs had been Rabbi White. It took twenty-one unwitting victims before Joe reluctantly donated the dog to the San Francisco Police Department, which retrained him for K-9 patrol duties.

In any event, Rabbi White took Susan under his wing and guided her through the entire conversion process. Despite the fact that her English was still only passable, she threw herself into her studies. He patiently explained what she must think and do, and she quickly realized that conversion was far more complicated than learning the Pledge of Allegiance. She would have to study basic Jewish beliefs, thousands of years of ancient history, and engage in a number of traditional rituals. She also would have to learn enough Hebrew to recite specific prayers at family gatherings. This could be a bit of a challenge, since English already was proving difficult, and Susan was afraid of compounding the issue by having to study yet another language that had its own distinct alphabet. Additionally, she had to pronounce her belief in God and the divinity of the Torah, accept all of its mitzvoth (commandments), and agree to live a Jewish life.

Susan embraced all of this with an open mind and a convivial spirit. In the fall of 1979, she spent hours each day studying with Rabbi White. She had no idea how she was doing, or how much work would be required in order for her to finish the process. She just went along with whatever he requested of her, figuring that after months of reading and cramming she must be getting close to the end.

She was; she just didn't know when—and in what manner—that end would arrive.

"On New Year's Eve we'd planned a big party at the house," she recalls:

> A lot of people were coming and I'd spent days preparing. That morning I'd had my hair done early, and I'd already painted my nails and done my makeup. Then Rabbi White showed up at the door to pick me up and take me to the place where I would convert. When we got there another rabbi looked at me and said, "Remove all that polish and makeup." I had to clean my face, take my hair down, and take a shower. All of this before I covered myself with a sheet and went to the fountain.

The fountain—actually a mikveh—is a bath used for the purpose of ritual immersion. In the Hebrew Bible, the word generally means "a collection of water," and full immersion in it is required for a convert to be ritually pure. Susan had known that her conversion would occur on New Year's Eve Day, but she had no idea what was involved until the very last minute.

"When we were finished Rabbi White commended me on doing a good job, then told me we had to go back to the synagogue," she says. After completing more ceremonial rituals, the rabbi told her she had passed. She was done. She had converted.

"Hallelujah—now I'm Jewish!" she remembers thinking. She exhaled a huge sigh of relief, amazed that, as a Korean woman who spoke limited English, she actually had converted to Judaism in America. "Rabbi White called Joe and told him what I'd done. I heard him on the other end; he laughed and laughed so hard that he made me angry. I had worked so hard, studied every morning, and I'd taken it all very seriously. Yet he was laughing. Then I realized it was a laughter of joy and love, and I felt relieved."

The New Year's Eve party went on as planned. Susan did not have time to get her hair done again, nor did she bother with painting her nails. She felt she had just achieved something magnificent, and suddenly all the makeup and nail polish didn't seem to matter. Joe had asked her to join him in his Jewish faith, and she had. Interestingly, he had not regularly attended synagogue for years, not since Stephanie had become ill. Now that he had Susan by his side, they began to go every week. They celebrated Shabbat, and other Jewish holidays regained greater importance in the house. Susan took great pride not only in being Jewish, but she also was comforted that she knew all the different ceremonial prayers by heart. "Joe always had to read the prayer for the bread, candle, wine," she says. "He had never memorized them, but I had to when I converted."

At the time, she didn't realize there was another reason Joe wanted her to convert. Not only did he wish to have a Jewish wife by his side, but he also wanted the Jewish community of San Francisco to welcome her. "The entire community looked at us in a different, very positive way," Susan observes. "He didn't tell me at the time, but he eventually was going to become heavily involved with his foundation, and the Jewish community would look at the two of us very critically. It was important to them, and to him, for me to convert."

Joe Koret and Susan McClain were married several weeks later in a modest ceremony held at the local synagogue, surrounded by friends and family. The reception that followed was anything but small; Joe rented the exclusive Concordia Club and filled it with food and music for the new couple's guests to enjoy. Since Joe was widely considered a member of San Francisco's elite social sphere, the event was bound to garner a lot of media attention, and it did. Herb Caen, the *San Francisco Chronicle*'s venerable gossip columnist, plied his pun-laden craft in writing a typically corny squib in advance of the ceremony:

> Joseph Koret, the 79-year-old clothing magnate, is getting married January 16 to a Korean-born beauty named Susan McClain who, he says wryly, "is younger than I am." Abe Battat and John Stafford, hired to make music at the Concordia Club reception, had this conversation earlier this week: Abe: "Know any Korean songs?" John: "Only 'Body and Seoul.'" Perhaps Mr. Koret should have hired Chick Korea. Yeah, I know it's Corea, but anything for a crummy joke.[1]

"I never, ever expected that we were going to marry," Susan says today. "I didn't think he was going to follow his long marriage of fifty-five years with another wife. Nor did I expect him to be a romantic guy. But once we got married, he started giving me very intimate cards on my birthday and Valentine's Day."

Over the six years that Susan had been in the Koret home her English had improved, but it still was not where she had wanted (or expected) it to be. She was able to communicate to Joe and others just fine, although typically in sentences punctuated by misplaced modifiers and incorrect verb tenses. She was painfully aware of this shortcoming, but Joe assured her that he didn't care. He loved her for the woman she was, not for the linguist she wasn't. If someone looked dubiously at her when she spoke, he would shoot them a disapproving glare that suggested, *You have a problem with that? It's how she talks.*

"Joe had very little formal education, but he'd built a very successful business, so that sort of thing wasn't important to him," Susan observes. "He didn't judge others, and he didn't like others judging him—or me. He just wanted me to be close to him, no matter where we went. He wanted me to be there. He totally relied on me."

DESPITE HIS MILLIONS OF DOLLARS IN ASSETS and a hefty annual income, Joe Koret—like many folks whose roots had been deeply entrenched in poverty—was characterized by his thrift. Generous to a fault and willing to pay good money for quality goods, he regularly sought out bargains and tried to save pennies whenever he could. For a man who paradoxically would sign a letter of credit for $25,000 worth of overvalued Asian trinkets, he spent hours looking for the best deal on canned beans. His fondness for Chinese food stemmed from his ability to quickly determine the best value of a plate of sweet-and-sour chicken as triangulated by portion, proximity, and price.

Another of Joe's idiosyncrasies was his adamant refusal to be seen in public paying for anything. JoAnne Vente had learned this lesson halfway through her first week as Joe's executive assistant, and she made sure she always carried plenty of cash to cover whatever expenses her boss might incur. Evidently, she had not shared this information with her husband, Ken Moline, who learned it the hard way while traveling with the Koret posse on a Baltic cruise.

"On the first trip we all took together, we were in Copenhagen and we went into a furrier," he recalls today. "He bought Susan a white coat with a brown collar, then picked out a coat for himself. He turned to me and said, 'Okay, Ken, pay for it.' I said, 'I can't. My credit card limit doesn't go that high.' He said, 'What do you mean? Where's the money you were supposed to bring?' He hadn't told JoAnne or me that we were supposed to bring his money and carry it with us. He seemed like he was staring right through me, then pulled out his billfold and took out a credit card. He had to pay for the coats himself."

Ken had hoped that was the end of the situation, but it wasn't. "When we got back to the ship he told me, 'Don't you ever come on these cruises without a credit card.' So the next cruise I carried $10,000 worth of travelers checks."

As the boss, Joe always expected to have all his needs met by his employees. He booked the best stateroom suite; he enjoyed dining with the captain; and if he needed something from the kitchen he expected it to be brought to him posthaste. That meant currying favor with members of the ship's crew, who always seemed eager to please. "On these cruises, Susan, Ken, and I all tried to make sure he got what he wanted and he was very comfortable," JoAnne Vente says. "We knew our lives would be miserable if we couldn't do that. At the end of that first trip he called us all to his room, where he had some white envelopes. He said, 'Okay, let's figure out the tips for everybody. Who do we have to tip?' We told him who deserved one, and he said, 'Okay—ten dollars for that steward, ten dollars for this porter.' Son-of-a-bitch, he could be cheap."

Once the money was stuffed in the white envelopes, JoAnne and Ken went back to their room and scrounged up as much extra cash as they could find. "Fortunately, he hadn't sealed the envelopes, so we could put in a proper tip," JoAnne says. "This was a man who'd been sitting at the captain's table, and we had his image to protect. Joe never forgot his upbringing. Yes, he had multimillions, but to him ten dollars was a huge amount."

On one of these cruises, Joe's sense of frugality was overshadowed by a lingering paranoia about his family origins. On the excursion through the Baltic Sea, one of the ports of call was Leningrad. Following the fall of the Soviet Union, the city was returned to its original name of St. Petersburg, but at this point the Cold War was still very real. When the cruise ship pulled into port, the entire Koret entourage disembarked for a sightseeing tour around the second-largest city in the country where which Joe had been born almost eighty years before.

None of the Americans in the tiny group noticed immediately, but pedestrian traffic was channeled much like vehicle traffic. People walked north-to-south on one side of the street, and south-to-north on the other side. "You weren't supposed to walk against them, but we did, until we learned," Ken Moline says. "Nobody really paid attention to us because everybody seemed to walk with their eyes on the sidewalk. The only reason they would look at us was because of the way we were dressed. Our winter Olympics team wore Western wear in 1980, and Mr. Koret insisted we wear Western clothing everywhere. Western hats and sheepskin vests—the whole thing."

"The Russians were fascinated by the four of us," adds JoAnne Vente. "We would come out of a store and there would be a group of them watching us. Mr. Koret began to get very nervous because he was afraid the government would force him to stay there because that's where he came from." At one point, the four wary travelers realized how far they had wandered from the ship, and Joe began to feel a suffocating desire to get back before the KGB realized who he was and apprehended him. JoAnne managed to flag down a taxi driven by a tired man in a drab gray coat. The group piled into the car, and suddenly scenes from old spy movies began flashing through Joe's mind.

"As we rode back to the ship, Mr. Koret was really frightened," JoAnne continues. "I was sitting up front with the driver and having a great time, but Mr. Koret was so afraid that he was going to be taken somewhere and maybe imprisoned. I gave the driver a pack of cigarettes and he immediately became part of the Koret family. Mr. Koret sighed a huge sigh of relief, and when we got to the ship we gave him more money for cigarettes."

JOE'S PERSISTENT THRIFTINESS CARRIED OVER to his household shopping. Despite the millions of dollars he had gained from the sale of Koracorp, every Sunday morning he would sit at the dining room table and pore over the colorful supermarket flyers in the *Chronicle*. Most people simply set them aside, but Joe scoured these FSIs—free-standing inserts—as if they contained the secrets of the universe. And perhaps they did, because from time to time he would pick up a pair of scissors and cut the page to shreds.

"Joe loved to clip coupons," Susan recalls:

> He was always thinking about how much money he could save on a can of beans, but didn't think twice about how much gas it would take to drive his Cadillac to the store. I was shocked that he cut out all these coupons for beans and discount meats. He collected pork. He didn't eat it, and we never served it. But he bought it because it was a bargain. He would always be so happy when he got pork for a good price. He didn't care that no one was going to eat it; with Joe Koret it didn't matter as long as it was food. And that he was saving money.

"Sundays were Joe's shopping days," Ken Moline adds. "He always had his coupons organized store by store. He would go to Walgreens, where they had beans for twelve cents a can, then drive to Albertson's, because they had a special on canned vegetables. He'd bring all these groceries home. He might have forty cans of beans in the house but he would buy two more because they were on sale."

One day Ken asked him about this strange obsession, and Joe said, "You have to understand: when I was young I had nothing to eat but maybe half a potato. I'm not apologizing for the way I am; I just like to find the cheapest price for all these things."

DURING THE PEAK YEARS WHEN RUNNING KORET of California was an all-encompassing endeavor, Joe Koret had been an ambitious and determined force within the company. He conveyed the image of a gruff, hard-edged businessman singularly focused on the bottom line. He worked hard and spent long hours in the office, and he expected the same from his executive staff. He was a perfectionist to a fault, and was quick to point out when a design or garment didn't live up to his personal expectations. He insisted that every product be of the highest quality, and expected that every person along the merchandising chain would be as meticulous as he was.

He also had a reputation for being blunt and sarcastic. "One time, a manufacturer brought some sweaters into the office, hoping Mr. Koret would carry their line," JoAnne Vente says. "He took a long, hard look at them and decided he didn't like what he saw. He took a pencil and poked a big hole in one of the sweaters and told the sales rep, 'This is crap. You can't sell that to a bug.' "

Stubborn and inflexible as he could be, Joe had every right to be proud of what his hard work and patience had created. "Mr. Koret would have been a great mentor, and it would have been nice to spend a lot more time around him," says Ken Moline. "You could learn so much—not just about business but about life, because he had endured so much. Think about it: he was born in Russia, and he came to the U.S. when he was one year old. His childhood was rough, and food was of primary importance to him. Even when he was much older, food was his top priority."

AS HE NEARED HIS EIGHTIETH BIRTHDAY, JOE began to mellow. The company he had built now belonged to someone else, and his bank account was flush with cash. He no longer had an office that beckoned him; he had a beautiful and loving wife at home; and he still spent several days a week out on his boat in pursuit of salmon. He was able to breathe deeply, reflect on the past, and find contentment in all that he had done.

Joe and Stephanie had never had any children, and it did not seem likely he was going to start down that path now. He began to realize how much he had missed having children to play with, to teach, and just to enjoy. That had always been Stephanie's role at family gatherings, but now he embraced the squeals of laughter that followed other people's children into his home.

Ron Brown, Merv Brown's son, was one of them. "As a small child I remember standing by the door to leave," he says. "Joe was wearing a sweater, and he reached into his pocket and found a hundred dollar bill in it. To a small child a hundred dollar bill was like having Wells Fargo in your hand. I stared at that bill in wonderment." No, Joe did not give him the Benjamin—combined with a wad of coupons it could buy a lot of pork and beans—but just seeing one gave the young boy a thrill.

Joe also quickly took to Susan's young relatives, some of whom were now living in California. "When I was a little girl it seemed to me Joe was always singing," says Denise Kim, Susan's niece. "He taught me the words to 'You Are My Sunshine,' and he loved another crazy song about a Japanese maid. Even today I remember how it goes: 'She was a maid of Japan / He was the son Choo Lee / She had a comb and a fan / And he had two chests of tea.' He would go crazy on that tune. I thought of him as this fuzzy, sweet old man who wore a gold chain."

AS CONTENTED AS JOE SEEMED, HE STILL HAD one last business venture in him. In the spring of 1980, a few months after he and Susan were married, they decided to go to the movies. Joe had always enjoyed a good film, and for years he and Stephanie would take his mother to the theater to see the latest releases. On this particular evening, the multiplex was showing a new flick starring John Travolta and Debra Winger as two Texas dreamers who fall in love in a Houston roadhouse.

The film was *Urban Cowboy*, which had just opened to positive reviews and a strong box office. All of a sudden, country music was taking America by storm. The movie's soundtrack was selling millions of copies, and Nashville recording studios began to buzz again after a long dry spell. The Urban Cowboy craze swept the nation from coast to coast. Dance clubs that had been "all disco all the time" suddenly shifted from Donna Summer and the Bee Gees to Kenny Rogers and Eddie Rabbit. Mirrored dance balls were replaced by mechanical bulls. Sequins, jumpsuits, and gold lamé abruptly hit the Goodwill bins as gingham shirts and black Stetsons rang the cash registers. Cowboy culture and all things Western gripped the retail world, and apparel manufacturers—Levi Strauss & Company particularly—could hardly keep up with the demand.

This obsession hit at a time when Joe Koret was most vulnerable. He was still smarting from the closure of Far East Traders and, aside from fishing three days a week, he was bored. His entire world had been tied to fashion, and the new owners of Koret of California had their own plans that no longer required his input. Still, he felt unsettled. He wasn't enjoying life the way he had expected, and except for Terok Properties, he wasn't making money. Work had been the constant driver throughout his life, and Joe Koret didn't feel complete unless he was running a business and generating a profit.

"I don't *have* to make money," he would tell his friends. "I just *want* to make money. I need something to do."

In the late sixties, Koracorp president Jere Helfat had engineered the acquisition of the Byer-Rolnick Corporation, which manufactured Resistol Hats. Joe was always a hat aficionado, and for a time he insisted that all his male executives and sales reps—any corporate employee who interacted with the public—wear a hat while on the job. This was at a time when hats were beginning to go out of fashion, but to Joe a piece of quality "headwear" presented a look of sophistication and style. Owning Byer-Rolnick had allowed Joe to be on the front line of American "hat couture," and when the Urban Cowboy wave swept across America, Resistol was perfectly positioned to take advantage of this cultural tsunami.

Even though Joe no longer owned Resistol, he had remained friends with John Milano, who had managed the firm for years. Milano's simple philosophy was, "I will always have a customer if I make the best product," and quality was what initially drew Joe to the company. One day, the two gentlemen met for lunch, and Milano, who also had suddenly seen his beloved firm engulfed by Levi Strauss—the "denim giant"—raised the concept of opening a high-end Western store. There wasn't a city in the States that hadn't been engulfed by the craze, yet not one store in San Francisco catered to this trend. While there may have been a good reason for this, Joe heard opportunity knocking, loud and hard.

The more Joe thought about it, the more he liked the idea of being a purveyor of fine Western wear. He watched the evening news and read the newspapers and trade publications. This trend was real, and by all accounts there was little risk and considerable upside. It was much different from the rationale behind opening an Asian art emporium, where he was somewhat blinded by his own passion for antiques and collectibles. This time, he had the taste of the entire American public on his side.

After consulting with Tad Taube and Eugene Friend, another of his Terok Property associates, Joe settled on a worn-out building at 969 Market Street. The property was owned by the parent company of Howard's Clothing, an apparel firm that Friend's parents had founded in the late 1930s. Over the years, the structure had fallen into disrepair, and Friend wanted to get rid of it.

Once again, the location should have been a dead giveaway for what was to come. The address was much closer to the downtown business area than Far East Traders had been, just fifty yards down the street from the noted Emporium department store. Still, it was forty-nine yards farther than most people cared to venture in the early 1980s. Market Street had an almost invisible line that separated the reputable retail businesses from the caged storefronts and peep shows where shady business was done on the sidewalks and in doorways.

The 969 building was on the wrong side of this line.

Turning a deaf ear to friends and colleagues who warned him about the dubious address, Joe acquired the building in a real estate exchange that partially included an interest in Fair Oaks West Properties, another real estate venture in which he was involved. Perhaps he liked the location because it was just a stone's throw from where the old Crystal Palace Market had sat at the corner of Market and Eighth Street, where he had opened his hosiery stall in December 1922. Whatever the motivation, Joe defended his decision to a *Chronicle* reporter who questioned him about the purchase. "The next area to make money is that part of Market Street," he said. "[It] is a beautiful street, and I have a lot of faith that bigger and better things are happening there. You get a different feeling walking down that block today than you did a year ago."[2]

Cassidy's Western Outfitters—named in honor of the legendary outlaw Butch Cassidy from the 1969 Paul Newman–Robert Redford film—debuted to considerable fanfare in June 1981. Mayor Dianne Feinstein was on hand to help celebrate the grand opening of the sixteen-thousand-square-foot store, which cost Joe Koret slightly over $3 million to develop. He hired Michael Box, a former partner of Tener's Western Outfitters of Oklahoma City, to run the upscale enterprise. Stocked with moderate- to higher-priced boots, hats, leatherwear, and a range of Western apparel, the store was designed to appeal to every taste and budget. As Joe later observed, Cassidy's was the kind of retail outlet that he'd always wanted to open but was prevented from doing so by "our good people who, from financial angles, were right not to let me."[3]

By 1981—just in time for the grand opening—the Urban Cowboy craze had begun to fade. The movie earned a phenomenal $53 million in box office receipts in the States alone, which translates to about $200 million in 2018. Country-style pickup trucks rolled off new car lots by the millions, and billions of dollars' worth of Western wear was purchased in the first eighteen months of the craze. Unfortunately, very little of that merchandise was sold at Cassidy's, and within just a few months, Joe realized the store was yet another failure. Koret of California veteran Warren Logan was brought in to replace Box as manager, but it was too little, too late. Timing is everything, and Joe had completely missed the Western trend—if there ever had been one in San Francisco in the first place. He hated to admit it, but he had violated one of his own biggest fashion principles: get in on a trend early, and stay clear of fads at all costs. Unfortunately, throwing a lot of money at the Urban Cowboy fad cost Joe millions of dollars.

"There was no market for a Western store in San Francisco," observes JoAnne Vente, who stood by him every step of the way. "It was a beautiful store, but toward the end it was losing money. Eventually, Mr. Koret said 'I don't want it anymore.' The big thing on his agenda was to give away all the inventory. Even at the very end, he was thinking about taking care of his friends and employees."

KORET PLAZA

DEDICATED TO JOSEPH & STEPHANIE KORET

FOUNDERS, KORET FOUNDATION, SAN FRANCISCO, CALIFORNIA IN HONOR OF

THEIR COMMITMENT TO ALLEVIATE HUNGER THROUGH EDUCATION & RESEARCH

כיכר קורט

מוקדש ליוסף וסטפני קורט

In 1981 the Koret Foundation provided $250,000 in "seed funding" to agriculture programs at Hebrew University in Israel, which eventually led to the creation and funding of the Koret School of Veterinary Medicine. Pictured at the dedication of the university's Koret Plaza are (far right) Joe and Susan Koret. [Koret private collection]

15

A Foundation of Trust

IN THE MID-1960S, JOE AND STEPHANIE'S personal estate planners recommended that the couple establish a nonprofit foundation that, on their eventual passing, would use their substantial assets to provide funding for charities and community causes of their choosing. The couple had no children of their own, Joe's parents and siblings were all deceased, and Stephanie could count her immediate family on two hands—with a few fingers left over. With no direct heirs, federal and state inheritance taxes would devour their fortune, something the attorneys firmly counseled against.

Rather than see their many millions of hard-earned dollars be handed over to tax collectors in Washington and Sacramento, the Korets chose to put that money to work for causes in which they personally believed. Joe was committed to assisting those truly in need within the greater San Francisco community, and especially in trying to help allevi- ate the growing issue of world hunger. Those early-childhood memories of an empty stomach had guided him his entire life, and now he wanted to ensure that as few people as possible had to suffer the emptiness of starvation ever again. He also felt a close bond with the San Francisco

Jewish community, which, over the years, had served as a reminder of his ancestry and the footing of his deep-rooted cultural heritage.

The Koret Foundation was officially chartered as a California 501(c)3 organization in 1966. At that point, both Korets appeared hale and hearty, although Stephanie was beginning to show the first signs of memory loss. Nothing much happened for the next decade as the foundation remained inert, waiting for the first of the Korets to pass away. That eventuality occurred on February 22, 1978, with Stephanie's death. At that point, her half of the community property contained in the Koret Trust legally shifted to the Koret Foundation, although pro-bate and other issues delayed the actual transfer for another year. Nonetheless, by mid-1979 the Koret Foundation became an active charitable entity funded with many millions of dollars.

In its early years, the Koret Foundation was located above Cassidy's Western Wear on Market Street. Joe served as the chairman of the board of directors and personally approved all grant-making decisions. He brought on board his trusted adviser and executive assistant JoAnne Vente as grants administrator, and made good on his pledge to Ken Moline to install him as the foundation's chief financial officer. The rest of the board consisted of Tad Taube, who had reversed Koracorp's ailing fortunes and sold it to Levi Strauss & Company; Eugene Friend, with whom Joe had made the questionable real estate exchange that left him with the property at 969 Market Street; tax attorney Richard Greene; and Koret of California veteran manager Stanley Herzstein, who was one of Joe's closest friends and allies.

After Joe married Susan, he also named her to the board, and appointed her the successor chairman for life.

Unlike many nonprofit organizations, the Koret Foundation derived about half of its working capital from real estate investments, many of which had been engineered by Joe Koret and Tad Taube. The assets acquired through Terok Properties—most of which were purchased fol-lowing the Koret of California IPO in 1966—were producing generous income on a steady, reliable basis. Stephanie's share of those real estate investments now accounted for approximately half of the Foundation's annual revenue; the other half had been invested in stocks and bonds which, because of high interest rates in the late seventies and early eighties, also were producing reliable cash flow.

A man who had spent his entire life amassing a fortune, Joe Koret now found himself faced with giving it away. Neither he nor anyone on the board had much, if any, experience doing that sort of thing, nor did they possess the professional expertise required to make the initial process flow smoothly. What they didn't know inherently, however, they quickly learned organically, and within months the foundation began tackling its first grants.

Charitable organizations are never faced with a shortage of potential beneficiaries, and this was true of the Koret Foundation from day one. Because he was chairman of the board, Joe made it quite clear that he wanted the foundation's grants to be split fifty-fifity between causes that helped the general community and those that benefitted Jewish needs. In those early years, every member of the board was Jewish, so the latter decisions usually were unanimous, while there tended to be some discord about the "general community" designation.

"Privately, Mr. Koret was more focused on the general community," JoAnne Vente recalls. "Yes, he was Jewish, but he was always so grateful to those little Asian ladies with their sewing machines, who really built Koret of California. Giving back to a city that had given him so much was of great importance to him, no matter their religion or ethnicity."

From all outward appearances, Joe was the epitome of the generous philanthropist who savored the prospect of "paying forward" his hard-earned fortune. Civic groups honored him for his generosity, while many of the early beneficiaries of that largess hailed him as a super-hero in the community. Joe readily welcomed the accolades, which, over time, eased the initial pain of signing away all those dollars he had worked so hard to amass.

"Joe really wanted to help poor people, but he was not accustomed to giving money away," Susan Koret says today. "His whole life he needed money, so making money was his priority. But giving it away? He didn't get that kind of education until late in life. It was painful. At those first meetings, he didn't even want to look at the foundation agenda, because it showed how much money he would be signing away."

Former Foundation CFO Ken Moline concurs. "We would go to board meetings with proposals for $5,000 grants, and after they were approved Mr. Koret signed the checks," he says with a chuckle. "He really had a hard time parting with all that money. 'It's my money!' he would say. He enjoyed the process and the thrill it gave him, but he was still giving away all this money he had worked so hard to accumulate."

THAT COLD MORNING IN EARLY 1980 WHEN JOE visited the Little Sisters of the Poor changed his perspective forever. The genuine humility expressed by the Mother Superior and the other sisters at St. Anne's pulled him back to his own humble beginnings. In an instant, the value of money took on a whole new meaning. No longer were zeroes, commas, and dollar signs as important as helping those dedicated women and their simple cause of providing care to elderly people in need.

Not since Stephanie had died two years earlier had JoAnne Vente seen a tear on Joe's face. Until now.

"Those sisters are going to get their new wing," he told her as they cruised back down Lake Street toward the Foundation headquarters on Market Street.

When they returned to the office, he immediately directed JoAnne and Ken to begin their due diligence on Little Sisters of the Poor. He asked them to develop a detailed proposal for the construction plan and identify how the foundation's money would be used. He also let the board of directors know that the Koret Foundation was going to fund this project—no ifs, ands, or buts. At that early stage, the organization's unofficial guidelines prohibited capital grants that funded construction projects, but Joe insisted they make an exception in this case.

The board of directors realized how serious Joe was about this gift, and the grant was approved with no opposition. Even if the board members had rejected the proposal, Joe was so enamored with the Little Sisters and their cause that they would have received their money anyway. "Mr. Koret would have taken it out of his own pocket if he'd had to," JoAnne Vente says. "Of all our early grants, that one excited him the most. Those sisters swept him off his feet. They were very humble, and they made him feel like he could really make a difference."

During the months that followed, Susan drove her husband to the foundation office almost every morning. Their regular route would take them down Lake Street, past the new construction that he had helped to finance. As they neared the entrance for St. Anne's Home, he often would tell her to slow down.

"I gave them the money for that," he would tell her, pointing at the framework that was going up.

"Yes, you did," she would reply. "It's so wonderful that you were able to help them."

OVER TIME, JOE CAME TO ENJOY GIVING HIS money to those who truly needed it. Susan encouraged him in this personal growth, reminding him that if he hadn't done so well in life, he wouldn't be in any position to help others. "People will respect you for giving back to the community," she assured him. "You have the money to give away, so you should be proud of yourself."

And he was.

Because of the poverty that had marked his early childhood, world hunger was always a primary issue for Joe, and he viewed the Koret Foundation as a way to help eradicate it. Not by giving everyone a fish, but rather by metaphorically teaching as many people to fish as possible. If he could help researchers find new ways to produce food and then distribute it efficiently, fewer people around the globe would go to bed hungry every night. He began researching the issue and eventually found a scientist named Dr. Walter Falcon at the Food Research Institute at Stanford University. Dr. Falcon was conducting groundbreaking studies on the availability of food around the planet and was developing some innovative theories about why some people had plenty to eat, while others had nothing.

Falcon was convinced that the problem was not a shortage of food, but rather how it was being distributed to—or withheld from—certain populations. One day, he and Joe had a long meeting on the Stanford campus in Palo Alto, and Joe decided to use foundation funds to help alleviate hunger through education and research. He was enthusiastic about the program he and Dr. Falcon had conceived, but when he presented it to the rest of the board it fell on deaf ears.

The more Joe pushed, the more they pushed back. As JoAnne Vente recalls, not everyone on the board was as committed to easing the very real problem of hunger as Joe was. "They didn't have a clue what he really wanted," she says. "But he was patient, and he was persistent."

In the end Joe won out, and the Koret Foundation gave $2 million to the Food Research Institute, dedicated to alleviating hunger through education and research. The Stanford grant also included funds for developing the Center of Economic and Policy Research, whose goal was to provide scholarships to study the challenges facing businesses and governments around the globe.[1]

"Joe tried to do whatever he could to help with hunger," Susan remembers. "He wanted to support hunger and homeless causes, and education causes. Education and food programs were his top priorities."

A TURNING POINT IN THE EARLY DAYS OF THE foundation came one day when an Israeli professor who was visiting the University of California-Davis campus near Sacramento traveled down to San Francisco to meet with Joe. That professor, Nachum Shapir, was chairman of the Department of Animal Sciences at Hebrew University in Israel, and had shown some success in a program that bred goats with ibexes. An ibex is a mountain goat closely related to antelopes, and Dr. Shapir believed that by cross-breeding these two species he could create an animal that could live off the rough terrain of Israel. "He actually had a number of them," JoAnne Vente says. "The big challenge was to get the Chief Rabbinate to approve it."

A naturally curious and inquisitive man, Joe wanted to see these goat-ibex crossbreeds in person. He decided that the entire board and foundation staff would travel to Israel to better understand these new creatures. In a week-long mission, they visited the campuses of Hebrew University, toured historic Jewish sites, and met with educators, researchers, and politicians. The group also visited a traditional Israeli kibbutz, which Joe found particularly fascinating. The hard work those young people contributed to the nation's common good struck a deep chord that resonated long after his return home to San Francisco.

Additionally, Joe was interested in learning more about the efficient use of water in farming, and for human consumption. "They're doing a marvelous job in water usage," he observed when he returned from the fact-finding trip. "The world is so wasteful of water, but they've developed systems gradually being used in many areas of the world."[2]

The trip to Israel opened Joe's eyes—and those of the rest of the foundation—to the phenomenal advances Israeli researchers were achieving in the field of animal science. The dry, arid climate of the region was less than ideal for growing crops and raising food animals, which the country needed in order to be self-sustaining. The government's push toward economic autonomy made imports less and less desirable, and any support in achieving this independence was roundly appreciated. To that end, Hebrew University was embarking on groundbreaking endeavors designed to guarantee the "food sovereignty" of an entire nation, and Joe felt compelled to contribute.

Shortly after the tour of Israel, the Koret Foundation board voted unanimously to assist in Hebrew University's far-reaching goal. It directed that $250,000 in "seed funding" go to initial programs dedicated to the alleviation of hunger through education and research, as well as the Israel-Egypt Agricultural Cooperative project. At a time when both those countries were striving to create political harmony in that troubled corner of the world, the Koret Foundation wanted to become involved with what it viewed as a groundbreaking enterprise.

That initial investment eventually led to the creation of the Koret School of Veterinary Medicine, the first of its kind in Israel. Established through the efforts of Professor Kalman Perk, the school today is part of the Robert H. Smith Faculty of Agriculture, Food, and Environment of the Hebrew University of Jerusalem. The stated objectives of the school, initiated with a $2 million donation from the Koret Foundation, were to "educate and train highly qualified veterinary students, with special emphasis on the specific needs of Israel, so that they will be able to meet the present and future challenges of the veterinary profession." Today, the Koret School conducts research in clinical veterinary medicine, with "a special responsibility to provide professional practical, ethical, and educational support."[3]

Unfortunately, Joe Koret died before he could see this dream fully visualized. The Koret School opened its doors in 1983, at which point the entire Koret Foundation board returned to Israel to attend the dedication of the new facility. The inaugural classes began in 1985, and three years later the first graduates walked out the doors as freshly minted veterinarians, researchers, and scientists. Over the ensuing years these men and women have gone on to practice veterinary medicine, participate in animal husbandry research, and engage in food and hygiene inspection. They also are active in regulating veterinary services for the Israeli police and army, promoting animal welfare, and providing veterinary care and the management of wildlife.[4]

IN 1982, AS THE FOUNDATION GREW MORE comfortable with its grant-making, Joe began to consider his own legacy. He realized that the 501(c)3 that bore his name possessed the financial assets that would allow it to evolve into a major source of institutional giving, and since it was his money that was being earmarked for specific causes and projects, he wanted to ensure that his personal vision would guide the board in future years. While he had absolute veto power over any decision the board made, he knew that after his death this would not be the case. He trusted and respected his new wife Susan's commitment to carrying his dreams forward, and insisted that when he died she be named lifetime chairman of the board.

With this in mind, Joe began to structure a document that would both define the nature of the foundation and set in stone the causes he believed in. During the summer of 1982, he worked with JoAnne Vente and board member/general counsel Richard Greene to develop a charter that would clarify his wishes and provide continuity for the foundation on this death. Joe insisted that one of its primary focuses would always be providing for the needs of working class folks who lived in the greater San Francisco community. For example, he had a particular fondness for the Asian seamstresses who had made the clothes that made him millions, and he wanted to give back to that segment of the community. While not all of the board agreed, he was adamant that they approve a donation to the On Lok Development Corporation to build a new residential facility and medical center for elderly low-income people in Chinatown and North Beach.

Joe also turned a sympathetic ear toward minority concerns, specifically focusing on parenting and adoption challenges. Following a meeting with Robert DeBolt, founder of the AASK (Aid to Adoption for Special Kids) program, he personally directed the board to approve an unspecified amount of funding to "to initiate a program to let minority parents know that they are, indeed, good adoptive parent material very much in need as a resource for minority children." At a ceremony held at the foundation's office on Market Street, DeBolt lauded the Koret Foundation as "the first in the Bay Area to feel so strongly about the recruitment of minority parents for adoptive children to make an investment in that cause. The Koret Foundation donation will help to expand the AASK program dedicated to placing 'special kids' with minority parents."[6]

Similarly, Joe spearheaded grants that funded cancer research at the Linus Pauling Institute, and insisted that money be given to Interplast, a group of medical volunteers who transported children from under-developed countries to Stanford for medical care they couldn't receive in their homelands. He ensured that Donaldina Cameron House in Chinatown received a grant to teach English to Chinese children, and funded special projects for the Light of Buddha Temple in Oakland. He also established Terok of California, a facility for senior citizens in the Russian River community of Monte Rio, about ninety minutes north of San Francisco. The project had begun when Joe purchased a fishing camp in the area, and quickly learned that many senior citizens were pursuing less-than-healthy social endeavors. "They were spending their time in saloons because there was no other social place for them," he told the *Examiner*. To rectify the situation, the Korets bought a house and presented it to the town's recreational district.[7]

The foundation also contributed $250,000 to the University of San Francisco to retire a mortgage and to establish a permanent chair in Jewish Studies. Initial seed money of $250,000 was given to Family House, which provided temporary housing for the families of out-of-town children being treated at the University of California San Francisco medical center. Numerous smaller grants were directed to programs that benefitted children throughout the Bay Area, including Big Brothers of the East Bay, Eden Youth Center, Oakland Youth Works, Alameda Boys Club, Stepping Stones, and the San Francisco Mayor's Youth Fund.[8]

As mentioned previously, Joe was an active member of the San Francisco Jewish community, widely respected for his philanthropy and generosity. When he asked his future wife Susan to convert to Judaism, he was guided by the knowledge that their marriage would be viewed as a commitment of faith. He served on the boards of several Jewish organizations in the city and strongly believed in the nation of Israel and its right to exist and prosper. He had been horrified by the atrocities wrought by Hitler and his Nazi forces in the 1930s and forties—during the early years of Koret of California—and for that reason never purchased a German automobile. It was important to Joe that half of the grants made by the Koret Foundation be directed to Jewish organizations whose purpose was to provide for the improvement of life for all, whether it was the Jewish Home for the Aged in San Francisco or the Koret School of Veterinary Medicine in Israel.

Joe also requested that an early grant be provided to the Jewish Home for the Aged to fund an adult day-care program and to help with the construction of a new hospital wing. When the Koret Foundation's grant fell short of the organization's goal, Joe donated $750,000 of his own personal funds. "They deserve it," he told the *San Francisco Examiner*.[5]

Joe's goal was clear: he wanted to make sure that the bulk of the Koret Foundation's grants be directed toward causes that had a direct impact on people, rather than provide funds to entities that were more focused on political ideology. He often would speak about how important it was to split the foundation's giving fifty-fifty to "general community" and "Jewish community" causes, a resolve that eventually resulted in the creation of a draft document that would state this preference in no uncertain terms.

In the summer of 1982, Joe was diagnosed with an esophageal tumor, which doctors strongly recommended be removed. It was causing him problems while swallowing and would only continue to grow if it remained in place. At the same time, he was preoccupied with the closure of Cassidy's Western Outfitters, and thus shifted the creation of a long-term charter to a back burner. Other than his immediate medical issues, he believed he was in good health, and he assumed he could revisit the foundation's core principles and other challenges when he was feeling better.

In late October, Joe underwent surgery to remove the tumor, after which Susan drove him home to recuperate. The surgical procedure was declared a success, and his doctors predicted a full recovery. Over the next few days, various friends and family members stopped by the house, where they found him propped up in bed contemplating who should get which pair of boots or hats from the liquidation of Cassidy's. It was his wish that everyone—friends, family, employees, former colleagues—receive some of the unsold merchandise.

Tragically, in the early-morning hours of November 3, Joe suffered a massive brain hemorrhage, from which he would not recover. He died later that day, just eight days shy of his eighty-second birthday. The official charter for the Koret Foundation never was formalized.

WITHIN MONTHS, THE TENOR OF THE KORET Foundation began to change. Having mellowed over his eighty-two years, Joe had introduced a warm, folksy demeanor to his position as foundation board chairman. He personally studied the human aspects of every cause with an eye toward understanding the real impact any grant would have in true philanthropic terms. He wanted to know how many people would be affected by a gift and how they might benefit. Was it a cause that he felt strongly about personally? How did it touch either the general public or the Jewish community? How would a grant help an organization achieve a specific goal? When meeting with potential grant recipients for the first time, he sized them up in human terms and listened closely to their words so he understood what they were saying. From his first days as a traveling sweater salesman, Joe Koret had learned that listening was much more important than talking, and no skill was more critical when determining how the Koret Foundation should spend its money.

Now that Joe was gone, the foundation's approach changed quickly and, some would say, radically. The foundation bylaws stated that Susan Koret would become the chairman of the board for life after her husband's death, while Tad Taube was elected president and CEO. His management style clearly differed from Joe's and—as it quickly became apparent to some of the board and staff—so were some of his priorities. Not long after he assumed day-to-day control, it became obvious he intended to steer a greater portion of the foundation's grants to Jewish causes. Taube met with the Jewish Community Foundation to determine what new, and larger, role the Koret Foundation might have as a major funding source for Jewish programs and institutions.

This shift was rather predictable, and as a recent convert herself, Susan knew that the Jewish community in San Francisco would be supportive of what Taube was trying to do. Still, Joe had specifically emphasized that he wanted grants to be split evenly, and this policy change was highly political—and anything but subtle. At least one member of the board had previously suggested that JoAnne Vente and Ken Moline convert to Judaism in order to remain on the staff. When Joe learned of this he became outraged and addressed the matter immediately. He assured JoAnne that one of the reasons he wanted Ken and her on the staff was to balance out the Jewish influence. It was clear that the remaining board members were attempting to shift the foundation's focus now that Joe Koret was no longer alive to ensure that the board would follow his wishes. A major transition loomed on the horizon.

Even when Joe was alive, several board members had begun forming personal alliances along two parallel lines, and this division progressed steadily after his death. Stanley Herzstein, a longtime friend and ally of Joe's, supported Susan's contention that the foundation should continue to follow the funding wishes of her late husband. By contrast, Richard Greene and Eugene Friend sided with Tad Taube's assessment of the foundation's priorities. In a three-against-two competition—with Susan representing the minority side—it was evident that the Koret Foundation was shifting onto a new track.[9]

While these changes were simmering out of public view, the Koret Foundation went about business as usual. During the first few years following Joe's death, the $2 million award for the Koret School of Veterinary Medicine was finalized, and the board approved a $2.4 million challenge grant for the construction of the Koret Vision Research Laboratory at UCSF. A gift of $3.85 million was made to construct the Koret Health and Recreation Center at the University of San Francisco. Meanwhile, Taube approached Rabbi Brian Lurie, the executive director of the Jewish Community Federation serving San Francisco, Marin, and Sonoma Counties, with a proposal that essentially would have linked the policy-making agendas of the two organizations. The federation balked at giving the Koret Foundation too much influence and power over its long-standing affairs, and gave the proposal a polite thumbs-down. Despite what has been described as "ruffled feathers," the Koret Foundation continued to provide financial assistance to the federation and numerous other Jewish organizations around the Bay Area.[10]

LESS THAN A YEAR AFTER JOE'S DEATH, STANLEY Herzstein was removed from the board by Taube, Greene, and Friend following a series of policy disputes. The triumvirate also stripped Susan Koret of her board chairmanship. She had attempted several times to reinstate Herzstein, but the new majority wouldn't hear of it. She and Herzstein represented obstacles to how they wanted to position the foundation, and the board majority boxed them both out.

Believing she had her late husband's best interests in mind, Susan filed a lawsuit to remove the other three members of the foundation from the board. Citing letters of resignation that her husband had required they all sign when appointed to the board, she wanted the three men gone. Taube, Greene, and Friend promptly countersued in order to maintain control of the board.

Superior Court Judge Raymond Williamson initially turned down Susan's request, ruling that the three men had the proper authority to remove her as board chair. He did not rule on whether the undated letters of resignation gave Susan the power to fire the other directors. The lawsuit in part concerned director compensation. Susan, who was due the same compensation as the other board members, had declined to receive hers.[9] Susan also alleged that foundation money had been used to promote personal interests of some of the other directors. Susan's lawsuit insisted this was improper use of foundation funds, and requested that money be paid back.

In June of 1986, all parties agreed to settle the matter out of court. Under terms of the settlement, Susan was reinstated as chairman of the board, and all the other members remained as directors. The settlement also expanded the board from four directors to ten. New members included investment banker Richard Blum, married to then-mayor Dianne Feinstein; civic leader and attorney William Coblentz; financier Bernard Osher; and real estate investor Mel Swig. Stanley Herzstein also returned to the board, and a tenth member was to be named later. Confident the new board could work together, Herzstein told the *Chronicle*, "You're dealing with a group of very mature adults who can put it all behind them."[10]

William Coblentz echoed this sentiment, saying, "The foundation has great potential for growth and good. I'm sure reasonable people can work together to carry out the wishes of Mr. Koret."[11]

The board expansion was seen as a power deterrent, intended to make it harder for any single board director—or alliance of directors—to control the foundation's decision-making. Additionally, the legal settlement formally ratified the fifty-fifty split between Jewish and non-Jewish grants that Joe had stipulated from the beginning. A third major change was the implementation of an independent counsel who would oversee all legal matters.

The settlement instituted some smaller changes, as well. It allowed a financial audit into directors' personal financial dealings. Also, prior to the legal skirmishes, the board had earmarked a small amount of its budget to pay for personal expenses, such as tickets to the San Francisco Opera. Additionally, the foundation previously had paid for the personal vehicles of several board members, which they were forced to either give back or purchase out of their own personal assets.

TODAY, FORTY YEARS SINCE ITS INCEPTION IN 1978, the Koret Foundation has contributed more than $500 million to causes that promoted "a higher quality of civic and Jewish community life."[12] Some of those years clearly were more discordant than others, but disagreement had been an element of its heritage almost since day one. Joe Koret had trusted that the foundation that bore his name—and was funded by his and his late wife's wealth—would act according to his wishes after his death, even though he never had time to properly codify them in a legal charter. During his years in business he had come to know that money meant power, and this was why Joe Koret had required each board member to sign a letter of resignation to be utilized if and when the chairman deemed it appropriate to make a change. While those letters never actually were used, their existence helped all parties involved in the 1986 litigation to resolve their differences outside the courtroom and carry on the foundation's work.

In more recent years, much-publicized conflict stemming from continued board-level acrimony produced a less amicable outcome, resulting in the departure of both Tad Taube and Susan Koret from the board of directors. Serious disagreements exposed major differences between Susan, who remained intent on following Joe Koret's original intentions, and a board of directors that over the years had departed from her late husband's wishes for the Foundation's objectives and tenor. Much has been written about that dispute and its resolution, and those accounts will serve as the public record of what transpired. While Joe obviously anticipated some discord among the individuals he selected to guide (and guard) his hard-earned money, he most certainly could not have ever envisioned—or appreciated—the spectacle that ensued.

Fortunately, the Koret Foundation lives on. Despite the period of dissonance and dissension, most of the recipients of its grants— both within the greater San Francisco community and the Jewish community—have been consonant with Joe Koret's initial intentions. While disagreements about the foundation's mission have from time to time threatened to derail the original intentions of the foundation's founders, it is nearly impossible to venture anywhere in the San Francisco Bay Area and not see a plaque stating "Gift of the Koret Foundation." Joe's goal had always been a selfless intention to "pay it forward" to those in need and, as his widow Susan has always said, his focus was on helping the "little guy" rather than self-aggrandizement.

As Susan Koret says today:

> Joe thought the foundation would be protected by putting me on the board, and he believed I would protect his legacy. I fought for what he wanted, and he trusted me. Joe wanted to help needy people—it was always about the people, not some policy group. His goal was to help the needy, but he adamantly believed it was vital to then equip them with an education so they could eventually help themselves. Joe didn't believe in only providing handouts; he wanted something more. That is why Joe loved the saying "give a man a fish and he will eat for one day, teach a man to fish, and you feed him for a lifetime" That sentiment came from deep within him, and that's what the foundation was supposed to be all about. I'm very proud of who Joe was . . . and what he tried to do with his money."

SOURCES

PREFACE

1. Stephen Pearson, "The Year 1980." *The People History*, accessed September 8, 2017, www.thepeoplehistory.com/1958.html

1 NEW YORK, NEW YORK

1. "The Immigrant Journey," accessed March 3, 2017, www.ohranger.com/ellis-island/immigration-journey
2. Alan Kraut, *The Huddled Masses: The Immigrant in American Society: 1880–1921* (Wheeling, IL: Harlan-Davidson, 1982)
3. Howard M. Sachar, "The International Ladies Garment Worker's Union and the Great Revolt of 1909," in *Modern History: A History of the Jews in America* (New York, NY: Alfred Knopf, 1992)
4. Ibid.
5. Ibid.
6. Stephen Mark Dobbs, *The Koret Foundation: 25 Years as a Catalyst for Positive Change* (Berkeley, CA: Western Jewish History Center, 2004)

2 THE STREETS OF SAN FRANCISCO

1. Federal Reserve Bank of Minneapolis Community Development Project, "Consumer Price Index (estimate) 1800," Federal Reserve Bank of Minneapolis, retrieved September 18, 2017
2. Carl Nolte, "The Great Quake, 1906–2006: Rising from the Ashes," *San Francisco Chronicle*, accessed March 25, 2017, www.sfgate.com/news/article/The-Great-Quake-1906-2006-Rising-from-the-ashes-2537103.php
3. Ibid.
4. "Scourge of the City: Looking Back at UCSF's Battle with Tuberculosis," UCSF, 2014, www.ucsf.edu/news/2014/11 /120926/scourge-city
5. Gus Lee, "China Boy," Crystal Palace Market clipping file, 1991, San Francisco Public Library History Room, as referenced in "Crystal Palace Market," by Gail MacGowan, accessed March 29, 2017, http://www.sfcityguides.org/public_guidelines.html?article=369&submitted=TRUE&srch_text=&submitted2=&topic=B
6. Crystal Palace Market advertisement, *San Francisco Chronicle*, December 14, 1922

3 CALIFORNIA DREAMING

1. Advertisement, *San Francisco Chronicle*, February 11, 1940
2. Funding Universe, "United Merchants & Manufacturers, Inc. History," accessed April 2, 2017, www.fundinguniverse.com/company-histories/united-merchants-manufacturers-inc-history
3. Ibid.
4. United States Patent Office, design patent No. 135,819, filed by Arthur Heyman October 13, 1941; approved June 15, 1943
5. United States Patent Office, patent No. 2,344,462, filed by Joseph Koret March 15, 1943; approved March 14, 1944
6. *San Francisco Examiner*, February 2, 1982

4 THE POSTWAR BOOM

1. Lee Kennett, *For the Duration: The United States Goes to War, Pearl Harbor–1942* (New York: Scribner, 1985)
2. *Women's Wear Daily*, December 3, 1943
3. Karen L. LaBat and Carol J. Salusso, *Classifications & Analysis of Textiles: A Handbook* (Minneapolis, MN: University of Minnesota, 2003)
4. *WWD*, May 27, 1946
5. *WWD*, October 24, 1945
6. *WWD*, April 14, 1945
7. Kerry Segrave, *Product Placement in Hollywood Movies* (Jefferson, NC: McFarland & Company, 2004)
8. Koret of California archives, Bancroft Library, University of California-Berkeley
9. *Betty Co-Ed* (review), Turner Classic Movies, accessed July 27, 2017, www.tcm.com/tcmdb/title/68527/Betty-Co-ed/
10. Fashion Archives, "A Look at the History of Culottes: September 19, 2015," accessed June 29, 2017, www.startupfashion.com/fashion-archives-history-of-culottes/
11. *San Francisco Chronicle*, May 12, 1946
12. Ibid.
13. *WWD*, November 11, 1947
14. *WWD*, May 14, 1947
15. *Chronicle*, December 20, 1947
16. *WWD*, May 25, 1949
17. Ibid.
18. Sol Koret death certificate, Los Angeles County. Filed November 10, 1943. Personal Koret family archives

5 THE BIRTH OF THE CONSUMER

1. Stephen Pearson, "The Year 1950," in *The People History*, accessed May 5, 2017, http://www.thepeoplehistory.com/1950.html
2. Koret of California archives, Bancroft Library, University of California-Berkeley

3. Megan D. Wessel, "Advertising, Post–World War II," in *Encyclopedia of American History: Postwar United States, 1946 to 1968*, Allan M. Winkler, Charlene Mires, and Gary B. Nash, eds., rev. ed, IX (New York: Facts on File, 2010)

4. Dawn Spring, *Advertising in the Age of Persuasion: Building Brand America 1941–1961* (Basingstoke, U.K.: Palgrave MacMillan, 2011)

5. *San Francisco Chronicle*, May 24, 1952

6. *Women's Wear Daily*, April 30, 1952

7. *WWD*, October 28, 1952

8. The Council of Fashion Designers of America, Inc. (CFDA), accessed April 14, 2017, https://www.cfda.com/about-cfda

9. *A Survey of Race Relations in South Africa* (Johannesburg, South Africa: South African Institute of Race Relations, 1973)

10. *Chronicle*, March 8, 1951

11. *Chronicle*, August 21, 1953

12. *Chronicle*, December 12, 1953

13. Ibid.

14. *Women's Wear Daily*, April 23, 1955

15. Ibid.

6 THE FIFTIES: A NEW GENERATION

1. Advertisement, *San Francisco Chronicle*, July 17, 1954

2. *Chronicle*, November 10, 1959

3. United States Patent Office, application for Patent No. 2,974,432, filed Feb. 20, 1956, serial No. 566,748

4. *Women's Wear Daily*, July 28, 1959

5. *WWD*, September 18, 1959

6. *Christian Science Monitor*, April 14, 1959

7. Ibid.

8. *Monitor*, April 15, 1959

9. *Monitor*, April 16, 1959

10. *Monitor*, April 17, 1959

11. *WWD*, March 4, 1960

7 THE SIXTIES: A DECADE OF TURMOIL

1. *Vogue*, November 11, 2013

2. Debbie Sessions, accessed May 17, 2017, www.vintagedancer.com/1960s/1960s-fashion-womens/

3. *Women's Wear Daily*, September 20, 1960

4. *WWD*, July 13, 1960

5. *San Francisco Chronicle*, April 28, 1963

6. *Life*, December 6, 1963

7. Debbie Sessions, accessed May 17, 2017, www.vintagedancer.com/1960s/1960s-fashion-womens/

8. Marcellous Jones, *Fashion Insider*, February 11, 2014, accessed May 21, 2017, http://thefashioninsider.com/2014/02/11/supermodel-biography-top-model-twiggy-marcellous-l-jones/

9. *Newsweek*, April 4, 1967

10. *Chronicle*, December 30, 1963

11. *Chronicle*, July 22, 1965

12. *Chronicle*, May 19, 1965

13. Ibid.

14. *Vogue*, January 1, 1966

15. Koret of California archives, Bancroft Library, University of California-Berkeley

16. *Chronicle*, March 12, 1966

17. *Chronicle*, September 14, 1966

18. *Women's Wear Daily*, September 7, 1967

19. *WWD*, July 18, 1967

20. *WWD*, August 29, 1967

21. *Chronicle*, June 20, 1967

22. *WWD*, January 17, 1968

8 KORATRON: HOLD THE PRESS

1. *San Francisco Chronicle*, November 10, 1964

2. *Chronicle*, January 9, 1966

3. *Chronicle*, October 21, 1965

4. *Chronicle*, August 18, 1966

5. Ibid.

6. *Women's Wear Daily*, April 21, 1966

7. M. Zinamon et al., Method of Permanently Pleating Fabrics, filed Feb. 9, 1954, U.S. Patent No. 2,769,584

8. W. K. Warnock et al.; Press-Free Crease Retained Garments and Method of Manufacture Thereof, filed Feb. 20, 1956, U.S. Patent No. 2,974,432

9. *Chronicle*, December 15, 1966

10. *Chronicle*, February 14, 1967

11. *Chronicle*, February 7, 1967

12. *Chronicle*, February 11, 1967

13. *Chronicle*, June 20, 1967

14. *Chronicle*, June 24, 1967

15. *WWD*, November 30, 1967

16. *Chronicle*, October 10, 1968

17. *Chronicle*, March 7, 1974

9 KORACORP: IN THE PUBLIC EYE

1. Conversation adapted from an article in *Women's Wear Daily*, April 12, 1967
2. *New York Times*, September 5, 1967
3. Ibid.
4. "Eight Unforgettable Ways 1968 Made History," accessed May 29, 2017, www.cnn.com/2014/07/31/us/1968-important-events/
5. Susan Froyd, *Four Fashion Trends That Defined Style in 1968* (Denver, CO: Westword, 2015)
6. *San Francisco Chronicle*, May 9, 1968
7. *Chronicle*, June 13, 1969
8. Ibid.
9. *Women's Wear Daily*, June 17, 1969
10. *Chronicle*, May 25, 1969
11. *Chronicle*, May 25, 1969
12. *New York Times*, May 3, 1970
13. *NYT*, May 3, 1970

10 THE SEVENTIES: THE END OF AN ERA

1. "With Flowers in Their Hair," *U.K. Daily Mail*, May 30, 2012, accessed June 3, 2017
2. *San Francisco Chronicle*, May 24, 1972
3. *New York Times*, January 13, 1972
4. *Women's Wear Daily*, May 16, 1973
5. *WWD*, May 16, 1973
6. *Chronicle*, February 20, 1973
7. *Chronicle*, April 29, 1973
8. *Chronicle*, October 27, 1974
9. *Chronicle*, May 4, 1973
10. *WWD*, August 28, 1973
11. *WWD*, October 4, 1972
12. Ibid.
13. *SEC News Digest*, January 23, 1974
14. Louis P. Weil and Beatrice Weil v. Commissioner, United States Tax Court, Docket No. 36115-83, accessed June 8, 2017, www.leagle.com
15. *WWD*, December 5, 1973
16. *Los Angeles Times*, February 19, 1973
17. *Chronicle*, July 1, 1976
18. *Chronicle*, November 24, 1976
19. *Chronicle*, December 27, 1978
20. *Chronicle*, August 2, 1978
21. Ibid.

22. Charles Fracchia, Levi Strauss Historical Essay, accessed June 12, 2017, http://www.foundsf.org/index.php?title=Levi Strauss
23. Chris Carlsson, "Levi's Blue Jean Kings Historical Essay" (with thanks to Charles Fracchia), accessed June 12, 2017, www.foundsf.org/index.php?title=LEVI%27S:_Blue_Jean_Kings
24. *Chronicle*, May 19, 1979
25. Ibid.
26. Ibid.

11 THE OLD MAN AND THE SEA

1. *San Francisco Chronicle*, February 10, 1953
2. *Chronicle*, May 10, 1953
3. *Chronicle*, November 11, 1968
4. E. Clement Chute, Jr., and Ailetta d'A. Belin, Regulations Report for Richardson Bay Special Area Plan (Report), San Francisco Bay Conservation and Development Commission, 1983

13 WEDDING BELL BLUES

1. Koret of California archives, Bancroft Library, University of California-Berkeley

14 URBANE COWBOY

1. *San Francisco Chronicle*, December 26, 1980
2. *Chronicle*, August 17, 1981
3. *Women's Wear Daily*, April 21, 1981

15 A FOUNDATION OF TRUST

1. Institute for Economic Policy Research, Stanford University, accessed September 13, 2017, https://siepr.stanford.edu
2. *San Francisco Sunday Examiner & Chronicle*, March 15, 1981
3. Koret School of Veterinary Medicine, Hebrew School of Jerusalem, accessed July 19, 2017. http://ksvm.agri.huji.ac.il/en/
4. Ibid.
5. *Sunday Examiner & Chronicle*, March 15, 1981
6. *Oakland Post*, October 26, 1980
7 *Sunday Examiner & Chronicle*, March 15, 1981
8. Stephen Mark Dobbs, *The Koret Foundation: 25 Years as a Catalyst for Positive Change* (Berkeley, CA: Western Jewish History Center, 2004)
9. Ibid.
10. Ibid.

= ACKNOWLEDGMENTS =

As a young boy growing up in California, I was oblivious of the fact that no matter how much wear and tear I put my trousers and shirts through, my mother could just throw them in the washer and dryer and put them away in my closet. No wrinkles, no ironing. I had no understanding that something called Koratron "permanent press" had made this profound impact on her life possible, and I certainly had no clue that the stylish sportswear she sometimes purchased at the Emporium department store very likely was manufactured by Koret of California. Young boys take little notice of such things, and the sizable influence Joe and Stephanie Koret had on the fashion world remained outside my awareness for more than a half-century.

Then, one day several years ago, I learned of a potential book project involving a notable entrepreneur, philanthropist, and fashion industry titan in San Francisco. After much discussion and consideration, I flew out to California to explore the project and see what contribution I might be able to make.

That's how I came to meet a magnificent woman named Susan Koret, who stands out in my mind as the most decent, generous, considerate, and respectful person I have ever come to know. On a cold, rainy December morning I sat down with Susan and Denise Kim, who is her personal attorney and also her niece. She was there to advise her aunt on the legal aspects of the project. And to vet me as its author.

Three weeks later I began the task of dissecting the life of Joseph Koret. The word "task" is a bit misleading, since every moment of this project quickly became an enjoyable and challenging mission. Aside from various newspaper and magazine articles, very little had ever been written about the poor Russian immigrant who had built a global empire in women's sportswear. Over the ensuing weeks and months, I had the great fortune to meet some of Joe's surviving friends and family, all of whom generously gave of their time and helped me piece together the man they had known and loved.

These include, in no particular order:

JoAnne Vente and Ken Moline, both of whom worked with Joe Koret during the last years of his business and his life. Without hesitation they provided rich and colorful memories of the man and those around him, contributing invaluable insights and anecdotes that became critical to the overall thread of the Koret story.

Merv Brown—nephew of Joe's wife Stephanie—graciously opened the doors of his home to me and, along with his wife Joyce and son Ron, shared many old stories and reminiscences of times gone by. Arlene Bernstein, daughter of Joe's best friend Bob Upright, and her husband Paul similarly had many great stories to tell, as did Susan Behr, Stephanie's sister's granddaughter. I thank them all for sharing their loving memories and their candid observations.

Many other people contributed to this book in various ways, and I am indebted to them for their invaluable assistance:

Steve Miller, a professional genealogist based in Oakland who helped me decipher the deaths of Solomon and Harold Koret. Similarly, I thank Kenneth Marks, who clarified much of the background of his great-uncle Arthur Heyman's initial patent of the Trikskirt.

Christina Moretta at the San Francisco History Center/San Francisco Public Library, who helped me dig out several of the photographs that were used in this book.

Charles Fracchia, founder of the San Francisco Historical Museum and Historical Society, for his advice and guidance in the latter stages of this project.

Judith Geary, who took a first look at the manuscript and provided serious editorial guidance prior to submission to the publisher.

Lorna Kirwan, Michael Maire Lange, Susan McElrath, Jennie Hinchcliff, and Peter E. Hanff at the Bancroft Library in Berkeley, whose assistance in hastening the photo reproduction and permissions process was a lifesaver as we were pulling together the graphic elements of the book.

Dana Marie Knapp, for her enthusiasm and diligence in scanning dozens of photos from the Koret family archives.

Sohaila Braam, who provided invaluable assistance in walking me through the San Francisco Public Library's online archives system.

Nion McEvoy, Catherine Huchting, Beth Weber, Pamela Geismar, Carolyn Miller, Freesia Blizard, and Amy Treadwell at Chronicle Books.

Tina Frank, who brought so much insight and wisdom to this project from the very beginning.

Sam Singer, who worked so much unbelievable magic pulling strings and making so many seemingly impossible things come to fruition.

Denise Kim, whose innate intelligence, casual demeanor, and easygoing approach helped to make this entire project seamless and enjoyable.

My wife Diana who, as usual, threw all of her love and encouragement my way in support of this endeavor.

And last, Susan Koret: Your boundless generosity, unyielding respect, and continued dedication to the memory of your late husband clearly reflects the content of your character. More than any single person, you have defined and guided his commitment to the overall San Francisco community, and ensured that the legacy of the foundation that bears his name remains committed to the causes that were important to him throughout his life. I am so grateful to have been able to tell Joe Koret's story in the pages of this book, and I could not be more thankful to have been given that opportunity.

INDEX

AASK (Aid to Adoption for Special Kids), 315–16
Aljean Sportswear, 128, 141
Allanius, Ray, 86
Alvarez, Lilí, 82
Arthur Andersen & Company, 199, 200, 206

Bab'nart, 67
Back, S. R., 107–8
Bates, John, 143
Battery Street Enterprises, 213
Behr, Susan, 252
Berghold, Joseph, 202
Bernstein, Arlene, 231–32, 235, 251–52, 253
Bernstein, Paul, 229, 231–34
Betty Co-Ed, 81
Bickel, Joyce, 134, 145, 186
Blairmoor Knitwear Corp., 154
Blum, Richard, 321
Box, Michael, 304, 305
Brand Names Foundation, 99
Broadway Knitting Mills, 150, 153, 182
Broidy, Steve, 80
Brown, Bernard, 195–96
Brown, Leo, 99, 127
Brown, Merv, 105, 107, 122, 123, 196, 235, 253
Brown, Ron, 252, 301
Brown, Stephanie Diana. *See* Koret, Stephanie
Burlington Industries, 149, 164–67, 169–71
Byer-Rolnick Corporation, 154–55, 158, 195, 302
Byrne, Kiki, 143

Caen, Herb, 295
Cain, Charles, 127, 178, 204, 206
Carter, John, 242–43, 244, 246–47
Carter, Oliver, 111
Cassidy's Western Outfitters, 290, 304–5, 317
Chan, Charles, 274, 281
Christopher, George, 119
Citron, Al, 81, 100, 105, 107
Clarence Rainess & Company, 202
Coblentz, William, 321
Cohn-Hall-Marx Company, 63–65, 71
Cold War, 94, 113
Columbia Studios, 81
Crystal Palace Market, 36, 43–44, 46
Cunningham, Arthur, 173–74, 201, 202, 206

Davis, Jacob, 210
DeBolt, Robert, 315–16
Deering, William, 171

Deering Milliken, 114, 171–73, 175, 176
Donaldina Cameron House, 316

Emberly, Gordon, 196
Establissments Fra-For, 194

Falcon, Walter, 312
Far East Traders, 268, 272–74, 276–77, 279–83, 286, 302
Feinstein, Dianne, 290, 304, 321
Field, Charlotte, 100
Fleischmann, Jay, 201, 202
Food Research Institute, 312
Ford, Henry, 129, 162
Friend, Eugene, 303, 308, 320–21

Garment Industries Ltd., 88
GEM Realty, 121, 133, 246
Giannini, A. P., 71
Goldberg, Abe, 99
Golson, Harry, 99
Gorewitz, Sarah. *See* Koret, Sarah
Grand'Mere Knitting Company, 88
Great Depression, 55, 56
Greenberg, Herman, 164, 165, 170, 173
Greene, Richard, 308, 315, 320–21

Haas, Walter A., Jr., 210–12
Hampton, Mary (Ninon), 101, 102, 105
H.C.A. Industries, 194–95
Head, Edith, 80
Hebrew University, 306, 313–14
Heim, Jacques, 95
Helfat, Jere, 141, 151–58, 171, 178, 180–84, 189–90, 194–95, 199, 201, 206, 241, 302
Herzstein, Stanley, 158, 308, 319, 320, 321
Heyman, Arthur and Bebe, 67–69
High School Hero, 80
Hollywood Preview, 79
Homemaking with a Flair, 189–91, 199–203, 204, 206, 208, 241
Hubener, Frank, 124

International Ladies Garment Workers Union (ILGWU), 30, 61, 75

Jewish Home for the Aged, 317
J.E.Z. Textile Corporation, 167–68, 169, 171, 180
Jugan, St. Jeanne, 14

Keller, Helen, 46
Kennedy, Jackie, 136–37, 139, 142–43
Kennedy, John F., 136, 138–39, 142
Kidder, Peabody & Company, 63
Kim, Denise, 301
Kittelberger, Raymond, 199–200
Kline, Benjamin, 227–28
Kolortron, 195–96
Koracorp
    renaming of company to, 159, 182
    in the sixties, 182–84, 187, 189
    in the seventies, 194–209, 211, 241–42
    sale of, to Levi Strauss, 211–13, 285, 308
Koraset process, 125–26, 132, 139, 140–41,
    144–45, 162–63. *See also* Koratron
Koratec Communications, 190, 199–201, 206
Koratron, 144, 146–49, 152–53, 155–59, 162–77,
    181, 182, 186, 187, 189, 204, 212
Koret, Abram
    as immigrant, 21–30
    as union organizer, 30–31, 58
    grocery stores of, in New York, 31, 32, 33
    moves family to California, 34, 37–39
    clothing store of, in San Francisco, 39
    as tailor, 41
    death of, 108–9, 140
    personality of, 34
    photograph of, 20
Koret, Alexander, 20, 22, 29, 33, 39, 40, 90, 132,
    158
Koret, Harold, 31, 40–41, 90, 140
Koret, Joe. *See also individual business ventures*
    childhood of, 20, 22, 29–33
    early employment of, 39, 42, 46–47, 53
    hosiery stall of, in Crystal Palace Market, 36,
        43–44, 46
    romance between Stephanie and, 44–46
    marries Stephanie, 46, 286
    learns about women's fashion, 44, 47–48,
        53–54, 59
    Sportswear Manufacturing Company
        started by, 54–55
    during the Great Depression, 55–57, 58
    Younger Set Sportswear started by, 60
    Koret of California started by, 61
    income tax problems of, 109–12, 120
    hires Susan as home caregiver, 230, 255–61
    romance between Susan and, 262–66,
        269–72, 276–79
    Far East Traders started by, 268, 272–75,
        276–77
    marries Susan, 286–88, 295–96
    Cassidy's Western Outfitters started by, 290,
        304
    illness and death of, 317–18
    "butterfly buying" and, 114–16
    "fear psychology" concept of, 87
    fishing and, 32–33, 214–38, 283, 285
    as gin rummy player, 284–85

Judaism and, 291–92
    motivational maxims of, 45–46, 155
    personality of, 15, 42, 44, 188, 235–36,
        249–51, 299–301
    as philanthropist, 10–11, 14–18, 309–19, 323
    photographs of, 2, 12, 20, 34, 50, 92, 118,
        160, 178, 192, 214, 240, 290, 306
    physical appearance of, 249
    real estate and, 246, 248
    thriftiness of, 296–99
    travel and, 237, 269–72, 296–98
Koret, Lenore, 90
Koret, Richard, 60
Koret, Sarah (Gorewitz), 20, 22, 29–30, 31,
    40–41, 118, 140
Koret, Solomon, 31, 40, 90
Koret, Stephanie (Brown). *See also* Koret of
    California
    romance between Joe and, 44–46
    marries Joe, 286
    Hollywood Preview developed by, 78–79
    retirement of, 153, 156, 254
    health issues of, 153, 208, 237, 254, 260–61,
        262, 269
    death of, 274, 282, 308
    design skills of, 53, 54, 60, 83–85, 95–96,
        122–23, 275
    personality of, 45, 77, 84, 123–24, 251–54,
        275
    photographs of, 50, 118, 275
    physical appearance of, 253
    pleated skirts and, 66–67, 69–70
    travel and, 237, 269–71
Koret, Susan (McClain)
    hiring of, as home caregiver, 230, 255–61
    romance between Joe and, 262–66, 269–72,
        276–79
    conversion of, to Judaism, 291–95, 317
    marries Joe, 286–88, 295–96
    on board of Koret Foundation, 308, 311, 315,
        319–21, 322–23
    memories of, 230, 233, 236, 238, 284, 285,
        287–88, 299, 311, 312, 323
    personality of, 255–56
    photographs of, 240, 290, 306
    travel and, 269–72, 296–97
Koret Foundation, 10, 15–16, 158, 213, 248,
    282, 306–23
Koretigan, 83
Koret Knits, 60
Koret Manufacturing Company, 90, 132–33, 158
Koret of California
    founding of, 61
    early financial challenges of, 61–65
    during World War II, 71, 74–75
    in the postwar period, 72, 76–88, 94–95, 97
    in the fifties, 98–100, 102–7, 113–14, 120,
        122–33

in the sixties, 137–41, 144–59, 162–64, 178, 179–82, 188
becomes division under Koracorp, 159, 182
in the seventies, 195, 197–98, 203–4, 205
Koret of California-Canada, 128, 141, 150–51
Koret School of Veterinary Medicine, 10–11, 306, 314, 320

LaPlanche, Rosemary, 81
Lasky, Moses, 167, 170, 172, 175
Levi Strauss & Company, 144, 162–63, 174–75, 210–13, 285, 288, 302, 303, 308
Light of Buddha Temple, 316
Little Sisters of the Poor, 14–18, 310–11
Logan, Warren, 156, 305
Lundgren, Harold, 169
Lurie, Brian, 320

Marilyn Inc., 99–100
McClain, Susan. See Koret, Susan
McClennan, Ronald, 133, 134, 141, 202, 206
McMillan, Robert, 110
Menzin, Sam, 99
Messing, Leon, 154
Milano, John, 302–3
Milliken, Seth, 171
Mitsubishi, 194
Moline, Ken, 15, 16, 177, 229–30, 231, 246–48, 250, 273, 281–83, 296–99, 300, 308, 310, 319
Monogram Pictures, 79–81
Murphy, Edward, 110

Ninon. See Hampton, Mary

On Lok Development Corporation, 315
Osher, Bernard, 321

Parker, Edna, 202, 203
Pausan, 254, 258–59, 260, 264, 271, 278, 279
Perawicki, Stanley, 212
Perk, Kalman, 314
Pinsky, Norman, 201, 202
Porter, Jean, 81
Preisser, June, 80, 81

Quant, Mary, 143

Renfrew, Charles, 175, 176
Robert Bruce, 208, 211, 212
Roosevelt, Franklin, 57, 58, 73, 87
Rosenberg, Maurice, 90
Rousseau, Charles, 43
Rousseau, Oliver and Arthur, 42–43

Sebro Knit Sportswear, 53
Semlitz, Edward, 167
Shapir, Nachum, 312–13
Silverstone, Herschel, 109–11
Simon, Sam, 63–64

Snyder Brothers, 46–47, 53, 54, 55
Sommer, Charles, 157
Sportswear Manufacturing Company, 54–55, 59
St. Anne's Home for the Elderly, 14–18, 310–11
Stephanie K brand, 253
Stewart, Freddie, 80, 81
Strauss, Levi, 209–10
Sue J, 153, 182
Sweigert, William, 206
Swig, Mel, 321

Taube, Tad, 201–2, 204, 205, 206, 207, 208, 211, 212, 241, 303, 308, 319–21, 322
Terok of California, 316
Terok Properties, 201–2, 229, 242, 246–48, 272, 281, 283, 302, 308
Three Star Manufacturing Pty., 88
Triangle Shirtwaist Company, 28–29, 30–31
Trikskirt, 66–71, 72, 76, 82, 102
Trikulotte, 83
Trune, Dan, 171
Turnbull, George, 247
Twiggy, 143–44

United Merchants & Manufacturers, 63, 64
University of California San Francisco (UCSF), 316, 320
Upright, Robert, 217–24, 226–29, 231–34, 292
Urban Cowboy, 301, 304

Vacation Days, 80–81
Vente, JoAnne, 14–18, 242–46, 248, 250–51, 283–85, 296–98, 300, 305, 308, 309, 310, 311, 312, 313, 315, 319
Vietnam War, 147, 151, 184, 193

Warnock, William, 124, 141, 158, 164, 178, 181, 182, 187–88, 189, 206
Weil, Henry, 103–4, 134, 138, 141
Weil, Phillip, 190, 201, 202–3
Weinberg, Jacob and Louis, 154
Weiss, Bob, 106
Westwood Knitting Mills, 55
White, Rabbi Saul, 140, 292–94
World War I, 51, 218
World War II, 69, 70–71, 73–76, 88, 90
Worth, Bernard, 134
Wrobbel, Richard, 158

Younger Set Sportswear, 60, 61

Zaharin, Henry, 75
Zinamon, Martin, 167, 168
Zirpoli, A. J., 110